GOSPEL STUDIES SERIES
Volume I

Isaiah

Made Easier

In the Bible and the Book of Mormon

Books
by David J. Ridges

The *Gospel Studies Series:*

- Volume 1: Isaiah Made Easier
- Volume 2: The New Testament Made Easier, Part 1
- Volume 3: The New Testament Made Easier, Part 2
- Volume 4: Your Study of The Book of Mormon Made Easier, Part 1

Upcoming volumes in the *Gospel Studies Series*:

- Your Study of The Book of Mormon Made Easier: Parts 2 and 3 (2004)
- Your Study of The Doctrine & Covenants Made Easier (2005)
- Your Study of The Pearl of Great Price Made Easier (2006)
- The Old Testament Made Easier—Selections from the Old Testament (2006)

Additional titles by David J. Ridges:

- The Proclamation on the Family: The Word of the Lord on More Than 30 Current Issues
- 50 Signs of the Times and the Second Coming
- From Premortality to Exaltation: Doctrinal Details of the Plan of Salvation (2004)

Watch for these titles to also become available through Cedar Fort as e-books and on CD.

GOSPEL STUDIES SERIES
Volume I

Isaiah

Made Easier

In the Bible and the Book of Mormon

by

David J. Ridges

Springville, Utah

ISBN: 1-55517-615-1
e. 2

Published by Cedar Fort Inc.
www.cedarfort.com

Distributed by:

Typeset by Kristin Nelson
Cover design by Adam Ford
Cover design © 2002 by Lyle Mortimer

Printed in the United States of America
10 9 8 7 6 5 4 3 2 1

Printed on acid-free paper

Library of Congress Control Number: 2002101333

Table of Contents

FOREWORD

As the title of this book implies, Isaiah has been made "easier" (not necessarily "easy") for us in the latter days because of the excellent resources listed below as well as many others. My intent has been to create a sort of "digest" that would help students of the scriptures quickly get a basic understanding of Isaiah chapters in the Bible and Book of Mormon. Then, it is hoped, with the help of more in-depth and scholarly books on Isaiah, they might continue to pursue their studies of the words of this great Prophet of God.

The King James Version of the Bible and The Book of Mormon are the basic documents. Sources for the explanatory notes in parentheses are: the footnotes in the new LDS Scriptures, the JST (Joseph Smith Translation), Book of Mormon, Doctrine and Covenants, *Teachings of the Prophet Joseph Smith*, compiled by Joseph Fielding Smith, (Deseret Book Company, 1977), *Isaiah: Prophet, Seer and Poet*, by Victor L. Ludlow, (Deseret Book Company, 1982), *"Great are the Words of Isaiah"*, by Monte S. Nyman, (Bookcraft, Inc., 1980), various dictionaries, the Religion 302 Student Manual published by the Church Educational System and the Martin Luther edition of the German Bible.

One purpose of this manual is to provide readers with help in making notes in their own scriptures as they study Isaiah. The notes in parentheses are notes I have made in my own large-print copies of the new LDS Scriptures (often using all available space between lines, margins etc.). Another major goal of this "digest" is to show members of the Church that Isaiah really can be understood and enjoyed. We have been blessed with much help, including the above-named resources, and by using them, we too can say, "Great are the words of Isaiah." (3 Nephi 23:1).

In order to keep the notes in parentheses brief and somewhat conversational, considerable license has been taken with respect to capitalization and punctuation. These explanations and interpretations are not intended to be the final word on Isaiah. Hopefully, readers will begin to see many other possibilities for interpretation and application of Isaiah, for the symbolism and messages of Isaiah do indeed lend themselves to multiple interpretations in various settings. The text comes from the King James Version of the Bible. Maps referred to are those in the 1991 edition of the LDS Bible.

David J. Ridges

ISAIAH 1

(Chapter 1 is a preface to the whole book of Isaiah, much like D&C, section one, is to the whole Doctrine and Covenants.)

1 The vision of Isaiah the son of Amoz, which he saw concerning Judah and Jerusalem in the days of Uzziah, Jotham, Ahaz, and Hezekiah, kings of Judah (an introduction to the whole book—a superscription similar to "An account of Lehi..." at the beginning of First Nephi. The kings mentioned above reigned from about 740 BC to 701 BC).

2 Hear, O heavens, and give ear, O earth: for the Lord hath spoken, I have nourished and brought up children, and they have rebelled against me (the main problem).

3 The ox knoweth his owner, and the ass his master's crib (manger): but Israel doth not know (know God), my people doth not consider (think seriously, i.e., Israel, you are acting dumber than animals!).

4 Ah sinful nation, a people laden with iniquity (loaded with wickedness), a seed of evildoers, children that are corrupters: they have forsaken the Lord, they have provoked the Holy One of Israel unto anger, they are gone away backward (retrogressing; they are "in the world" and "of the world").

5 Why should ye be stricken any more (why do you keep asking for more punishment)? ye will revolt more and more: the whole head (leadership) is sick, and the whole heart (the people) faint (is diseased).

6 From the sole of the foot even unto the head there is no soundness in it (you are completely sick); but wounds, and bruises, and putrifying sores: they have not been closed, neither bound up, neither mollified with ointment (you are sick and you don't even care; you won't try the simplest first aid).

7 Your country is desolate (prophecy of coming destruction), your cities are burned with fire: your land, strangers devour it in your presence, and it is desolate as overthrown by strangers (foreigners, specifically the Assyrians).

8 And the daughter of Zion (Israel) is left as a cottage (temporary shade structure built of straw and leaves) in a vineyard, as a lodge (same as cottage) in a garden of cucumbers, as a besieged city (you are about as secure as a flimsy shade shack in a garden).

9 Except the Lord of hosts had left unto us a very small remnant (if God hadn't intervened and saved a few of Israel), we should have been as Sodom, and we should have been like unto Gomorrah (totally destroyed).

10 Hear the word of the Lord, ye rulers of Sodom ("Listen up, you wicked leaders!"); give ear unto the law of our God, ye people of Gomorrah (Sodom and Gomorrah symbolize total wickedness).

11 To what purpose is the multitude of your sacrifices unto me (what good are your insincere, empty rituals)? saith the Lord: I am full ("I've had it to here!") of the burnt offerings of rams, and the fat of fed beasts; and I delight not in the blood of bullocks, or of lambs, or of he goats.

12 When ye come to appear before me, who hath required this at your hand, to tread my courts (who authorized you to be such hypocrites)?

13 Bring no more vain (useless) oblations (offerings); incense is an abomination unto me; the new moons (special Sabbath ritual at beginning of month—Bible Dictionary p. 738 under "New Moon") and sabbaths, the calling of assemblies, I cannot ("I can't stand it!") away with; it is iniquity, even the solemn meeting (solemn assembly).

14 Your new moons and your appointed feasts my soul hateth: they are a trouble unto me; I am weary to bear them.

15 And when ye spread forth your hands (pray), I will hide mine eyes from you: yea, when ye make many prayers, I will not hear: your hands are full of blood (bloodshed; murder, see verse 21).

16 Wash you (be baptized), make you clean; put away the evil of your doings from before mine eyes (repent); cease to do evil;

17 Learn to do well (don't just cease to do evil, but replace evil with good); seek judgement (be fair), relieve the oppressed, judge the fatherless (be kind and fair to them), plead for the widow.

18 Come now, and let us reason together, saith the Lord: though your sins be as scarlet (cloth dyed with scarlet, a color-fast dye), they shall be as white as snow (even though you think your sins are "colorfast", the Atonement can cleanse you); though they be red like crimson, they shall be as wool (a long process is required to get wool white, but it can be done).

19 If ye be willing and obedient, ye shall eat the good of the land (you will prosper):

20 But if ye refuse and rebel, ye shall be devoured with the sword: for the mouth of the Lord hath spoken it.

21 How is the faithful city (Jerusalem) become an harlot (unfaithful to the Lord; a willful sin)! it was full of judgement (justice); righteousness lodged in it; but now murderers.

22 Thy silver is become dross (surface scum on molten metal) thy wine mixed with water (you are polluted!).

23 Thy princes (rulers) are rebellious, and companions of thieves: every one loveth gifts (bribes), and followeth after rewards: they judge not (do not justice to) the fatherless, neither doth the cause of the widow come unto them (never penetrates their hearts).

24 Therefore saith the Lord, the Lord of hosts, the mighty One of

Israel, Ah, I will ease me of (be rid of) mine adversaries, and avenge me of mine enemies:

25 And I will turn (return; i.e., repeatedly chastise) my hand upon thee, and purely purge away thy dross, and take away all thy tin (slag, i.e., I will refine thee):

26 And I will restore thy judges as at the first, and thy counsellors as at the beginning: afterward thou shalt be called, The city of righteousness, the faithful city (gathering).

27 Zion shall be redeemed (a fact!) with judgment, and her converts with righteousness (message of hope).

28 And the destruction of the transgressors and of the sinners shall be together (at the same time; Second Coming), and they that forsake the Lord shall be consumed.

29 For they shall be ashamed of (shamed because of) the oaks (trees and gardens used in idol worship) which ye have desired, and ye shall be confounded for the (because of the) gardens (used in idol worship) that ye have chosen.

30 For ye shall be as an oak whose leaf fadeth, and as a garden that hath no water (drought; destruction).

31 And the strong shall be as tow (as a tuft of inflammable fibers), and the maker of it as a spark, and they shall both burn together, and none shall quench them (destruction of the wicked is sure to happen).

ISAIAH 2

Note: Chapters 2, 3 and 4 go together.

1 The word that Isaiah the son of Amoz saw concerning Judah and Jerusalem.

2 And it shall come to pass in the last days, that the mountain ("high place", i.e., temples will be established; also, the Church will be established in the tops of the mountains in the last days) of the Lord's house shall be established in the top of the mountains, and shall be exalted above the hills (you can get higher, closer to God in the temples than on the highest mountains); and all nations shall flow unto it.

3 And many people shall go and say, Come ye, and let us go up to the mountain of the Lord, to the house (temples) of the God of Jacob; and he will teach us of his ways, and we will walk in his paths: for out of Zion shall go forth the law, and the word of the Lord from Jerusalem ("law" and "word" are synonyms).

4 And he shall judge among the nations, and shall rebuke many people: and they shall beat their swords into plowshares, and their spears into pruninghooks (there will be peace): nation shall not lift up sword against nation, neither shall they learn war any more (millennium).

5 (Isaiah now switches from the

future back to his own time and people.) O house of Jacob (Israel), come ye, and let us walk in the light of the Lord.

6 Therefore (this is why) thou (the Lord) hast forsaken thy people the house of Jacob (the Israelites), because they be replenished from the east (are adopting false eastern religions), and are soothsayers (are into witchcraft, sorcery etc.) like the Philistines, and they please themselves in the children of strangers (are mixing with and marrying foreigners, people not of covenant Israel).

7 Their land also is full of silver and gold, neither is there any end of their treasures (they have become materialistic); their land is also full of horses, neither is there any end of their chariots (horses and chariots represent machines of war):

8 Their land also is full of idols; they worship the work of their own hands, that which their own fingers have made (an absurd thing to do):

9 And the mean (poor, low in social status) man boweth (not, see 2 N. 12:9) down, and the great man humbleth himself (not): therefore forgive them not (no one is humble).

10 Enter into the rock (you wicked people), and hide thee in the dust, for fear of the Lord and for (2 Nephi 12:10 does not have "for") the glory of his majesty (shall smite thee).

11 The lofty looks of man (pride) shall be humbled, and the haughtiness of men shall be bowed down, and the

Lord alone shall be exalted in that day (i.e., the Lord will demonstrate power over all things at the 2nd Coming).

12 For the day of the Lord of hosts (2nd Coming) shall be upon (against) every one that is proud and lofty, and upon (against) every one that is lifted up; and he shall be brought low:

13 And upon all the cedars (people) of Lebanon, that are high and lifted up, and upon all the oaks (people) of Bashan,

14 And upon all the high mountains, and upon all the hills that are lifted up,

15 And upon every high tower, and upon every fenced wall (man-made defenses),

16 And upon all the ships of Tarshish (noted for ability to travel long distances, carry large cargos and strength as warships), and upon all pleasant pictures (pleasure craft upon which the wealthy traveled).

17 And the loftiness (pride) of man shall be bowed down, and the haughtiness of men shall be made low: and the Lord alone shall be exalted in that day.

18 And the idols he shall utterly abolish.

19 And they shall go into the holes of the rocks (caves), and into the caves of the earth, for fear of the Lord, and for the glory of his majesty, when he ariseth to shake terribly the earth.

20 In that day (2nd Coming) a man shall cast his idols of silver, and his idols of gold, which they made each one for himself to worship (totally

absurd), to the moles and the bats (live in darkness like wicked people do);

21 To go into the clefts of the rocks, and into the tops of the ragged rocks, for fear of the Lord, and for the glory of his majesty, when he ariseth to shake terribly the earth.

22 Cease ye from man, whose breath is in his nostrils: for wherein is he to be accounted of (why trust in man)?

ISAIAH 3

Note: In this chapter, Isaiah uses "chiasmus", a poetic writing form in which the author says certain things, then repeats them in reverse order for emphasis.

1 For, behold, the Lord, the Lord of hosts, doth take away from Jerusalem (chiasmus A) and from Judah the stay (supply) and the staff (support), the whole stay of bread (chiasmus B), and the whole stay of water (the Lord is going to pull the props out and the whole thing will collapse),

2 The mighty man (chiasmus C), and the man of war (your military power will crumble), the judge, and the prophet, and the prudent, and the ancient,

3 The captain of fifty, and the honorable man (chiasmus D), and the counsellor (no competent leaders), and the cunning artificer (skilled craftsman), and the eloquent orator (all the stable, dependable people will be gone).

4 And I will give children to be their princes (leaders), and babes (chiasmus E) shall rule over them (immature, irresponsible leaders will take over).

5 And the people shall be oppressed, everyone (chiasmus F) by another, (this is the pivot point of this chiasmus) and every one by his neighbour (anarchy): the child shall behave himself proudly against the ancient (chiasmus E'), and the base against the honourable (no respect for authority; departing from common sense, wisdom).

6 When a man shall take hold of his brother of the house of his father, saying, Thou hast clothing, be thou our ruler (chiasmus D'), and let (not) this ruin be under thy hand (be our leader, don't let this happen to us):

7 In that day shall he swear (protest), saying, I will not be (chiasmus C') an healer (I can't defend and protect you!); for in my house is neither bread (chiasmus B') nor clothing: make me not a ruler of the people (I can't solve your problems. I've got my own problems).

8 For Jerusalem is ruined (chiasmus A'), and Judah is fallen: because their tongue and their doings are against the Lord, to provoke the eyes of his glory (in word and actions, the people are completely against the Lord).

9 The shew of their countenance doth witness against them; and they

declare their sin as Sodom, they hide it not (blatant sin...no shame!). Woe unto their soul! for they have rewarded evil unto themselves.

10 Say ye to the righteous, that it shall be well with him; for they shall eat the fruit of their doings (righteousness will pay off).

11 Woe unto the wicked! it shall be ill with him: for the reward of his hands shall be given him ("As ye sow, so shall ye reap.")

12 As for my people, children are their oppressors, and women rule over them (breakdown of traditional family; men are weak leaders). O my people, they which lead thee cause thee to err, and destroy the way of thy paths (leadership without basic gospel values).

13 The Lord standeth up to plead, and standeth to judge the people.

14 The Lord will enter into judgment with the ancients of his people,, and the princes (leaders) thereof: for ye have eaten up the vineyard; the spoil of the poor is in your houses (you were supposed to protect them, but, instead, you prey on them).

15 What mean ye (what have you got to say for yourselves) that ye beat my people to pieces, and grind the faces of the poor? saith the Lord God of hosts.

16 (Isaiah now says that society is lost when women also turn to evil.) Moreover the Lord saith, Because the daughters of Zion are haughty (full of pride), and walk with stretched forth necks and wanton eyes (lustful),

walking and mincing as they go, and making a tinkling with their feet (so people will notice them):

17 Therefore (for these reasons) the Lord will smite with a scab the crown of the head (take away their beauty) of the daughters of Zion, and the Lord will discover their secret parts (expose their evil deeds).

18 In that day the Lord will take away the bravery (beauty) of their tinkling ornaments about their feet, and their cauls, and their round tires like the moon (female ornamentations),

19 The chains, and the bracelets, and the mufflers (veils),

20 The bonnets, and the ornaments of the legs, and the headbands, and the tablets (perfume boxes), and the earrings,

21 The rings, and nose jewels,

22 The changeable suits of apparel (beautiful clothing), and the mantles, and the wimples (shawls), and the crisping pins (money purses),

23 The glasses (see-through clothing, Isa. 3:23, footnote a), and the fine linen, and the hoods (turbans), and the vails. (Isaiah has described female high-society fashions, arrogance and materialism in terms of such things in his day).

24 And it shall come to pass, that instead of sweet smell there shall be stink (from corpses of people killed by invading armies); and instead of a girdle a rent (rags), and instead of well set hair baldness (slaves had shaved heads); and instead of a stom-

acher (nice robe) a girding of sackcloth; and burning (branding, a mark of slavery) instead of beauty.

25 Thy men shall fall by the sword, and thy mighty in the war (invasion).

26 And her (Jerusalem's) gates shall lament and mourn; and she being desolate (empty, defeated) shall sit upon the ground.

ISAIAH 4

1 (The Joseph Smith Translation and the Hebrew Bible put this verse at the end of chapter 3, which puts this verse in the context of Jerusalem's destruction and the scarcity of men resulting from that invasion.) And in that day seven women shall take hold of one man, saying, We will eat our own bread, and wear our own apparel (we will pay our own way): only let us be called by thy name (please marry us), to take away our reproach (the stigma of being unmarried and childless).

2 (This verse starts a new topic, namely conditions during the Millennium.) In that day shall the branch of the Lord (often refers to Messiah in Hebrew) be beautiful and glorious, and the fruit of the earth shall be excellent and comely (pleasant to look at) for them that are escaped of Israel (those who have escaped wickedness, i.e., the righteous remnant of Israel).

3 And it shall come to pass, that he that is left in Zion, and he that remaineth in Jerusalem, shall be called holy, even every one that is written among the living (those saved by approval of the Messiah) in Jerusalem:

4 When the Lord shall have washed away the filth of the daughters of Zion (when the Lord has cleansed the earth), and shall have purged the blood of Jerusalem from the midst thereof by the spirit of judgement, and by the spirit of burning (earth will be cleansed by fire).

5 (Note: Angel Moroni quoted verses 5 & 6 to Joseph Smith in reference to the last days. See Messenger and Advocate, April 1835, p. 110.) And the Lord will create upon every dwelling place of mount Zion, and upon her assemblies, a cloud and smoke by day (represents the presence of the Lord as in Exodus 19:16-18), and the shining of a flaming fire by night (presence of God): for upon all (everyone) the glory shall be a defence.

6 And there shall be a tabernacle (shelter) for a shadow (shade) in the daytime from the heat, and for a place of refuge, and for a covert (protection) from storm and from rain (Millennial peace and protection).

ISAIAH 5

1 Now will I sing (Isaiah composes a song or poetic parable of a vineyard, showing God's mercy and Israel's unresponsiveness) to my wellbeloved a song of my beloved (Christ) touching his vineyard (Israel). My

wellbeloved hath a vineyard in a very fruitful hill:

2 And he fenced it, and gathered out the stones thereof, and planted it with the choicest vine, and built a tower (set prophets) in the midst of it, and also made a winepress therein (for a good harvest): and he looked that it should bring forth grapes (the desired product, faithful people), and it brought forth wild grapes (apostasy).

3 And now, O inhabitants of Jerusalem, and men of Judah, judge, I pray you, betwixt me and my vineyard (I'll give you the facts; you be the judge).

4 What could have been done more to my vineyard, that I have not done in it (the main question)? wherefore (why), when I looked (planned) that it should bring forth grapes (the desired result), brought it forth wild grapes (apostasy)?

5 And now go to; I will tell you what I will do to my vineyard (Israel): I will take away the hedge (divine protection) thereof, and it shall be eaten up; and break down the wall (protection) thereof, and it shall be trodden down:

6 And I will lay it waste: it shall not be pruned, nor digged (the Spirit withdraws, no prophets); but there shall come up briers and thorns (apostate doctrines and behaviors): I will also command the clouds that they rain no rain upon it.

7 For the vineyard of the Lord of hosts is the house of Israel, and the men of Judah his pleasant plant: and he looked for judgement (fairness,

etc.), but behold oppression; for righteousness, but behold a cry (riotous living).

8 Woe unto them (the powerful, wealthy) that join house to house, that lay field to field, till there be no place, that they (the poor) may be placed alone in the midst of the earth (those in power push the poor farmers off their land).

9 In mine ears said the Lord of hosts, Of a truth many houses shall be desolate, even great and fair, without inhabitant (troubles are coming because of your wickedness).

10 Yea, ten acres of vineyard shall yield one bath (about 8 1/4 U.S. gallons), and the seed of an homer (6 1/2 bushel of seed) shall yield an ephah (1/2 bushel of harvest; famine is coming!).

11 Woe unto them that rise up early in the morning, that they may follow strong drink; that continue until night, till wine inflame them!

12 And the harp, and the viol (lyre), the tabret (drums), and pipe (instruments associated with worship of the Lord), and wine, are in their feasts: but they regard not the work of the Lord (their worship is empty, hypocritical), neither consider the operation of his hands (they do not actually acknowledge God).

13 Therefore (that is why) my people are gone into captivity, because they have no knowledge (Amos 8:11-12 famine of hearing words of the Lord); and their honourable men are famished, and

their multitude dried up with thirst.

14 Therefore (that is why) hell hath enlarged herself (they've had to add on to hell to make room for you!), and opened her mouth without measure: and their glory, and their multitude, and their pomp, and he that rejoiceth (in riotous living), shall descend into it.

15 And the mean (poor) man shall be brought down, and the mighty man shall be humbled, and the eyes of the lofty shall be humbled (everyone needs humbling):

16 But the Lord of hosts shall be exalted in judgment, and God that is holy shall be sanctified in righteousness (the Lord will triumph).

17 Then shall the lambs feed (graze where the Lord's vineyard once stood, ie, destruction is complete) after their manner, and the waste places of the fat ones shall strangers (foreigners) eat.

18 Woe unto them that draw iniquity with cords of vanity, and sin as it were with a cart rope (you are tethered to your sins; they follow you like a cart follows the animal pulling it!):

19 That say, Let him (the Lord) make speed, and hasten his work, that we may see it (it is up to God to prove to us that he exists): and let the counsel (plans) of the Holy One of Israel draw nigh and come, that we may know it!

20 Woe unto them that call evil good, and good evil; that put darkness for light, and light for darkness; that put bitter for sweet, and sweet for bitter!

21 Woe unto them that are wise in their own eyes (full of evil pride), and prudent in their own sight!

22 Woe unto them that are mighty to drink wine, and men of strength to mingle strong drink:

23 Which justify the wicked for reward (bribes, i.e., corrupt judicial system), and take away the righteousness of the righteous from him (deprive the innocent of his rights)!

24 Therefore as the fire devoureth the stubble, and the flame consumeth the chaff, so their root shall be as rottenness, and their blossom shall go up as dust (not bear fruit, no posterity in the next life and destruction of many in this life): because they have cast away the law of the Lord of hosts, and despised the word of the Holy One of Israel.

25 Therefore (for these reasons) is the anger of the Lord kindled against his people, and he hath stretched forth his hand against them, and hath smitten them: and the hills did tremble, and their carcases were torn in the midst of the streets (great destruction). For all this his anger is not turned away, but his hand is stretched out still (you can still repent, Jacob 6:4).

26 And he will lift up an ensign (flag, rallying point; the true gospel) to the nations from far, and will hiss (whistle; a signal to gather) unto them from the end of the earth: and, behold, they shall come with speed swiftly (modern transportation?):

27 None shall be weary nor stumble among them; none shall slumber nor sleep; neither shall the girdle of their loins be loosed, nor the latchet of their shoes be broken (they will travel so fast that they won't need to change clothes or even take their shoes off):

28 Whose arrows are sharp, and all their bows bent, their horses' hoofs shall be counted like flint, and their wheels like a whirlwind (trains, airplanes?):

29 Their roaring shall be like a lion (airplanes etc?), they shall roar like young lions: yea, they shall roar, and lay hold of the prey (passengers in modern types of transportation?), and shall carry it away safe, and none shall deliver it (the converts, i.e., none will stop the gathering in the last days).

30 And in that day (the Last Days) they shall roar against them like the roaring of the sea: and if one look unto the land, light is darkened in the heavens thereof (conditions in the last days, war, smoke, pollutions etc.?)

ISAIAH 6

1 (This chapter deals with Isaiah's call, either his initial call or a subsequent call to a major responsibility.) In the year (about 740 BC) that king Uzziah died I (Isaiah) saw also the Lord (Jesus) sitting upon a throne, high and lifted up ("exalted"), and his train (skirts of his robe; authority, power; Hebrew: wake, light) filled the temple.

2 Above it (the throne) stood the seraphims (angelic beings): each one had six wings (symbolic of power to move, act etc. in God's work, D&C 77:4); with twain he covered his face (showing respect toward God), and with twain he covered his feet, and with twain he did fly.

3 And one cried unto another, and said, Holy, holy, holy (repeated three times is the superlative, means the very best in Hebrew), is the Lord of hosts: the whole earth is full of his glory.

4 And the posts of the door moved (shook) at the voice of him that cried, and the house was filled with smoke (symbolic of God's presence, as at Sinai, Ex. 19:18).

5 Then said I, Woe is me! for I am undone (completely overwhelmed); because I am a man of unclean lips (I am so imperfect!), and I dwell in the midst of a people of unclean lips: for mine eyes have seen the King, the Lord of hosts.

6 Then flew one of the seraphims unto me, having a live coal (the Holy Ghost cleanses by fire and makes us equal to callings) in his hand, which he had taken with the tongs from off the altar (the atonement; i.e., Christ was sacrificed for us on the "altar" cross):

7 And he laid it upon my mouth (inadequacies, sins, imperfections), and said, Lo, this (the Atonement) hath touched thy lips; and thine iniquity is taken away, and thy sin purged (results of the Atonement).

8 Also I heard the voice of the Lord, saying, Whom shall I send, and who will go for us? Then said I (Isaiah), Here am I; send me (the cleansing power of the Atonement and help of the Spirit gave Isaiah the needed confidence to accept the call).

9 And he said, Go, and tell this people, Hear ye indeed, but understand not; and see ye indeed, but perceive not (Isaiah's task will not be easy with that kind of people).

10 (I.e., Isaiah, get a clear view of the type of people you will be dealing with.) Make the heart (chiasmus A) of this people fat (unfeeling), and make their ears (chiasmus B) heavy (deaf to spiritual matters), and shut their eyes (chiasmus C) (i.e., spiritually blind); lest they see with their eyes (chiasmus C'), and hear with their ears (chiasmus B'), and understand with their heart (chiasmus A'), and convert and be healed (compare with Matt. 13:15).

11 Then said I, Lord, how long (will people be like this)? And he answered, Until the cities be wasted without inhabitant, and the houses without man, and the land be utterly desolate (i.e., as long as people are around).

12 And the Lord have removed men far away (people are gone), and there be a great forsaking (many deserted cities) in the midst of the land.

13 But yet in it (the land) shall be a tenth (remnant), and it (Israel) shall return (includes concept of repenting), and shall be eaten (pruned—as by animals eating the limbs, leaves and branches—i.e., the Lord "prunes" his vineyard, cuts out old apostates etc.; destroys old unrighteous generations so new may have a chance): as a teil (lime?) tree, and as an oak, whose substance (sap) is in them, when they cast their leaves (shed the old, non-functioning leaves and look dead in winter): so the holy seed shall be the substance thereof (Israel may look dead, but there is still life in it).

ISAIAH 7

1 And it came to pass in the days of Ahaz (about 734 BC) the son of Jotham, the son of Uzziah, king of Judah, that Rezin the king of Syria, and Pekah the son of Remaliah, king of Israel (the 10 Tribes in northern Israel), went up toward Jerusalem to war against it, but could not prevail against it (didn't win, but they did kill 120,000 men of Judah and take 200,000 captives in one day; see 2 Chr. 28:6-15).

2 And it was told the house of David (Jerusalem), saying, Syria is confederate (joining forces) with Ephraim (Israel, Northern Ten Tribes). And his (Ahaz's) heart was moved (shaken), and the heart of his people, as the trees of the wood are moved with the wind (they were "shaking in their boots", scared).

3 Then said the Lord unto Isaiah, Go forth now to meet Ahaz (king in Jerusalem), thou, and Shear-jashub

("the remnant shall return") thy son, at the end of the conduit of the upper pool in the highway of the fuller's field (where the women wash clothes; i.e., Ahaz is hiding among the women);

4 And say unto him, Take heed, and be quiet; fear not, neither be faint-hearted (don't worry about continued threats from Syria and Israel) for (because of) the two tails of these smoking firebrands (smoldering stubs of firewood), for (because of) the fierce anger of Rezin with Syria, and of the son of Remaliah.

5 Because Syria, Ephraim (the Ten Tribes), and the son of Remaliah (the Ten Tribes' king), have taken evil counsel (have evil plans) against thee, saying,

6 Let us go up against Judah, and vex it, and let us make a breach therein for us, and set a king in the midst of it (set up our own king in Jerusalem), even the son of Tabeal:

7 Thus saith the Lord God, It shall not stand, neither shall it come to pass (the plot will fail so don't worry about it).

8 For the head (capital city) of Syria is Damascus, and the head (leader) of Damascus is Rezin; and within three-score and five years (65 years) shall Ephraim (the Ten Tribes) be broken, that it be not a people (in 65 years, the Ten Tribes will be lost).

9 And the head (capital city) of Ephraim is Samaria, and the head (leader) of Samaria is Remaliah's son. If ye (Ahaz and his people, the tribe of Judah) will not believe (in the Lord), surely ye shall not be established (not be saved by the Lord's power).

10 Moreover the Lord spake again unto Ahaz, saying,

11 Ask thee a sign (to strengthen your faith) of the Lord thy God; ask it either in the depth or in the height above.

12 But Ahaz said, I will not ask, neither will I tempt (test) the Lord (refuses to follow prophet's counsel; is deliberately evasive, secretly depending on Assyria for help).

13 And he said, Hear ye now, O house of David (Ahaz and his people, Judah); Is it a small thing for you to weary men, but will ye weary my God also (try the patience of God)?

14 Therefore (because of your disobedience) the Lord himself shall give you a sign; Behold, a virgin shall conceive, and bear a son, and shall call his name Immanuel (the day will come when the Savior will be born).

15 Butter and honey (curd and honey, the only foods available to the poor at times) shall he eat, that he may know to refuse the evil, and choose the good.

16 For before the child shall know to refuse the evil, and choose the good (before old enough to choose right from wrong, i.e., in just a few years), the land (both Israel and Syria) that thou abhorrest shall be forsaken of both her kings.

17 The Lord shall bring upon thee (Ahaz), and upon thy people, and upon thy father's house, days that

have not come (trouble like never before), from the day that Ephraim departed from Judah (when Israel split into the Northern Kingdom under Jeroboam I, and the tribes of Judah and Benjamin under Rehoboam, about 975 BC); even the king of Assyria.

18 And it shall come to pass in that day, that the Lord shall hiss (signal, call for) for the fly (associated with plagues, troubles etc.) that is in the uttermost part of the rivers of Egypt, and for the bee that is in the land of Assyria.

19 And they shall come, and shall rest all of them in the desolate valleys, and in the holes of the rocks, and upon all thorns, and upon all bushes (will overrun the land).

20 In the same day shall the Lord shave with a razor (fate of captives, slaves who are shaved—for humiliation, sanitation, identification) that is hired (Assyria will be "hired" to do this to Judah), namely, by them beyond the river, by the king of Assyria, the head, and the hair of the feet: and it shall also consume the beard (they will shave you clean, i.e., conquer you).

21 And it shall come to pass in that day (after much devastation in Judah), that a man shall nourish a young cow, and two sheep;

22 And it shall come to pass, for the abundance of milk that they (the domestic animals) shall give he shall eat butter: for butter and honey shall every one eat that is left in the land (not many people left, so a few animals can supply them well).

23 And it shall come to pass in that day, that every place shall be, where there were a thousand vines at a thousand silverlings (worth a thousand pieces of silver), it shall even be for briers and thorns (uncultivated land where it used to be cultivated and productive; apostasy).

24 With arrows and bows shall men come thither; because all the land shall become briers and thorns (previously cultivated land will become wild and overgrown so hunters will hunt wild beasts there).

25 And on all hills that shall be digged (that were once cultivated) with the mattock (hoe), there (you) shall not come thither (because of) the fear of briers and thorns: but it shall be for the sending forth (pasturing) of oxen, and for the treading of lesser cattle (sheep or goats).

ISAIAH 8

1 Moreover the Lord said unto me, Take thee a great (large) roll (scroll), and write in it with a man's pen concerning Maher-shalal-hash-baz (to speed to the spoil, he hasteneth the prey).

2 And I (Isaiah) took unto me faithful witnesses to record, Uriah the priest, and Zechariah the son of Jeberechiah.

3 And I went unto the prophetess (Isaiah's wife); and she conceived, and bare a son. Then said the Lord to

me, Call his name Maher-shalal-hash-baz.

4 For before the child shall have knowledge to cry, My father, and my mother, the riches of Damascus (Syria) and the spoil of Samaria (Northern Israel, ie, the Ten Tribes) shall be taken away before the king of Assyria (before Isaiah's son is old enough to say "Daddy", "Mommy", Assyria will attack Northern Israel and Syria).

5 The Lord spake also unto me again, saying,

6 Forasmuch as this people (Jerusalem) refuseth the waters of Shiloah (the gentle help of Christ, John 4:14) that go softly, and rejoice in Rezin (heed Syria instead of the Lord) and Remaliah's son (Northern Israel's king);

7 Now therefore, behold, the Lord bringeth up upon them the waters of the river, strong (terrifying) and many, even the king of Assyria, and all his glory (his pomp, armies etc.): and he shall come up over all his channels, and go over all his banks (you'll be "flooded" by Assyrians):

8 And he (Assyria) shall pass through Judah; he shall overflow and go over, he shall reach even to the neck; and the stretching out of his wings shall fill the breadth of thy land, O Immanuel (ie, the land of the future birth of Christ).

9 Associate yourselves (if you form political alliances for protection rather than turning to God), O ye people, and ye shall be broken in pieces; and give ear, all ye of far countries (foreign nations who might rise against Judah): gird yourselves (prepare for war), and ye shall be broken in pieces; gird yourselves, and ye shall be broken in pieces (note that "broken in pieces" is repeated three times for emphasis; 3 times = Hebrew superlative).

10 Take counsel together, and it shall come to nought (your plans to destroy Judah will not succeed ultimately); speak the word, and it shall not stand: for God is with us (Judah won't be destroyed completely).

11 For the Lord spake thus to me (Isaiah) with a strong hand (with power), and instructed me that I should not walk in the way of this people (Judah), saying,

12 Say ye not, A confederacy, to all them to whom this people shall say, A confederacy; neither fear ye their fear, nor be afraid ("Isaiah, don't endorse Judah's plan for confederacy with Assyria. Don't tell them what they want to hear.").

13 Sanctify the Lord of hosts himself; and let him be your fear, and let him be your dread ("Isaiah, you rely on the Lord, not public approval.").

14 And he shall be for a sanctuary (for you, Isaiah); but for a stone of stumbling and for a rock of offence (rock that makes them fall) to both the houses of Israel (Northern and Southern), for a gin (a trap) and for a snare to the inhabitants of Jerusalem.

15 And many among them shall

stumble, and fall, and be broken, and be snared, and be taken.

16 Bind up the testimony (record your testimony, Isaiah), seal the law among my disciples (followers).

17 And I (Isaiah) will wait upon the Lord (I will trust the Lord), that hideth his face from the house of Jacob (Israel), and I will look for him.

18 Behold, I and the children whom the Lord hath given me are for signs and for wonders in Israel from the Lord of hosts, which dwelleth in mount Zion.

19 And when they (the wicked) shall say unto you, Seek unto them (spiritualists, mediums etc.) that have familiar spirits, and unto wizards that peep (into their crystal balls etc.), and mutter: should not a people seek unto their God? for the living to the dead (why consult the dead on behalf of the living)?

20 To the law and to the testimony (the scriptures): if they speak not according to this word (the scriptures), it is because there is no light in them (the mediums etc).

21 And they (Israel; will be taken into captivity) shall pass through it (the land) hardly bestead (much distressed) and hungry: and it shall come to pass, that when they shall be hungry, they shall fret themselves (become enraged), and curse their king and their God, and look upward (cockey, defiant).

22 And they shall look unto the earth (will look around them); and behold (see only) trouble and dark-

ness, dimness of anguish (gloom); and they shall be driven to darkness (thrust into utter despair; results of wickedness).

ISAIAH 9

1 (Note: This verse is the last verse of chapter 8 in the Hebrew Bible. King Ahaz of Judah ignored Isaiah's counsel and made an alliance with Assyria.) Nevertheless the dimness (referred to in 8:22) shall not be such as was in her vexation, when at the first (Assyrian attacks in Isaiah's day) he lightly afflicted the land of Zebulun (in Northern Israel) and the land of Naphtali (in Northern Israel), and afterward did more grievously afflict (Hebrew: gloriously bless; German: bring honor to) her by the way of the sea, beyond Jordan, in Galilee of the nations (blessed her via Jesus walking in Galilee).

2 The people that walked in darkness (apostasy and captivity) have seen a great light (the Savior and his teachings): they that dwell in the land of the shadow of death, upon them hath the light shined.

3 Thou hast multiplied the nation, and not ("not" is a mistake in translation and doesn't belong here; see 2 Nephi 19:3) increased the joy: they joy before thee according to the joy in harvest, and as men rejoice when they divide the spoil (Christ and his faithful followers will ultimately triumph).

4 For thou hast broken the yoke of

his burden, and the staff of his shoulder, the rod of his oppressor, as in the day of Midian (with Gideon and his 300; Judges 7:22).

5 For every battle of the warrior is with confused noise, and garments rolled in blood; but this shall be with burning (the burning at the 2nd Coming) and fuel of fire.

6 For unto us a child (Christ) is born, unto us a son is given: and the government shall be upon his shoulder: and his name shall be called Wonderful, Counselor, The mighty God, The everlasting Father, The Prince of Peace.

7 Of the increase of his government and peace there shall be no end, upon the throne of David, and upon his kingdom, to order it, and to establish it with judgment (fairness) and with justice from henceforth even for ever. The zeal of the Lord of hosts will perform this.

8 The Lord sent a word into Jacob (continued message to Northern Israel), and it hath lighted upon Israel.

9 And all the people shall know, even Ephraim (Northern Israel) and the inhabitant of Samaria (Northern Israel), that say in the pride and stoutness of heart,

10 The bricks are fallen down, but we will build with hewn stones (boastful Northern Israel claims they can't be destroyed, but would simply rebuild with better materials than before): the sycomores are cut down, but we will change them into cedars.

11 Therefore (this is why, ie,

because of wicked pride) the Lord shall set up the adversaries of Rezin (Syria) against him, and join his enemies together;

12 The Syrians before (on the East), and the Philistines behind (on the West); and they shall devour Israel with open mouth. For all this his anger is not turned away, but his hand is stretched out still (the Lord will still let you repent if you will turn to him. Compare with Jacob 6:4&5).

13 For the people turneth not unto him (the Lord) that smiteth them, neither do they seek the Lord of hosts (the people won't repent).

14 Therefore the Lord will cut off from Israel head (leaders) and tail (false prophets), branch (Hebrew: palm branch = triumph) and rush (reed = people low in social status) in one day.

15 The ancient and honourable, he is the head; and the prophet that teacheth lies, he is the tail.

16 For the leaders of this people cause them to err; and they that are led of them are destroyed.

17 Therefore the Lord shall have no joy in their young men, neither shall have mercy on their fatherless and widows (all levels of society have gone bad): for every one is an hypocrite and an evildoer, and every mouth speaketh folly. For all this his anger is not turned away, but his hand is stretched out still (please repent!).

18 For wickedness burneth as the fire (wickedness destroys like wildfire): it shall devour the briers and

thorns, and shall kindle in the thickets of the forest, and they shall mount up like the lifting up of smoke.

19 Through the wrath of the Lord of hosts is the land darkened (awful conditions), and the people shall be as the fuel of the fire: no man shall spare his brother.

20 And he shall snatch on the right hand, and be hungry; and he shall eat on the left hand, and they shall not be satisfied: they shall eat every man the flesh of his own arm (the wicked will turn on each other):

21 Manasseh, Ephraim; and Ephraim, Manasseh: and they together shall be against Judah. For all this his anger is not turned away, but his hand is stretched out still (you can still repent; please do!)

ISAIAH 10

1 Woe unto them that decree unrighteous decrees (unrighteous laws), and that write grievousness (oppression) which they have prescribed;

2 To turn aside the needy from judgment (fair treatment), and to take away the right from the poor of my people, that widows may be their prey (victims), and that they may rob the fatherless!

3 And what will ye do in the day of visitation (punishment), and in the desolation which shall come from far (from Assyria)? to whom will ye flee for help? and where will ye leave your glory (wealth etc.)?

4 Without me (God) they shall bow down under the prisoners ("huddle among the prisoners"), and they shall fall under the slain. For all this his anger is not turned away, but his hand is stretched out still (you can still repent).

5 O Assyrian, the rod (tool of destruction used by the Lord to hammer Israel) of mine anger, and the staff in their hand is mine indignation.

6 I will send him (Assyria) against an hypocritical nation (Israel), and against the people of my wrath will I give him a charge, to take the spoil, and to take the prey, and to tread them (Israel) down like the mire of the streets.

7 Howbeit he meaneth not so, neither doth his heart think so (king of Assyria doesn't realize he is a tool in God's hand, thinks he's very important on his own); but it is in his heart to destroy and cut off nations not a few.

8 For he (Assyrian king) saith, Are not my princes (commanders) altogether kings (just like kings in other countries)?

9 Is not Calno as Carchemish? is not Hamath as Arpad? is not Samaria as Damascus (Assyria has already taken these cities)?

10 As my hand hath found the kingdoms of the idols, and whose graven images did excel them of Jerusalem and of Samaria:

11 Shall I not, as I have done unto Samaria and her idols, so do to Jerusalem and her idols (a boast; I'll

do the same to Jerusalem)?

12 Wherefore it shall come to pass, that when the Lord hath performed his whole work upon mount Zion and on Jerusalem, I will punish the fruit of the stout heart of the king of Assyria, and the glory of his high looks (when I'm through using Assyria against Israel, then Assyria will get its just punishments).

13 For he (Assyrian king) saith, By the strength of my hand I have done it, and by my wisdom; for I am prudent: and I have removed the bounds of the people, and have robbed their treasures, and I have put down the inhabitants like a valiant man (bragging):

14 And my hand hath found as a nest the riches of the people: and as one gathereth eggs that are left, have I gathered all the earth; and there was none that moved the wing, or opened the mouth, or peeped (everybody is afraid of me!).

15 Shall the axe (Assyria) boast itself against him (the Lord) that heweth therewith? or shall the saw magnify itself against him that shaketh it (uses it)? as if the rod should shake itself against them that lift it up, or as if the staff should lift up itself, as if it were no wood (i.e.,. how foolish for people to say they don't need the Lord).

16 Therefore shall the Lord, the Lord of hosts, send among his fat ones (Assyria's powerful armies) leaness (trouble is coming); and under his (Assyria's) glory he shall kindle a burning like the burning of a fire (the fate of Assyria).

17 And the light of Israel shall be for a fire, and his Holy One for a flame: and it shall burn and devour his (Assyria's) thorns and his briers (armies) in one day (Example: 185,000 Assyrians died of devastating sickness in one night as they prepared to attack Jerusalem; see 2 Kings 19:35-37);

18 And shall consume the glory of his forest, and of his fruitful field, both soul and body: and they shall be as when a standardbearer fainteth (as when the last soldier falls and the flag with him, i.e., you will waste away, be destroyed).

19 And the rest of the trees (people) of his forest shall be few, that a child may write them (a little child can count them).

20 And it shall come to pass in that day (the last days), that the remnant of Israel, and such as are escaped of the house of Jacob (Israel), shall no more again stay (depend) upon him (Assyria; Satan) that smote them; but shall stay upon the Lord, the Holy One of Israel, in truth.

21 The remnant shall return, even the remnant of Jacob, unto the mighty God (1. A remnant remains in the land after Assyrian destruction. 2. A future righteous remnant).

22 For though thy people Israel be as the sand of the sea, yet a remnant of them shall return: the consumption decreed (at end of the world) shall overflow with righteousness (Christ).

23 For the Lord God of hosts shall make a consumption, even determined, in the midst of all the land.

24 Therefore thus saith the Lord God of hosts, O my people that dwellest in Zion, be not afraid of the Assyrian: he shall smite thee with a rod, and shall lift up his staff against thee, after the manner of Egypt (like Egypt did in earlier times).

25 For yet a very little while, and the indignation shall cease, and mine anger in their (Assyrians) destruction.

26 And the Lord of hosts shall stir up a scourge for him according to the slaughter of Midian at the rock of Oreb: and as his rod was upon the sea, so shall he lift it up after the manner of Egypt (God will stop Assyria like he stopped the Egyptians).

27 And it shall come to pass in that day, that his burden shall be taken away from off thy shoulder, and his yoke from off thy neck, and the yoke shall be destroyed because of the anointing (i.e., the Savior).

28 He (Assyria) is come to Aiath, he is passed to Migron: at Michmash he hath laid up his carriages (symbolic of military might).

29 They are gone over the passage: they have taken up their lodging as Geba; Ramah is afraid; Gibeah of Saul is fled.

30 Lift up thy voice, O daughter of Gallim: cause it to be heard unto Laish, O poor Anathoth.

31 Madmenah is removed; the inhabitants of Gebim gather themselves to flee.

32 As yet shall he (Assyria) remain at Nob that day (Assyria will take city after city, getting closer and closer to Jerusalem until they come to Nob, just outside Jerusalem): he shall shake his hand against the mount of the daughter of Zion (Jerusalem), the hill of Jerusalem.

33 Behold, the Lord, the Lord of hosts, shall lop the bough with terror (when Assyrian armies get right to Jerusalem, the Lord will "trim them down to size", "clip their wings" and stop them in their tracks): and the high ones of stature (leaders of Assyrian armies) shall be hewn down, and the haughty shall be humbled.

34 And he shall cut down the thickets of the forest with iron (an axe), and Lebanon shall fall by a mighty one (see 2 Kings 19:32).

ISAIAH 11

1 (Moroni quoted this chapter to Joseph Smith, saying that it was about to be fulfilled, JS-H 1:40.) And there shall come forth a rod (Hebrew: twig or branch) out of the stem (root) of Jesse (Christ), and a Branch shall grow out of his roots:

2 (Christ-like qualities of leadership are described.) And the spirit of the Lord shall rest upon him, the spirit of wisdom and understanding, the spirit of counsel and might, the spirit of knowledge and of the fear of the Lord;

3 And shall make him of quick understanding in the fear of the Lord:

and he shall not judge after the sight of his eyes, neither reprove after the hearing of his ears:

4 But with righteousness shall he judge the poor, and reprove with equity for the meek of the earth: and he shall smite the earth with the rod of his mouth, and with the breath of his lips shall he slay the wicked.

5 And righteousness shall be the girdle of his loins, and faithfulness the girdle of his reins (desires, thoughts).

6 The wolf also shall dwell with the lamb and the leopard shall lie down with the kid (young goat); and the calf and the young lion and the fatling together; and a little child shall lead (herd) them (Millennial conditions).

7 And the cow and the bear shall feed (graze); their young ones shall lie down together: and the lion shall eat straw like the ox.

8 And the sucking child shall play on the hole of the asp (viper), and the weaned child shall put his hand on the cockatrice' (venomous serpent) den.

9 They shall not hurt nor destroy in all my holy mountain: for the earth shall be full of the knowledge (Hebrew: devotion) of the Lord, as the waters cover the sea.

10 And in that day there shall be a root of Jesse (probably Joseph Smith), which shall stand for an ensign of the people; to it shall the Gentiles seek: and his rest shall be glorious.

11 And it shall come to pass in that day, that the Lord shall set his hand again the second time (dual: after Babylonian captivity; also last days) to recover the remnant of his people, which shall be left, from Assyria, and from Egypt, and from Pathros, and from Cush, and from Elam, and from Shinar, and from Hamath, and from the islands of the sea.

12 And he shall set up an ensign (the Church in the last days) for the nations, and shall assemble the outcasts of Israel, and gather together the dispersed of Judah from the four corners of the earth.

13 The envy also of Ephraim shall depart, and the adversaries of Judah shall be cut off: Ephraim shall not envy Judah, and Judah shall not vex Ephraim (USA and others will work with the Jews).

14 But they (the Jews with Ephriam's help) shall fly upon the shoulders of the Philistines toward the west (attack the western slopes that were Philistine territory); they shall spoil them of the east together: they shall lay their hand upon Edom and Moab; and the children of Ammon shall obey them (the Jews will be powerful in the last days rather than easy prey for their enemies).

15 And the Lord shall utterly destroy the tongue of the Egyptian sea (productivity of Nile River ruined? See Is. 19:5-10); and with his mighty wind shall he shake his hand over the river (perhaps the river referred to in rev. 16:12, Euphrates, symbolically representing preparation for the Battle of Armageddon), and shall smite it in the seven streams, and make men go over dryshod.

16 And there shall be an highway (i.e., God will prepare a way for them to return; gathering) for the remnant of his people, which shall be left, from Assyria; like as it was to Israel in the day that he came up out of the land of Egypt.

ISAIAH 12

1 (This chapter refers to the Millennium.) And in that day thou shalt say, O Lord, I will praise thee: though thou wast angry with me, thine anger is turned away, and thou comfortedst me.

2 Behold, God is my salvation; I will trust, and not be afraid: for the Lord JEHOVAH (Jesus) is my strength and my song: he also is become my salvation.

3 Therefore with joy shall ye draw water (John 7:38-39) out of the wells of salvation.

4 And in that day shall ye say, Praise the Lord, call upon his name, declare his doings among the people, make mention that his name is exalted.

5 Sing unto the Lord; for he hath done excellent things: this is known in all the earth.

6 Cry out and shout, thou inhabitant of Zion: for great is the Holy One of Israel (Christ) in the midst of thee.

ISAIAH 13

1 The burden of (message of doom to) Babylon, which Isaiah the son of Amoz did see.

2 (The Lord will gather his righteous forces, verses 2-5.) Lift ye up a banner upon the high mountain, exalt (raise) the voice unto them (the righteous), shake the hand (wave the hand, signal), that they may go into the gates of the nobles (i.e., gather with the righteous).

3 I have commanded my sanctified ones, I have also called my mighty ones for mine anger (2 N. 23:3, "is not upon them"), even them that rejoice in my highness.

4 The noise of a multitude in the mountains (gathering), like as of a great people; a tumultuous noise of the kingdoms of nations gathered together: the Lord of hosts mustereth the host of the battle.

5 They come from a far country, from the end of heaven, even the Lord, and the weapons of his indignation, to destroy the whole land (the wicked).

6 Howl ye (the wicked); for the day of the Lord (2nd Coming) is at hand; it shall come as a destruction from the Almighty.

7 Therefore shall all hands be faint (hang limp), and every man's (wicked men) heart (courage) shall melt:

8 And they shall be afraid: pangs and sorrows shall take hold of them; they shall be in pain as a woman that travaileth (like a woman in labor, they can't get out of it now): they shall be amazed (will look in fear) one at another; their faces shall be as flames (burn with shame).

9 Behold, the day of the Lord (2nd

Coming) cometh, cruel both with wrath and fierce anger, to lay the land desolate: and he shall destroy the sinners thereof out of it (a purpose of the 2nd Coming).

10 For the stars of heaven and the constellations thereof shall not give their light: the sun shall be darkened in his going forth, and the moon shall not cause her light to shine (signs of the times).

11 And I will punish the world for their evil, and the wicked for their iniquity; and I will cause the arrogancy of the proud to cease, and will lay low the haughtiness of the terrible (tyrants; typical Isaiah repetition to drive home a point).

12 I will make a man more precious (scarce) than fine gold; even a man than the golden wedge of Ophir (a land rich in gold, possibly in southern Arabia; ie, there will be relatively few survivors of the 2nd Coming).

13 Therefore I will shake the heavens, and the earth shall remove out of her place, in the wrath of the Lord of hosts, and in the day of his fierce anger.

14 And it (dual: Babylon; also the wicked in general) shall be as the chased roe (hunted deer), and as a sheep that no man taketh up (no shepherd, no defence): they shall every man turn to his own people, and flee every one into his own land (foreigners, who have had safety in Babylon, because of Babylon's great power, will return back to homelands because Babylon is no longer

powerful and safe).

15 Every one that is found ("proud", 2 N. 23:15) shall be thrust through (stabbed); and every one that is joined unto them (with the wicked in babylon) shall fall by the sword.

16 Their children also shall be dashed to pieces before their eyes (refers only to conditions in Babylon and among the wicked before the Second Coming, not at the Second Coming; young children will not be harmed by the Second Coming of the Savior); their houses shall be spoiled, and their wives ravished (fate of Babylon / wicked).

17 Behold, I will stir up the Medes against them (a very specific prophecy; Medes, from Persia conquered Babylon easily in 538 BC), which shall not regard silver; and as for gold, they shall not delight in it (you Babylonians will not be able to bribe the Medes to not destroy you).

18 Their bows also shall dash the young men to pieces; and they shall have no pity on the fruit of the womb (babies); their eye shall not spare children.

19 And Babylon (a huge cith with 335 ft. high walls; see Bible Dictionary, p. 618), the glory of kingdoms, the beauty of the Chaldees' excellency, shall be as when God overthrew Sodom and Gomorrah (Babylon will be completely destroyed and never inhabited again).

20 It shall never be inhabited, neither shall it be dwelt in from generation to generation: neither shall the

Arabian pitch tent there; neither shall the shepherds make their fold there.

21 But wild beasts of the desert shall lie there; and their houses (the ruins) shall be full of doleful creatures (such as owls); and owls shall dwell there, and satyrs (male goats) shall dance there.

22 And the wild beasts of the islands shall cry in their desolate houses, and dragons (hyenas, wild dogs, jackals) in their pleasant palaces: and her time is near to come, and her days shall not be prolonged (Babylon's time is up, her days are almost over; see 2 N. 23:22 for rest of verse).

ISAIAH 14

1 For the Lord will have mercy on Jacob (Israel), and will yet choose ("elect for eternal happiness", 1828 Noah Webster Dictionary) Israel, and set them in their own land: (One historical fulfillment was when Cyrus the Great of Persia allowed captives in Babylon to return, 538 BC; another group returned in 520 BC. This is also being fulfilled in our day.) and the strangers shall be joined with them (foreigners will live with them), and they shall cleave to the house of Jacob.

2 And the people (many nations who will help Israel return) shall take them (Israel) and bring them to their place: and the house of Israel shall possess them (nations who used to dominate Israel) in the land of the Lord for servants and handmaids: and they (Israel) shall take them (nations who used to dominate Israel) captives, whose captives they (Israel) were; and they shall rule over their oppressors (i.e., the tables will be turned in the last days).

3 And it shall come to pass in the ("that", 2 N. 24:3; Millennium) day that the Lord shall give thee rest from thy sorrow, and from thy fear, and from the hard bondage wherein thou wast made to serve (Israel will finally be free from subjection by foreigners, enemies),

4 That thou shalt take up this proverb (a taunting) against the king of Babylon (dual: literally King of Babylon. Refers to Satan also, plus any wicked leader), and say, How hath the oppressor ceased (what happened to you!)! the golden city ceased (your unconquerable city, kingdom, is gone!)!

5 The Lord hath broken the staff of the wicked, and the sceptre of the rulers.

6 He (Babylon; Satan) who smote the people in wrath with a continual stroke, he that ruled the nations in anger, is persecuted, and none hindereth (nobody can stop it).

7 The whole earth is at rest, and is quiet: they break forth into singing (during the millennium).

8 Yea, the fir trees (people) rejoice at thee, and the cedars (people) of Lebanon, saying, Since thou art laid down (since you got chopped down), no feller (tree cutter) is come up against us.

9 Hell (spirit prison) from beneath is moved for thee (is getting ready to receive you) to meet thee at thy coming: it stirreth up the dead for thee, even all the chief ones of the earth (wicked leaders); it hath raised up from their thrones all the kings of the nations.

10 All they shall speak and say unto thee, Art thou also become weak as we (What happened to your power Satan; King of Babylon)? art thou become like unto us (did you get your wings clipped too?)?

11 Thy pomp is brought down to the grave (was destroyed with you), and the noise of thy viols (royal harp music): the worm is spread under thee, and the worms cover thee (Maggots are destroying your dead body just like they destroyed ours. You're no better off here in Hell than we are, so hah, hah, hah! Refers to the King of Babylon since Satan has no physical body.).

12 How art thou fallen from heaven, O Lucifer (What happened to you?), son of the morning! how art thou cut down to the ground, which didst weaken the nations (you used to destroy nations, now your power is destroyed.)!

13 For thou hast said in thine heart (these were your motives), I will ascend into heaven, I will exalt my throne above the stars of God (I will be the highest): I will sit also upon the mount of the congregation, in the sides of the north (mythical mountain in the north where gods assemble):

14 I will ascend above the heights of the clouds; I will be like the most High (same motive as in Moses 4:1).

15 Yet thou (Lucifer) shalt be brought down to hell, to the sides of the pit (to the lowest part of the world of the dead, i.e., outer darkness).

16 They (residents of hell) that see thee (Lucifer; King of Babylon) shall narrowly look upon thee (mock, scorn you), and consider thee, saying, Is this the man that made the earth to tremble, that did shake kingdoms;

17 That made the world as a wilderness, and destroyed the cities thereof; that opened not the house of his prisoners (never freed his prisoners)?

18 All the kings of the nations, even all of them, lie in glory, every one in his own house (all other kings have magnificent tombs etc.).

19 But thou (dual: King of Babylon literally; Satan figuratively because he doesn't even have a physical body) art cast out of thy grave like an abominable branch (pruned off and thus worthless), and as the raiment of those that are slain, thrust through with a sword (ruined and discarded), that go down to the stones of the pit (the very bottom); as a carcase trodden under feet.

20 Thou (King of Babylon/Satan) shalt not be joined with them in burial, because thou hast destroyed thy land, and slain thy people: the seed of evildoers shall never be renowned (none of your evil family will survive).

21 Prepare slaughter for his (King

of Babylon) children for the iniquity of their fathers; that they do not rise, nor possess the land, nor fill the face of the world with cities (none of your children will rule the earth like you have).

22 For I will rise up against them, saith the Lord of hosts, and cut off from Babylon the name, and remnant, and son, and nephew (I will wipe out Babylon; Satan's kingdom on earth, completely), saith the Lord.

23 I will also make it (Babylon) a possession for the bittern (owls), and pools of water: and I will sweep it with the besom (broom) of destruction (a "clean sweep"), saith the Lord of hosts.

24 (A new topic now, the fate of Assyria) The Lord of hosts hath sworn (covenanted, promised) saying, Surely as I have thought (planned), so shall it come to pass (here is something else I will do); and as I have purposed, so shall it stand (It will happen):

25 That I will break the Assyrian in my land (Judah), and upon my mountains (the mountains of Judah) tread him (the Assyrians) under foot: then shall his yoke (bondage) depart from off them (my people), and his burden depart from off their shoulders (dual: the Assyrian downfall in Judah, 701 BC/the forces of wicked will be destroyed at the Second Coming and at the end of the earth).

26 This is the purpose (the plan) that is purposed upon the whole earth: and this is the hand that is stretched out

upon all the nations (the eventual fate of all wicked nations).

27 For the Lord of hosts hath purposed, and who shall disannul it (prevent it)? and his hand is stretched out, and who shall turn it back?

28 (Topic now switches to the Philistines) In the year that king Ahaz died (about 720 BC) was this burden (message of doom to the Philistines).

29 Rejoice not (don't get all happy and start celebrating), whole Palestina (Philistia), because the rod (power) of him (Shalmaneser, King of Assyria from 727-722 BC) that smote thee is broken: for out of the serpent's root ("snakes lay eggs", i.e., from the same source, Assyria) shall come forth a cockatrice (one "snake" is dead [Shalmaneser] and a worse one will yet come [Sennacherib, King of Assyria, 705-687 BC]. The Philistines rejoiced when Sargon, King of Assyria from 722-705 took over at Shalmaneser's death. Sargon was not as hard on them as his predecessor was.), and his (Sennacherib) fruit shall be a fiery flying serpent.

30 And the firstborn of the poor shall feed, and the needy shall lie down in safety (If you Philistines will join with the Lord, repent etc., you too can enjoy peace and safety, otherwise...): and I will kill thy (Philistines) root with famine, and he shall slay thy remnant (you will be utterly destroyed if you don't repent).

31 Howl, O gate; cry, O city; thou whole Palestina (Philistia), art dissolved (reduced to nothing): for

there shall come from the north a smoke (cloud of dust made by enemy army), and none shall be alone in his appointed times (the enemy army will have no cowards in it).

32 What shall one then answer the messengers of the nation (Philistia, i.e., what will one say when people ask, "What happened to the Philistines?")? (Answer:) That the Lord hath founded Zion, and the poor of his people shall trust in it (the Lord is the one who caused the destruction of the wicked and established Zion).

ISAIAH 15

1 The burden (message of doom) of Moab (descendants of Lot and his eldest daughter, Genesis 19:37). Because in the night (suddenly? unexpectedly?) Ar of Moab (a city in Moab) is laid waste, and brought to silence; because in the night, Kir (another city) of Moab is laid waste and brought to silence;

2 He (Moab, the country south and east of the Dead Sea) is gone up to Bajith (a city), and to Dibon, (a city), the high places (pagan places of worship), to weep: Moab shall howl over Nebo (Mt. Nebo, north of Moab), and over Medeba (a city): on all their heads shall be baldness (symbolic of slavery, captivity and mourning), and every beard cut off (slavery, captivity and mourning).

3 In their streets they shall gird (dress) themselves with sackcloth (symbolic of deep tragedy and mourning): on the tops of their houses (flat-roofed buildings used like we use decks etc.), and in their streets, every one shall howl, weeping abundantly.

4 And Heshbon (city in Moab) shall cry, and Elealeh (city): their voice shall be heard even unto Jahaz (city): therefore (for this reason) the armed soldiers of Moab shall cry out; his life shall be grievous (miserable) unto him.

5 My heart shall cry out for Moab; his fugitives shall flee unto Zoar (a border city just south of the Dead Sea), an heifer (young cow) of three years old (i.e., Moab, including Zoar, is being destroyed in its prime): for by the mounting up of Luhith (where you start climbing up to get to Luhith) with weeping shall they go it up; for in the way of Horonaim they shall raise up a cry of destruction.

6 For the waters of Nimrim shall be desolate (dried up): for the hay is withered away, the grass faileth, there is no green thing (there will be a drought).

7 Therefore the abundance they have gotten, and that which they have laid up, shall they carry away to the brook of the willows (probably the border between Moab and Edom— land directly south of Moab).

8 For the cry is gone round about the borders of Moab (they are completely surrounded); the howling thereof unto Eglaim, and the howling thereof unto Beer-elim.

9 For the waters of Dimon shall be

full of blood: for I will bring more upon Dimon, lions upon him that escapeth of Moab, and upon the remnant of the land (those who manage to escape the enemy armies will be destroyed by other means including lions.)

ISAIAH 16

Note: A mood change now occurs. Isaiah indicates the time will come when Moab will come under protection of Judah. This occurs under righteous King David. This is a great prophecy in light of the fact that in Isaiah's day, Judah and Moab were long-standing enemies.

1 Send ye the lamb (send an appeal for help) to the ruler of the land from Sela (about 60 miles south of the Dead Sea) to the wilderness, unto the mount of the daughter of Zion (Jerusalem).

2 For it shall be, that, as a wandering bird cast out of the nest, so the daughters of Moab shall be at the fords of Arnon (a river on the northern border of Moab). (Moab will have gone through some rough times.)

3 (Isaiah now prophesies that Moab will appeal to Judah for help.) Take counsel, execute judgement (kindness and fairness); make thy shadow (symbolic of protection and help) as the night in the midst of the noonday; hide the outcasts (protect the inhabitants of Moab); bewray (betray) not him that wandereth.

4 Let mine outcasts dwell with thee, Moab (should say Judah); be thou a covert (protection) to them (Moab's inhabitants) from the face of the spoiler (German: destroyer); for the extortioner (persecutor) is at an end, the spoiler ceaseth, the oppressors are consumed out of the land (thanks to help from Judah. Could also refer to destruction of wicked at Second Coming.)

5 And in mercy shall the throne be established: and he shall sit upon it in truth in the tabernacle of David, judging, and seeking judgement, and hasting righteousness. (Conditions during the Millennium. Could also refer to Judah in the last days.)

6 (Isaiah now returns to troubles to come upon Moab back then.) We have heard of the pride of Moab; he is very proud; even of his haughtiness, and his pride, and his wrath: but his lies shall not be so (Moab's unfounded boasts of strength and well-being will not work out in fact)

7 Therefore (because of these sins listed in verse 6) shall Moab (chiasmus A) howl for Moab, every one shall howl: for the foundations of Kir-hareseth shall ye mourn (chiasmus B); surely they are stricken.

8 For the fields of Heshbon (chiasmus C) languish, and the vine of Sibmah (chiasmus D): the lords of the heathen (enemy nations-Assyrians) have broken down the principal plants thereof (the Assyrians ruined terraced vineyards when they attacked Moab), they are come even unto Jazer

(chiasmus E), they wandered through the wilderness: her branches are stretched out, they are gone over the sea.

9 Therefore (this is why) I will bewail with the weeping of Jazer (chiasmus E') the vine of Sibmah (chiasmus D'): I will water thee with my tears, O Heshbon, and Elealeh: for the shouting for thy summer fruits and for thy harvest is fallen (chiasmus C').

10 And gladness is taken away and joy out of the plentiful field; and in the vineyards there shall be no singing, neither shall there be shouting: the treaders shall tread out no wine in their presses (because the grapes and vines have been destroyed by the enemy soldiers); I have made their vintage shouting to cease.

11 Wherefore my bowels (symbolic in Hebrew of the center of feeling and emotion) shall sound like an harp for Moab (chiasmus A'), and mine inward parts for Kir-haresh (Chiasmus B').

12 And it shall come to pass when it is seen that Moab is weary on the high place (places of worshipping false gods), that he shall come to his sanctuary to pray; but he shall not prevail (won't get the help he needs from his false gods).

13 This is the word that the Lord hath spoken concerning Moab since that time (the Lord has warned Moab through past prophets too).

14 But now the Lord hath spoken, saying, Within three years, as the years of an hireling, and the glory of Moab shall be contemned (scorned),

with all that great multitude; and the remnant shall be very small and feeble (in three years, there won't be much left of Moab).

ISAIAH 17

Note: Isaiah now tells what will happen to Syria and says a few more things about Israel.

1 The burden (message of doom) of Damascus (a major city in Syria). Behold, Damascus is taken away from being a city, and it shall be a ruinous heap (worthless pile of rubble).

2 The cities of Aroer (area near Damascus) are forsaken: they shall be for flocks, which shall lie down, and none shall make them afraid (animals will graze where cities now stand).

3 The fortress (fortified city) also shall cease from Ephraim (northern Israel), and the kingdom from Damascus, and the remnant of Syria: they shall be as the glory of the children of Israel (cut down like Israel will be), saith the Lord of hosts.

4 (Topic now turns to Israel's coming troubles) And in that day it shall come to pass, that the glory of Jacob (Israel) shall be made thin, and the fatness of his flesh shall wax lean (bad times are coming).

5 And it shall be as when the harvestman gathereth the corn, and reapeth the ears with his arm; and it shall be as he that gathereth ears in the valley of Rephaim (a fertile valley northwest of Jerusalem well-known

for good harvests, i.e., Israel will be "harvested", plucked up).

6 Yet gleaning grapes shall be left in it (a small remnant will be left after Assyria's attack on Israel), as the shaking of an olive tree, two or three berries (olives) in the top of the uppermost bough, four or five in the outmost fruitful branches thereof, saith the Lord God of Israel (remnants scattered here and there).

7 At that day shall a man look to his Maker (people will repent), and his eyes shall have respect to the Holy One of Israel (Jesus).

8 And he shall not look to the altars, the work of his hands (idols he has made), neither shall respect (worship) that which his fingers have made, either the groves (locations used for idol worship), or the images (idols). (This probably refers also to the last days and into the Millennium.)

9 In that day shall his (Syria's) strong cities be as a forsaken bough, and an uppermost branch, which they left because of the children of Israel: and there shall be desolation (in Syria).

10 Because (this is why you have these problems) thou hast forgotten the God of thy salvation, and hast not been mindful of the rock of thy strength (the Lord), therefore shalt thou plant pleasant plants (continue idol worship), and shalt set it with strange slips (cuttings for grafting, symbolic of imported gods or idols).

11 In the day (while things are going well) shalt thou make thy plant to grow (continue worshiping idols), and in the morning shalt thou make thy seed to flourish: but the harvest (results of idol worship) shall be a heap (worthless) in the day of grief and of desperate sorrow (your false gods will not help you).

12 Woe to the multitude of many people (nations, including Assyria, who attack the Lord's people), which make a noise like the noise of the seas (powerful); and to the rushing of nations, that make a rushing like the rushing of mighty waters!

13 The nations shall rush like the rushing of many waters: but God shall rebuke them (will stop them), and they shall flee far off, and shall be chased as the chaff of the mountains before the wind, and like a rolling thing (tumbleweeds etc.) before the whirlwind (wicked enemy nations are nothing compared to God's power).

14 And behold at eveningtide trouble; and before the morning (unexpected, sudden disaster) he is not (wicked are destroyed. Can refer to the Second Coming also). This is the portion (what is coming to them) of them that spoil us (the Lord's people), and the lot of them that rob us.

ISAIAH 18

1 Woe (this is a mistranslation in King James version. The Hebrew word means "hark" or "greetings" and has no negative connotation) to the land (most likely America) shadowing

(overshadowed with God's protecting Spirit) with wings (wings often represent shelter, protection as in the hen gathering her chicks under her wings in Matt. 23:37 etc. Also represent power in D&C 77:4; Also, North and South America look like wings), which is beyond the rivers of Ethiopia (Africa, i.e., America is beyond the rivers or "oceans" beyond Africa).

2 That sendeth ambassadors (missionaries) by the sea, even in vessels of bulrushes upon the waters, saying, Go, ye swift (modern transportation?) messengers, to a nation scattered (scattered Israel) and peeled, to a people terrible from their beginning hitherto (German: once powerful, perhaps meaning once righteous); a nation meted out and trodden down, whose land the rivers (symbolic of enemy nations in Is. 8:7, 17:12) have spoiled!

3 All ye inhabitants of the world, and dwellers on the earth, see ye (pay attention) when he (the Lord) lifteth up an ensign (the restored gospel) on the mountains; and when he bloweth a trumpet (a clear, unmistakable sound, easy to distinguish from other sounds, i.e., the gospel message), hear ye.

4 For so the Lord said unto me, I will take my rest, and I will consider in my dwelling place like a clear heat (nourishing rays of light and truth) upon herbs, and like a cloud of dew (nourishing water) in the heat of harvest (right when it is needed).

5 For afore (before) the harvest, when the bud is perfect, and the sour grape (immature grape) is ripening in the flower, he (the Lord) shall both cut off the sprigs with pruning hooks, and take away and cut down the branches (just before the millennial harvest, a final "pruning" will take place, i.e., wicked destroyed, pruned away so the righteous can develop to their full potential).

6 They (the wicked) shall be left together (completely) unto the fowls of the mountains (birds of prey), and to the beasts of the earth: and the fowls shall summer upon them, and all the beasts of the earth shall winter upon them.

7 (Isaiah now prophesies that the remnant, scattered Israel, will be gathered and brought back to the Lord, a righteous nation. See verses 1-3.) In that time (probably the last days) shall the present (gift, gathered Israel) be brought unto the Lord of hosts of a people scattered and peeled, and from a people terrible from their beginning hitherto; a nation meted out and trodden under foot, whose land the rivers have spoiled (see verse 2), to the place of the name of the Lord of hosts, the mount Zion (The remnant, scattered Israel, will be gathered and brought back to the Lord a righteous nation; see verse 1).

ISAIAH 19

1 The burden (message of doom) of Egypt. Behold, the Lord rideth upon a swift cloud (trouble coming quickly), and shall come into Egypt: and the

idols (false religions) of Egypt shall be moved at his presence, and the heart (courage) of Egypt shall melt in the midst of it (they will be terrified).

2 And I will set the Egyptians against the Egyptians (civil war): and they shall fight every one against his brother, and every one against his neighbor; city against city, and kingdom against kingdom.

3 And the spirit of Egypt shall fail (great despair) in the midst thereof; and I will destroy the counsel (plans) thereof: and they shall seek to the idols (they will seek help from their false gods), and to the charmers, and to them that have familiar spirits, and to the wizards (the occult).

4 And the Egyptians will I give over into the hand of a cruel lord (hard masters); and a fierce king shall rule over them, saith the Lord, the Lord of hosts.

5 And the waters shall fail from the sea, and the river shall be wasted and dried up (the Nile River will be ruined).

6 And they (the Egyptians) shall turn the rivers far away (will ruin their own rivers); and the brooks of defence shall be emptied and dried up: the reeds and flags shall wither.

7 The paper reeds (papyrus) by the brooks, by the mouth of the brooks, and every thing sown (planted) by the brooks, shall wither, be driven away, and be no more (the papyrus industry, crops etc. will be devastated).

8 The fishers also shall mourn, and all they that cast angle (fish hooks) into the brooks shall lament, and they that spread nets upon the waters shall languish (fishing industry will be ruined).

9 Moreover (in addition) they that work in fine flax (linen fabric is made from flax plant fibers), and they that weave networks (fine linen), shall be confounded (textile industry will be ruined).

10 And they shall be broken in the purposes (will have no success) thereof, all that make sluices (dams) and ponds for fish.

11 Surely the princes (nobles; leaders) of Zoan (Tanis, ancient capital of the Nile Delta) are fools, the counsel of the wise counsellors of Pharaoh is become brutish (absurd): (Pharaoh has received bad counsel from those who are supposed to be wise) how say ye unto Pharaoh, I am the son of the wise, the son of ancient kings (How do you counselors to Pharaoh dare to claim to be wise?)?

12 Where are they? where are thy wise men? and let them tell thee now, and let them know what the Lord of hosts hath purposed upon (against) Egypt.

13 The princes of Zoan are become fools, the princes of Noph (Memphis, capital of Northern Egypt) are deceived; they have also seduced (led astray) Egypt, even they that are the stay (support) of the tribes thereof.

14 The Lord hath mingled a perverse spirit in the midst thereof: and they have caused Egypt to err in every work thereof, as a drunken man

staggereth in his vomit.

15 Neither shall there be any work for Egypt, which the head (leaders, high society) or tail (poor, low society), branch (palm branch, i.e., high society) or rush (papyrus reed, i.e., low society, poor), may do.

16 In that day (the last days) shall Egypt be like unto women (worst insult in Egyptian culture): and it (Egypt) shall be afraid and fear because of the shaking of the hand of the Lord of hosts, which he shaketh over it.

17 And the land of Judah shall be a terror unto Egypt (a complete turnabout; tremendous prophecy!), every one that maketh mention thereof shall be afraid in himself, because of the counsel (plan) of the Lord of hosts, which he hath determined against it (Egypt).

18 In that day (last days) shall five (several) cities in the land of Egypt speak the language of Canaan (Israel; a prophecy of greatly improved relationship between Egypt and Judah in the last days), and swear (make covenants) to the Lord of Hosts; one shall be called the city of destruction (not a good translation; could be "city of the sun").

19 In that day (last days) shall there be an altar (a temple?) to the Lord in the midst of the land of Egypt, and a pillar (symbolic of a temple) at the border thereof to the Lord.

20 And it (the altar and the pillar) shall be for a sign and for a witness (reminder) unto (of) the Lord of hosts in the land of Egypt: for they (Egyptians) shall cry (pray) unto the Lord because of the oppressors, and he shall send them a saviour, and a great one, and he shall deliver them (the Egyptians will hear and live the gospel).

21 And the Lord shall be known to Egypt, and the Egyptians shall know the Lord in that day (the last days), and shall do sacrifice (3 Nephi 9:20; broken heart and contrite spirit) and oblation (D&C 59:12); yea, they shall vow a vow (make covenants) unto the Lord, and perform it.

22 And the Lord shall smite Egypt: he shall smite and heal it (first humble it, then heal it): and they shall return even to the Lord, and he shall be intreated (prayed to) of (by) them, and shall heal them (wonderful blessings are in store for Egypt).

23 In that day shall there be a highway out of Egypt to Assyria (Iraq?), and the Assyrian shall come into Egypt, and the Egyptian into Assyria, and the Egyptians shall serve (the Lord; see verse 25) with the Assyrians.

24 In that day (the last days) shall Israel be the third with Egypt and with Assyria (all three will be allied, with Israel as a blessing in the midst of them), even a blessing in the midst of the land:

25 Whom the Lord of hosts shall bless, saying, Blessed be Egypt my people, and Assyria the work of my

hands, and Israel mine inheritance (all three nations will worship the true God and be part of the Lord's people).

ISAIAH 20

Note: Isaiah 20 seems to have no particular references to the future. Deals with ancient Egypt.

1 In the year (about 711 BC) that Tartan (an Assyrian general) came unto Ashdod (see map 3), (when Sargon the king of Assyria sent him,) and fought against Ashdod (the center of a revolt against Assyria), and took it;

2 At the same time spake the Lord by Isaiah the son of Amoz, saying, Go and loose the sackcloth (symbolic of mourning already) from off thy loins, and put off thy shoe from thy foot. And he did so, walking naked (without an upper garment, symbolic of slavery and exile) and barefoot (like a slave).

3 And the Lord said, Like as my servant Isaiah hath walked naked and barefoot three years (we don't know whether this means constantly during the three years, or occasionally during the three years to remind the people of the message) for a sign and wonder upon Egypt and upon Ethiopia (symbolic of what will happen to Egypt and Ethiopia);

4 So shall the king of Assyria lead away the Egyptians prisoners, and the Ethiopians captives, young and old,

naked and barefoot, even with their buttocks (upper thighs) uncovered, to the shame of Egypt.

5 And they (Judah) shall be afraid and ashamed of (disappointed by) Ethiopia their expectation (hope), and of Egypt their glory (Judah was hoping for protection by Egypt and Ethiopia, rather than repenting and turning to God.).

6 And the inhabitant of this isle (Jerusalem, Judah) shall say in that day, Behold, such is our expectation (our hope is destroyed!), whither we flee for help to be delivered from the king of Assyria: and how shall we escape (if that can happen to Ethiopia and Egypt, our "protection" from Assyria, what do we do now)?

ISAIAH 21

1 The burden (message of doom) of the desert of the sea (Babylon). As whirlwinds (devastating in the desert) in the south pass through; so it cometh from the desert, from a terrible land.

2 A grievous (this was extra hard for Isaiah to watch) vision is declared unto me (Isaiah); the treacherous dealer dealeth treacherously, and the spoiler spoileth. Go up, O Elam (Map 2. A country east of Babylon): besiege (attack), O Media (Map 2. A country northeast of Babylon); all the sighing thereof (groaning Babylon has caused) have I (the Lord) made to cease.

3 Therefore are my (Isaiah's) loins

(whole being) filled with pain: pangs have taken hold upon me, as the pangs of a woman that travaileth (is in labor): I was bowed down at the hearing of it (the vision); I was dismayed at the seeing of it (the vision overwhelmed Isaiah).

4 My heart panted (faltered), fearfulness affrighted me (made me tremble): the night of my pleasure hath he turned into fear unto me (I can't get to sleep at night).

5 Prepare the table, watch in the watchtower, eat, drink: arise, ye princes, and anoint the shield (oil your shields, get ready for action).

6 For thus hath the Lord said unto me (Isaiah), Go, set a watchman, let him declare what he seeth.

7 And he saw a chariot with a couple of horsemen, a chariot of asses, and a chariot of camels; and he hearkened diligently with much heed (paid very close attention to my instructions):

8 And he cried, A lion: My lord, I stand continually upon the watchtower in the daytime, and I am set in my ward whole nights (I am keeping watch constantly like you told me to):

9 And, behold, here cometh a chariot of men, with a couple of horsemen (messengers). And he answered and said Babylon is fallen, is fallen (dual meaning: Babylon has fallen; Satan's kingdom will likewise eventually fall); and all the graven images of her gods he hath broken unto the ground (the Medes joined the Persians and Elamites and conquered Babylon about 539 BC).

10 O my threshing (O my threshed one), and the corn of my floor (the son of my threshing floor, ie, the Israelites who will survive Babylon's downfall): that which I have heard of the Lord of hosts, the God of Israel have I declared unto you.

11 The burden (message of doom to the Edomites) of Dumah (a desert oasis about 250 miles southeast of the Dead Sea). He calleth to me out of Seir (mountain range southeast of the Dead Sea), Watchman, what of the night (how long until daylight? ie, how long will this oppression last)? Watchman, what of the night?

12 The watchman said, The morning cometh, and also the night (the end of Babylonian captivity will come but another oppressor will follow): if ye will enquire, enquire ye (ask for more information later): return, come.

13 The burden (difficulties caused Arabia by the Babylonian conquests) upon Arabia. In the forest (oasis) in Arabia shall ye lodge, O ye travelling companies of Dedanim (see Dedar, map 2).

14 The inhabitants of the land of Tema (map 2) brought water to him (Kedar, ie, refugees from Kedar) that was thirsty, they prevented (met; "prevent" is used 17 times in King James Bible, always in obsolete sense of "go before, meet, precede, etc. See Psalms 119:147 where "prevented" means "got up before dawn". See also Matt. 17:25 where Jesus spoke first, before Peter spoke.) with their bread

him that fled (refugees from Kedar, fleeing the Babylonians, ie, Dedan and Tema need to prepare to take care of refugees from Kedar).

15 For they (refugees from Kedar) fled from the swords, from the drawn sword, and from the bent bow, and from the grievousness of war.

16 For thus hath the Lord said unto me (Isaiah), Within a year, according to the years of an hireling (wage earner, can be fired for poor performance just as Kedar, in one year, will be "fired" for poor performance with respect to God), and all the glory of Kedar shall fail.

17 And the residue of the number of archers, the mighty men of the children of Kedar, shall be diminished (Kedar will be devastated and have few warriors left): for the Lord God of Israel hath spoken it.

ISAIAH 22

1 The burden of the valley of vision (message of doom to Jerusalem). What aileth thee now, that thou art wholly gone up to the housetops ("What's wrong with you! Can't you see what's coming? How can you be so insensitive, always partying when future is so bleak!")?

2 Thou that art full of stirs (noise), a tumultuous city, a joyous city (partying; false sense of security): thy slain men are not slain with the sword, nor dead in battle (easily captured).

3 All thy rulers are fled together, they are bound by the archers (captured easily; tied up by the archers who don't normally do the actual hand to hand combat and capturing): all that are found in thee are bound together, which have fled from far.

4 Therefore said I (Isaiah), Look away from me (don't try to get me to party with you); I will weep bitterly, labour not to comfort me (don't try to comfort me; I see what's coming), because of the spoiling of the daughter (Jerusalem) of my people.

5 For it is a day of trouble, and of treading down, and of perplexity by the Lord God of hosts in the valley of vision (Jerusalem), breaking down the walls, and of crying to the mountains.

6 And Elam bare the quiver with chariots (symbolic of war) of men and horsemen (horse = symbolic of conquering, victory), and Kir uncovered the shield (Jerusalemites hope the soldiers of Elam, map 2 in new LDS Bible, and Kir—on main road between Elam and Babylon—will defeat the Assyrians before they reach Jerusalem).

7 And it shall come to pass, that thy choicest valleys shall be full of chariots, and the horsemen shall set themselves in array at the gate (enemy soldiers will be everywhere in your land).

8 And he discovered (stripped off) the covering (defense) of Judah, and thou didst look in that day to the armour of the house of the forest (Jerusalem's defence is inadequate).

9 Ye have seen also the breaches

(cracks, breaks in the wall) of the city of David (Jerusalem), that they are many (Isaiah points out weaknesses in Jerusalem's defenses): and ye gathered together the waters of the lower pool (Hezekiah's tunnel; you dug a tunnel to bring water into the city during siege).

10 And ye have numbered (taken stock of things) the houses of Jerusalem, and the houses have ye broken down to fortify the wall (dismantled houses for stone to fortify city walls etc.).

11 Ye made also a ditch between the two walls for the water of the old pool: but ye have not looked unto the maker thereof (the Lord), neither had respect unto him that fashioned it long ago (you have not turned to the Lord and repented, wherein your only reliable protection lies).

12 And in that day did the Lord God of hosts call to weeping, and to mourning, and to baldness, and to girding with sackcloth (God said "Repent, humble yourselves!"):

13 And behold joy and gladness (partying), slaying oxen, and killing sheep, eating flesh, and drinking wine: let us eat and drink; for to morrow we shall die (people ignore God, don't repent, continue riotous living).

14 And it was revealed in mine ears by the Lord of hosts, Surely this iniquity shall not be purged from you till ye die, saith the Lord God of hosts (the way you're heading, you will die in your sins).

15 Thus saith the Lord God of hosts, Go, get thee unto this treasurer, even unto Shebna (leader of the king's court, probably a foreigner; perhaps symbolic of foreign religions, life styles etc. taking hold of Jews but eventually driven out by Messiah— see verses 19 & 20), which is over the house, and say,

16 What hast thou here? and whom hast thou here, that thou hast hewed thee out a sepulchre (foreign influences attempting to become permanent; Shebna is a vain man carving out a great monument to himself) here, as he that heweth him out a sepulchre on high, and that graveth an habitation for himself in a rock?

17 Behold, the Lord will carry thee away with a mighty captivity, and will surely cover thee (you won't be famous).

18 He will surely violently turn and toss thee like a ball into a large country: there shalt thou die (you will die in a foreign land, symbolic of fate of Jerusalem's inhabitants), and there the chariots of thy glory shall be the shame of thy lord's house.

19 And I will drive thee from thy station, and from thy state shall he pull thee down.

20 And it shall come to pass in that day, that I will call my servant Eliakim (a real person in Jerusalem, symbolic of the Messiah) the son of Hilkiah:

21 And I will clothe him with thy robe, and strengthen him with thy

The Savior opens the door to the Father's presence ✗

girdle (he will take your place), and I will commit thy government into his hand: and he (Messiah) shall be a father to the inhabitants of Jerusalem, and to the house of Judah.

22 And the key of the house of David will I lay upon his shoulder; so he shall open, and none shall shut; and he shall shut, and none shall open (Symbolic of Christ's power).

23 And I will fasten him as a nail in a sure place (Messiah); and he shall be for a glorious throne to his father's house (Dual: Eliakim's family depends on him for security as we depend on Christ's atonement).

24 And they shall hang upon him all the glory of his father's house, the offspring and the issue, all vessels of small quantity, from the vessels of cups, even to all the vessels of flagons (Dual: Eliakim's relatives, small and great, depend on him; Christ carries all mankind, small and great, upon the cross; Atonement).

25 In that day, saith the Lord of hosts, shall the nail that is fastened in the sure place be removed, and be cut down, and fall; and the burden that was upon it shall be cut off: for the Lord hath spoken it (Eliakim will eventually fall from office and his family with him).

ISAIAH 23

Note: This is the concluding prophecy against foreign nations of the set of prophecies starting with chapter 13.

1 The burden (prophecy of doom) of Tyre (see map 2, LDS Bible; a leading sea power of Isaiah's time). Howl, ye ships of Tarshish (large ships of trade); for it (Tyre) is laid waste, so that there is no house, no entering (harbor) in: from the land of Chittim (Cyprus) it is revealed to them.

2 Be still (stunned), ye inhabitants of the isle (seaport of Tyre or Cyprus?); thou whom the merchants of Zidon, that pass over the sea, have replenished (made rich).

3 And by great waters the seed (grain from the Nile) of Sihor (city in Egypt), the harvest of the river, is her revenue; and she is a mart (market-place) of nations.

4 Be thou ashamed (German: terri-fied; i.e., Sidon's commerce will be interrupted via Tyre's downfall), O Zidon: for the sea hath spoken, even the strength of the sea, saying, I travail not, nor bring forth children, neither do I nourish up young men, nor bring up virgins (Tyre is not producing anymore).

5 As at the report concerning Egypt (as the report comes to Egypt), so shall they (the Egyptians) be sorely pained at the report of Tyre (Egypt will be in anguish upon hearing what has happened to Tyre).

6 Pass ye over to Tarshish (probably in Spain); howl, ye inhabitants of the isle.

7 Is this your joyous (riotous revelry) city, whose antiquity is of ancient days? her own feet (she creates her own downfall like we do

when we go against God) shall carry her afar off to sojourn.

8 Who hath taken this counsel (who is planning this) against Tyre, the crowning city, whose merchants are princes (leaders), whose traffickers (traders) are the honourable (famous) of the earth.

9 The Lord of hosts hath purposed (planned) it, to stain the pride of all glory, and to bring into contempt (to humble) all the honourable (unrighteous famous) of the earth.

10 Pass through thy land as a river, O daughter of Tarshish: there is no more strength (you are ruined).

11 He (the Lord) stretched out his hand over the sea, he shook the kingdoms: the Lord hath given a commandment against the merchant city (Tyre), to destroy the strong holds thereof (merchandising networks; Tyre is doomed).

12 And he said, Thou shalt no more rejoice, O thou oppressed virgin, daughter of Zidon: arise, pass over to Chittim (Cyprus); there also shalt thou have no rest (Tyre's downfall ruins other economies too).

13 Behold (look at) the land of the Chaldeans (Babylon); this people was not, till (was not ruined, until) the Assyrian founded it for them (desert creatures) that dwell in the wilderness (the Assyrians destroyed Babylon to the point that it is now nothing more than a place for desert creatures to live): they set up the towers (siege towers) thereof, they raised (razed) up the palaces thereof; and he (Assyria) brought it to ruin.

14 Howl, ye ships of Tarshish: for your strength is laid waste (via Tyre's downfall).

15 And it shall come to pass in that day, that Tyre shall be forgotten seventy years, according to the days of one king: after the end of seventy years shall Tyre sing as an harlot (will "prostitute" the ways of God again).

16 Take an harp, go about the city, thou harlot that hast been forgotten; make sweet melody, sing many songs, that thou mayest be remembered.

17 And it shall come to pass after the end of seventy years, that the Lord will visit Tyre, and she shall turn (return) to her hire (wicked ways), and shall commit fornication (symbolic of intense and total disloyalty to God) with all the kingdoms of the world upon the face of the earth.

18 And her merchandise and her hire shall be holiness to the Lord (perhaps referring to the future when the wicked will be gone and the good things and wealth of the earth will be for the righteous): it shall not be treasured nor laid up; for her merchandise shall be for them that dwell before the Lord (the righteous), to eat sufficiently, and for durable clothing (righteousness blesses people for eternity).

ISAIAH 24

Note: Isaiah emphasizes the consequences of wickedness in this chapter.

1 Behold, the Lord (chiasmus A) maketh the earth empty (chiasmus B), and maketh it waste, and turneth it upside down, and scattereth abroad the inhabitants thereof.

2 And it shall be, as with the people (chiasmus C), so with the priest; as with the servant, so with his master; as with the maid, so with her mistress; as with the buyer, so with the seller; as with the lender, so with the borrower; as with the taker of usury (interest on loans), so with the giver of usury to him (no one who is wicked will escape, regardless of social status).

3 The land shall be utterly emptied (chiasmus B'), and utterly spoiled: for the Lord (chiasmus A') hath spoken this word.

4 The earth mourneth and fadeth away, the world languisheth and fadeth away, the haughty people of the earth do languish.

5 The earth also is defiled under the inhabitants thereof; because they have transgressed the laws, changed the ordinance, broken the everlasting covenant (this is the real problem!).

6 Therefore (this is why) hath the curse devoured the earth, and they that dwell therein are desolate: therefore (this is why) the inhabitants of the earth are burned, and few men left (at the Second Coming).

7 The new wine mourneth (fails, runs out), the vine languisheth (fails), all the merryhearted do sigh ("The party's over!").

8 The mirth (merriment) of tabrets (drums; tambourines) ceaseth, the noise of them that rejoice (party, revel) endeth, the joy of the harp ceaseth.

9 They shall not drink wine with a song; strong drink shall be bitter to them that drink it.

10 The city of confusion is broken down (towns are broken down): every house is shut up, that no man may come in.

11 There is a crying for wine in the streets (people still want their wicked lifestyle); all joy is darkened, the mirth of the land is gone.

12 In the city is left desolation, and the gate is smitten with destruction (Isaiah has "painted" a verbal picture in verses 7-12. This is an excellent example of his inspired brilliance and typical approach to prophesying.)

13 When thus it shall be in the midst of the land among the people (nations), there shall be as the shaking of an olive tree, and as the gleaning grapes when the vintage is done (a few righteous come out, ie, gleaned from the wicked).

14 They (the few righteous) shall lift up their voice, they shall sing for the majesty of the Lord, they shall cry aloud from the sea.

15 Wherefore glorify ye the Lord in the fires (probably should say

"islands"), even the name of the Lord God of Israel in the isles of the sea (a few righteous, a remnant, are scattered throughout the earth).

16 From the uttermost part of the earth have we heard songs, even glory to the righteous. But I (Isaiah) said, My leanness, my leanness (My inability to change things!), woe unto me! the treacherous dealers have dealt treacherously; yea, the treacherous dealers have dealt very treacherously (wickedness continues despite Isaiah's efforts to warn them and get them to change).

17 Fear (terror), and the pit (a trap), and the snare (a trap), are upon thee, O inhabitant of the earth.

18 And it shall come to pass, that he who fleeth from the noise of the fear shall fall into the pit; and he that cometh up out (escapes) of the midst of the pit shall be taken in the snare (ultimately, there is no escape for the wicked): for the windows from on high are open, and the foundations of the earth do shake.

19 The earth is utterly broken down, the earth is clean dissolved, the earth is moved exceedingly.

20 The earth shall reel to and fro like a drunkard, and shall be removed like a cottage (flimsy temporary shade structure built in a garden; see Is. 1:8); and the transgression thereof shall be heavy upon it; and it shall fall, and not rise again (German: not remain standing).

21 And it shall come to pass in that day, that the Lord shall punish the host of the high ones (wicked, proud) that are on high, and the kings of the earth upon the earth (the wicked will be punished).

22 And they shall be gathered together, as prisoners are gathered in the pit (spirit prison), and shall be shut up in the prison, and after many days shall they be visited (by missionaries in spirit prison; see D&C 138).

23 Then the moon shall be confounded, and the sun ashamed (moon and sun's majesty is nothing compared to radiant glory, majesty etc. of Christ when He comes; see D&C 133:49), when the Lord of hosts shall reign in mount Zion, and in Jerusalem, and before his ancients gloriously.

ISAIAH 25

1 (This chapter emphasizes that it is worth being righteous.) O Lord, thou art my God; I will exalt thee, I will praise thy name; for thou hast done wonderful things; thy counsels of old (plans made in council in Heaven) are faithfulness and truth.

2 For thou hast made of a (wicked) city an heap (pile of rubble); of a defenced city a ruin: a palace of strangers (symbolic of kingdoms of the wicked) to be no city; it shall never be built (rebuilt; symbolic of Babylon, wickedness).

3 Therefore (that is why) shall the strong people glorify (acknowledge) thee, the city of the terrible (tyrant; German: powerful gentile) nations

[handwritten margin notes: "— small and..."; "✗ The Savior wipes"; vertical left margin: "✗ The Savior will prepare a feast (spiritual feast) — the vail (spiritual darkness)"]

shall fear thee (God has power over the wicked).

4 For thou hast been a strength to the poor, a strength to the needy in his distress, a refuge from the storm, a shadow (shade; protection) from the heat, when the blast of the terrible ones (the wicked) is as a storm against the wall (you have helped the righteous poor and needy).

5 Thou shalt bring down (humble) the noise (unrighteous revelry) of strangers (foreigners; people whose lifestyle is "foreign" to the gospel), as the heat in a dry place (strangers who have been fierce like the heat in the desert against the righteous); even the heat with the shadow (shade) of a cloud (God subdues the wicked like He subdues desert heat with clouds): the branch (victory song of tyrants) of the terrible (tyrants) ones shall be brought low (humbled).

6 And in this mountain shall the Lord of hosts make unto all people (nations; the righteous) a feast of fat things (the best), a feast of wines on the lees (thickest, best part of the wine, ie, the best blessings of the gospel are made available to the righteous), of fat things full of marrow, of wines on the lees well refined.

7 And he will destroy in this mountain the face of the covering (veil) cast over all people, and the vail that is spread over all nations (veil of spiritual darkness will be taken away).

8 He will swallow up death in victory (the resurrection of all); and the Lord God will wipe away tears from off all faces (via Atonement come happiness and eternal life for the righteous; sharp contrast with the fate of wicked in verse 2, 10, 11, 12 etc.); and the rebuke of his people shall he take away from off all the earth: for the Lord hath spoken it (it will happen!).

9 And it shall be said in that day (future), Lo, this is our God; we have waited for him, and he will save (has saved) us: this is the Lord; we have waited for him, we will be (are) glad and rejoice in his salvation.

10 For in this mountain shall the hand of the Lord rest, and Moab (symbolic of the wicked) shall be trodden down under him, even as straw is trodden down for the dunghill (fate of the wicked).

11 And he shall spread forth his hands in the midst of them (the wicked), as he that swimmeth spreadeth forth his hands to swim: and he shall bring down their pride together with the spoils of their hands (he will humble the wicked and take away their ill-gotten gain).

12 And the fortress of the high fort (supposedly invincible domains of the wicked) of thy walls shall he (the Lord) bring down, lay low, and bring to the ground, even to the dust (kingdoms of the wicked destroyed completely!).

ISAIAH 26

1 In that day (last days) shall this song be sung in the land of Judah; We have a strong city; salvation will God appoint for walls and bulwarks ("salvation is all around us").

2 Open ye the gates (dual: implies peaceful times; "gate" can also mean baptism etc.), that the righteous nation (the righteous people) which keepeth the truth may enter in.

3 Thou wilt keep him (the righteous nation) in perfect peace, whose mind is stayed (based, supported, supplied by) on thee: because he trusteth in thee.

4 Trust ye in the Lord for ever: for in the Lord JEHOVAH (the Savior) is everlasting strength.

5 For he (JEHOVAH) bringeth down (humbles) them that dwell on high (the "high and mighty", ie, the proud wicked); the lofty city, he layeth it low; he layeth it low, even to the ground; he bringeth it even to the dust (will completely destroy the wicked).

6 The foot shall tread it (the lofty city, ie, the wicked) down, even the feet of the poor, and the steps of the needy (the tables are turned; the oppressed now triumph and the wicked get their just dues).

7 The way of the just (righteous) is uprightness: thou, most upright (Christ), dost weigh the path of the just (make the path smooth ie, bless the righteous).

8 Yea, in the way of thy judgments, O Lord, have we waited for thee ("We've been living righteously."); the desire of our soul is to thy name (our hearts are right; D&C 64:22), and to the remembrance of thee.

9 With my soul have I desired thee in the night; yea, with my spirit within me will I seek thee early (I seek thee day and night, ie, always); for when thy judgments (teachings and commandments) are in the earth, the inhabitants of the world will learn righteousness.

10 Let favour be shewed to the wicked, yet will he not (does not want to) learn righteousness: in the land of uprightness will (desires to) he deal unjustly, and will not (does not want to) behold the majesty of the Lord (even when the Lord shows kindness to the wicked, they don't repent because they don't desire righteousness, ie, their hearts are not right).

11 Lord, when thy hand is lifted up (when your power and existence is obvious), they (the wicked) will not see (don't want to see): but they shall see (every knee shall bow and every tongue confess, D&C 76:110 etc.), and be ashamed (put to shame) for their envy at the people (because of thy zeal for thy people); yea, the fire of (reserved for) thine enemies shall devour them (the wicked; Second Coming).

12 Lord, thou wilt ordain peace for us: for thou also hast wrought all our works in us (all we have is from thee; gratitude, D&C 59:21).

13 O Lord our God, other lords (wicked rulers) beside thee have had dominion over us: but by thee only will we make mention of thy name (you

The Saviour will bring the Resurrection

only do we honor and worship).

14 They (the wicked rulers) are dead, they shall not live (until the resurrection of the wicked, D&C 88:101); they are deceased, they shall not rise (their power is ended): therefore (because of their wickedness) hast thou visited (punished) and destroyed them, and made all their memory to perish.

15 Thou hast increased the nation (the righteous, vs. 2), O Lord, thou hast increased the nation: thou art glorified: thou hadst (hast) removed (spread) it far unto all the ends of the earth (Millennium).

16 Lord, in trouble have they (the righteous) visited thee (come unto thee), they poured out a prayer when thy chastening was upon them (righteous turn to God in times of trouble).

17 Like as a woman with child, that draweth near the time of her delivery, is in pain, and crieth out in her pangs: so have we been in thy sight, O Lord (when unavoidable trouble came, we turned to thee).

18 We have been with child (we have had pain and suffering as part of our mortal probation), we have been in pain, we have as it were brought forth wind (nothing, ie, sometimes we have turned from thee and pain and suffering have not produced desired results, fruits of righteousness in our lives), we have not wrought any deliverance in the earth (we have not brought salvation to people of the earth like we were called to do); neither have the inhabitants of the world fallen (been humbled).

19 Thy dead men shall live, together with my dead body shall they arise (resurrection). Awake and sing, ye that dwell in dust (lie in graves): for thy dew is as the dew of herbs, and the earth shall cast out the dead (resurrection).

20 Come, my people (the righteous, 19:25), enter thou into thy chambers, and shut thy doors about thee: hide thyself as it were for a little moment, until the indignation (cleansing of the earth) be overpast. (This verse is full of passover symbolism. The Israelites closed their doors and put lamb's blood [atonement] on door posts which provided them safety from the Lord's destructions among the Egyptians. Through righteous homes where the gospel is lived and the atonement used, we can be spared God's punishments. God punishes only those who merit punishment.)

21 For, behold, the Lord cometh out of his place to punish the inhabitants of the earth for their iniquity (Second Coming): the earth also shall disclose her blood, and shall no more cover her slain (the bloodshed and crimes of the wicked will be exposed and punishment given out).

ISAIAH 27

1 In that day the Lord with his sore (hard, fierce) and great and strong sword shall punish (Christ's forces will win!) leviathan (Satan; can also include all forces of evil, all who

serve Satan) the piercing serpent, even leviathan that crooked serpent; and he shall slay the dragon that is in the sea (leviathan was a legendary sea monster representing evil; see Revelation 12:9 for similar names for Satan).

2 In that day sing ye unto her (Israel), a vineyard of red wine.

3 I the Lord do keep it (my vineyard, Israel); I will water it every moment: lest any hurt it, I will keep it night and day (so that it will do verse 6).

4 Fury is not in me: who would set the briers and thorns against me in battle? I would go through them, I would burn them together (all).

5 Or let him (Israel) take hold of my strength, that he may make peace with me; and he shall make peace with me (prophetic!).

6 He (God) shall cause them (Israel) that come of Jacob to take root: Israel shall blossom and bud, and fill the face of the world with fruit (the blessings of righteousness and salvation).

7 Hath he (God) smitten him (Israel), as he (God) smote those (Israel's enemies) that smote him (Israel)? or is he (Israel) slain according to (like) the slaughter of them (Israel's enemies) that are slain by him (God)? (i.e., has God been as hard on his people, Israel, as on her enemies? Answer. No!)

8 In measure (moderation), when it (Israel) shooteth forth, thou wilt debate with it (prune it): he (God) stayeth his rough wind in the day of the east wind (God could destroy you with a really "rough" wind, but instead he sends the terrible east wind, a hot, dry wind off the Arabian Desert which devastates crops and helps humble you).(In German, this says "You mete to them what is needed to set them straight so you can set them free." Jeremiah 30:11 in the King James version says the same thing and is much more clear than the King James translation of verse 8 above.)

9 By this (the rough times, refiner's fire referred to in verse 8) therefore shall the iniquity of Jacob (Israel) be purged; and this is all the fruit (the product of Israel's wickedness, ie, the consequences designed by God to purge wickedness out of them) to take away his (Israel's) sin when he (God) maketh all the stones of the altar (used in idol worship) as chalkstones that are beaten in sunder (into pieces), the groves (used in idol worship) and images (used in idol worship) shall not stand up (ie, your false religions, upon which you have relied, will crumble).

10 Yet the defenced city (established wickedness) shall be desolate, and the habitation forsaken (abandoned), and left like a wilderness: there shall the calf feed, and there shall he (the calf) lie down, and consume the branches thereof (nothing will be left of you and your wickedness).

11 When the boughs thereof are withered, they shall be broken off: the women come, and set them on fire (women will use what is left for

cooking fires etc., ie, wickedness will be destroyed completely by fire): for it is a people of no understanding: therefore (that is why) he that made them will not have mercy on them, and he (God) that formed them will shew them no favour.

12 And it shall come to pass in that day, that the Lord shall beat (glean) off from the channel of the river (Mesopotamia) unto the stream of Egypt (the Nile River), (ie, the "whole world") and ye shall be gathered one by one, O ye children of Israel (the righteous shall be gathered from the whole earth).

13 And it shall come to pass in that day, that the great trumpet (ushers in the Millennium) shall be blown, and they shall come which were ready to perish in the land of Assyria (in the wicked world), and the outcasts in the land of Egypt (the righteous, who have been "outcasts" in the wicked world), and shall worship the Lord in the holy mount at Jerusalem (in the holy temples).

ISAIAH 28

Note: Isaiah speaks to Israel, ie, the Northern 10 Tribes in his day, verses 1-4. This message came probably somewhere around 724 BC, before the 10 Tribes were taken captive by the Assyrians in 722 BC.

1 Woe to the crown of pride (the haughty Ephraimites at Samaria, headquarters of Israel, who have not yet come under Assyrian control and have boasted about their invincibility), to the drunkards of Ephraim (Northern Israel is "drunk", out of control with wickedness), whose glorious beauty is a fading flower (on the way out), which are on the head of the fat valleys (rich, productive land area in Samaria) of them that are overcome with wine (you are out of control with wickedness)!

2 Behold, the Lord hath a mighty and strong one (Shalmaneser, the Assyrian king and his armies), which as a tempest of hail and a destroying storm, as a flood of mighty waters overflowing (see Isa. 8:7), shall cast down to the earth with the hand (the Assyrians will flood your land).

3 The crown of pride, the drunkards of Ephraim, shall be trodden under feet (Israel, the Northern Ten Tribes, will be destroyed; this happens in 722 BC via Assyria):

4 And the glorious beauty, which is on the head of the fat valley, shall be a fading flower, and as the hasty fruit (early fruit; the first ripe fruit on the tree) before the summer; which when he that looketh upon it seeth, while it is yet in his hand he eateth it up (it doesn't last long, once someone has spotted it, ie, you will be "gobbled up" quickly like the first ripe fig of the season).

5 In that day (last days or Millennium) shall the Lord of hosts be for a crown of glory, and for a diadem of beauty, unto the residue (the righteous who are left) of his

people (the Savior will lead you, as opposed to the proud, haughty drunkards referred to in verse 1),

6 And for a spirit of judgment to him that sitteth in judgment, and for strength to them that turn the battle to the gate (Christ will provide strength to overcome all enemies and "push them back to where they came from").

7 But they (Israel's leaders) also have erred through wine, and through strong drink are out of the way; the priest and the prophet have erred through strong drink, they are swallowed up of wine, they are out of the way through strong drink; they err in vision, they stumble in judgement (apostasy; out of control literally and symbolically).

8 For all tables are full of vomit and filthiness, so that there is no place clean (apostasy has completely penetrated the nation).

9 Whom shall he (the Lord) teach knowledge? and whom shall he make to understand doctrine: them that are weaned from the milk, and drawn from the breasts (start teaching them while very young).

10 For precept must be upon precept, precept upon precept; line upon line, line upon line; here a little, and there a little (a life-long process starting very young):

11 For with stammering (un-understandable) lips and another tongue (a tongue "foreign" to the wicked, i.e., the Holy Ghost) will he speak to this people.

12 To whom he said, This is the rest (peace of God) wherewith ye may cause the weary to rest; and this is the refreshing (available from God through righteous living): yet they would not (didn't want to) hear (in verse 10, the Lord tells them how he would help them bit by bit, not overwhelm them, but they don't want to hear such stuff!).

13 But the word of the Lord was unto them precept upon precept, precept upon precept; line upon line, line upon line; here a little, and there a little; that they might go, and fall backward (apostasy isn't just "falling"; it is retrogressing, ie, falling backward), and be broken, and snared, and taken (by Satan; ie, when ignored, the "word" condemns).

14 Wherefore hear the word of the Lord, ye scornful (scoffers) men, that rule this people which is in Jerusalem (Isaiah now speaks to the people in Jerusalem in his day).

15 Because ye have said (boasted), We have made a covenant with death, and with hell are we at agreement (we have an "agreement" with hell); when the overflowing scourge (which all the prophets keep saying will come) shall pass through, it shall not come unto us: for we have made lies our refuge (we have found that crime does pay!), and under falsehood have we hid ourselves (we will live wickedly and get away with it!):

16 Therefore (because of your wickedness, boasting, etc.) thus saith the Lord God, Behold, I lay in Zion for a foundation a stone (the Savior),

46

The Savior is our sure foundation

a tried (proven reliable) stone, a precious corner stone (Ephesians 2:20), a sure foundation (the Lord is the only one with whom you can strike agreements and have guaranteed results): he that believeth shall not make haste (flee; ie, he that lives righteously will not have to flee before the face of the Lord).

17 Judgement also will I lay to the line (carpenter's line used to build straight and true), and righteousness to the plummet (plumb bob; i.e., carpenter's tools used to build square etc.): and the hail shall sweep away the refuge of lies (ie, you won't get away with your boast in verse 15), and the waters (can refer to the Assyrians, see 8:7; could also refer to Christ as "living water", in John 7:38 etc.) shall overflow the hiding place (of the wicked).

18 And your covenant with death (verse 15) shall be disannulled (canceled), and your agreement with hell shall not stand; when the overflowing scourge (referred to boastfully in verse 15) shall pass through, then ye shall be trodden down by it (the wicked will be destroyed).

19 From the time that it (God's judgements) goeth forth it shall take you: for morning by morning shall it pass over, by day and by night (continuously): and it shall be a vexation (pure terror) only to understand the report (God's judgements).

20 (Isaiah now refers to the proud boast in verse 15 that they could be comfortable and protected in sin.) For the bed is shorter than that a man can stretch himself on it (you can't ever get completely comfortable in the bed of sin you've made for yourselves to lie in): and the covering (the blanket of lies you made for yourselves) narrower than that he can wrap himself in it (you can't hide under a blanket of sin!).

21 For the Lord shall rise up as in mount Perazim (David attacked and smote Philistines there, with the Lord's help), he shall be wroth as in the valley of Gibeon (where the Lord killed Joshua's enemies, the Amorites, with huge hailstones), that he may do his work, his strange work; and bring to pass his act, his strange (unusual) act.

22 Now therefore be ye not mockers (don't scoff at God's word), lest your bands be made strong (lest you be totally enslaved by wickedness): for I (Isaiah) have heard from the Lord God of hosts a consumption, even determined upon the whole earth (I've heard God will annihilate the wicked).

23 Give ye ear, and hear my voice; hearken, and hear my speech.

24 Doth the plowman (farmer; symbolic of God) plow all day to sow (getting ready to plant): doth he open and break the clods of his ground (continuously)? (Does the Lord just keep plowing, preparing, etc. forever, or does he go on to the next steps, planting, harvesting etc.? In other words, "Do you think judgement day will never come, that the Lord will

never get around to harvest time?")

25 When he (the farmer; the Lord) hath made plain the face thereof (has the ground plowed and leveled), doth he not cast abroad (plant, throw the seeds by hand) the fitches (dill seeds), and scatter the cummin, and cast in the principal wheat (the main crop) and the appointed (planned on) barley and the rie in their place (God plans carefully and carries it out)?

26 For his (the plowman's) God doth instruct him to discretion, and doth teach him.

27 For the fitches are not threshed with a threshing instrument, neither is a cart wheel turned about (around and around) upon the cummin (careful harvest methods); but the fitches are beaten out with a staff, and the cummin with a rod (God will use appropriate methods to "harvest" all the righteous out from the wicked).

28 Bread corn (cereal grain) is bruised (ground in a mill); because he will not ever (forever) be threshing it, nor break it with the wheel of his cart, nor bruise it with his horsemen. (In German, this verse says basically that cereal grain is ground to make bread, not threshed to the point of destruction when it is threshed with wagon wheels and horses.)

29 This also cometh forth from the Lord of hosts, which is wonderful in counsel (planning; see 19:3, 25:1 etc.), and excellent in working (German: "carries it out wonderfully").

ISAIAH 29

1 Woe to Ariel (Jerusalem; Zion in 2 N. 27:3), to Ariel, the city where David dwelt! add ye year to year; let them kill sacrifices (keep right on going as you are with your wickedness and empty rituals, it will do you no good!).

2 Yet I will (I will continue to) distress Ariel, and there shall be heaviness and sorrow: and it shall be unto me as Ariel (it shall become a proper Zion).

3 And I will camp against thee (Ariel) round about, and will lay siege against thee with a mount (mound of dirt), and I will raise forts against thee (as in a planned military action, i.e., you will be chastened until you repent).

4 And thou (Ariel) shalt be brought down (humbled), and shalt speak out of the ground, and thy speech shall be low out of the dust, and thy voice shall be, as of one that hath a familiar spirit (a dead relative speaking from the spirit world), out of the ground, and thy speech shall whisper out of the dust (the Book of Mormon came "out of the ground" and in it, the Nephites, our dead Israelite "relatives" who came from Ariel, i.e., Jerusalem, speak to us as from the dust).

5 Moreover the multitude of thy strangers (enemies) shall be like small dust (countless), and the multitude of the terrible ones (tyrants) shall be as chaff that passeth away (that blows

away in the wind, ie, countless): yea, it shall be at an instant suddenly (the things that humble you, see first part of verse 4, will catch you off guard so that you will hardly be able to believe they are happening so rapidly and nobody is stopping them).

6 Thou shalt be visited of (disciplined or punished by) the Lord of hosts with thunder, and with earthquake, and great noise, with storm and tempest, and the flame of devouring fire.

7 And the multitude of all the nations that fight against Ariel (Zion, 2 N. 27:3), even all that fight against her and her munition, and that distress her, shall be as a dream of a night vision.

8 It shall even be (unto them, 2 N. 27:3, i.e., enemy nations) as when an hungry man dreameth, and, behold, he eateth; but he awaketh, and his soul is empty: or as when a thirsty man dreameth, and, behold, he drinketh; but he awaketh, and, behold, he is faint, and his soul hath appetite: so shall the multitude of all the nations be, that fight against mount Zion (persecutors of the saints never feel satisfied, are still "hungry and thirsty" for more, can't leave us alone).

9 Stay yourselves (stop, you wicked!), and wonder (think); cry ye out, and cry: they (the wicked, 2 N. 27:4) are drunken, (out of control), but not with wine; they stagger (stumble around), but not with strong drink (no prophets to lead them, as mentioned in verse 10).

10 For the Lord hath poured out upon you the spirit of deep sleep (spiritual darkness), and hath closed (ye have closed, 2 N. 27:5) your eyes: the prophets and your rulers, the seers hath he covered (because of your iniquity, 2 N.27:5).

11 And the vision of all (German: the vision of all the prophets, i.e., scripture) is become unto you (Israelites who are spiritually dead) as the words of a book (Book of Mormon) that is sealed (because you refuse to hearken to the scriptures, they might just as well be sealed and unreadable to you like the copy of characters from the Book of Mormon plates), which men (Martin Harris) deliver to one that is learned (Professor Charles Anthon of Colombia College in N.Y. City, Feb. 1828), saying, Read this, I pray thee: and he (Charles Anthon) saith, I cannot; for it is sealed:

12 And the book is delivered to him (Joseph Smith) that is not learned, saying, Read this, I pray thee: and he saith, I am not learned (i.e., I can't read it without God's help).

13 Wherefore the Lord said, Forasmuch as this people draw near me with their mouth, and with their lips do honour me, but have removed their heart far from me (they are spiritually dead), and their fear toward me is taught by the precept (traditions) of men (people have gone far astray from truth):

14 Therefore, behold, I will proceed to do a marvellous work among this

*Restoration of the Gospel

(Dec 4:1; 6:1)

49

people, even a marvellous ("aston-ishing" as used in O.T. Hebrew) work and a wonder (the restoration of the gospel): for the wisdom of their wise men shall perish (revealed truth cuts through falsehood), and the under-standing of their prudent men shall be hid (false philosophies and false scientific conclusions etc., fade away via light of truth).

15 Woe unto them (the wicked) that seek deep to hide their counsel (plans) from the Lord, and their works are in the dark, and they say, Who seeth us? and who knoweth us? (We can get away with wickedness without getting exposed; typical thinking of wicked people.)

16 Surely your turning of things upside down (foolish perversion of the truth) shall be esteemed as (is the same as) the potter's clay: for shall the work (the pot) say of him that made it (the potter), He made me not? or shall the thing framed say of him that framed it, He had no understanding (he doesn't know me; I have success-fully hidden from God)? (You wicked are just as foolish as the potters clay that claims it made itself into a pot and has no responsibility to its maker.)

17 Is it not yet a very little while (after the Book of Mormon comes forth), and Lebanon (the Holy Land) shall be turned into a fruitful field, and the fruitful field shall be esteemed as a forest (Israel will blossom with forests etc. after the restoration)?

18 And in that day shall the deaf hear the words of the book, and the eyes of the blind shall see out of obscurity, and out of darkness (as a result of the Book of Mormon and restoration, the spiritually deaf and blind will be healed).

19 The meek also shall increase their joy in the Lord, and the poor among men shall rejoice in the Holy One of Israel (the righteous will know the Savior again).

20 For the terrible one (tyrant) is brought to nought, and the scorner (scoffer) is consumed, and all that watch for iniquity are cut off (the restored truth will expose wickedness and eventually overthrow it):

21 That make a man an offender for a word (via unjust lawsuits and corrupt judicial system etc.), and lay a snare for him that reproveth in the gate (try to eliminate honest people in government etc.), and turn aside the just for a thing of nought (replace truth and honesty with lies).

22 Therefore thus saith the Lord, who redeemed Abraham, concerning the house of Jacob (Israel), (Implies "I redeemed Abraham and I can and will redeem you.") Jacob shall not now be ashamed, neither shall his face now wax pale ("Father Jacob", i.e., Israel, will no longer have to be embarrassed by the behavior of his posterity).

23 But when he seeth his children (his posterity), the work of mine hands (who are now finally righteous, i.e., "my people"), in the midst of

*Restoration of the Gospel –

him, they shall sanctify my name, and sanctify the Holy One of Jacob (the Savior), and shall fear (respect) the God of Israel. (Isaiah here has said, in many ways, that in the last days Israel will return to God.)

24 They also that erred in spirit shall come to understanding, and they that murmured shall learn doctrine (via the Book of Mormon and the restoration of the Church).

ISAIAH 30

Note: Historical setting, 705-701 BC. Sargon II of Assyria has died. Judah joins Philistines and Phonecians in rebellion against Assyria. Judah makes treaty for protection with Egypt.

1 Woe to the rebellious children, saith the LORD, that take counsel (make political plans), but not of me; and that cover with a covering (alliance), but not of my spirit (not approved by God), that they may add sin to sin (add insult to injury; make things worse):

2 That walk to go down into Egypt (turn to Egypt for help), and have not asked at my mouth (haven't asked my permission); to strengthen themselves in the strength of Pharaoh, and to trust in the shadow (protection) of Egypt!

3 Therefore (because you have done this) shall the strength of Pharaoh be your shame (downfall), and the trust in the shadow (protection) of Egypt

your confusion (your pact with Egypt will lead to your ruin, i.e., you should have turned to God rather than man for help).

4 For his (Pharaoh's) princes (leaders) were at Zoan (Tanis), and his ambassadors came to Hanes (Leaders from one end of Egypt to the other worked out the treaty with Judah).

5 They (Judah) were (will be) all ashamed of (disappointed by) a people (Egypt) that could not (can not) profit them, nor be an help nor profit, but a shame, and also a reproach (this deal with Egypt will bring shame and scorn to Judah).

6 The burden of (message of doom for those of Judah who travel with loads of gifts on animals toward Egypt, verses 2-7) the beasts of the south: into the land of trouble and anguish, from whence come the young and old lion, the viper and fiery flying serpent, they (Judah) will carry their riches upon the shoulders of young asses, and their treasures upon the bunches of camels, to a people (Egypt) that shall not profit them.

7 For the Egyptians shall help in vain, and to no purpose: therefore have I cried concerning this, Their strength is to sit still (Egypt won't help you at all!).

8 Now go, write it before them in a table, and note it in a book (the scriptures), that it may be for the time to come for ever and ever (write this down as a witness against Israel):

9 That this (Judah) is a rebellious

people, lying children, children that will not hear the law of the LORD:

10 Which say to the seers, See not; and to the prophets, Prophesy not unto us right things, speak unto us smooth things (comfortable false doctrines), prophesy deceits:

11 Get you out of the way, turn aside out of the path, cause the Holy One of Israel to cease from before us (tell God to quit bothering us).

12 Wherefore thus saith the Holy One of Israel, Because ye despise (spurn, intentionally ignore) this word, and trust in oppression (German: wickedness) and perverseness, and stay (depend) thereon:

13 Therefore this iniquity shall be to you as a breach (broken section in a protective wall) ready to fall, swelling (bulging) out in a high wall, whose breaking cometh suddenly at an instant (you are living on borrowed time; you have broken the covenant that could protect you like a wall, by making covenants with Egypt rather than God).

14 And he (Christ) shall break it as the breaking of the potters' vessel that is broken in pieces; he shall not spare: so that there shall not be found in the bursting of it a sherd (fragment) to take fire from the hearth, or to take water withal out of the pit (nothing useable remains).

15 For thus saith the Lord GOD, the Holy One of Israel; In returning (to God) and rest shall ye be saved (German: you could be saved); in quietness (peacefulness) and in confi-

dence (faith in God) shall be your strength: and ye would not.

16 But ye said (bragged), No; for we will flee (into battle against Assyria) upon horses (symbolize victory); therefore (because of your rebellion) shall ye flee (from Assyria's armies): and, We will ride upon the swift (Judah bragged); therefore shall they (Assyrians) that pursue you be swift (it will be exactly opposite of what you brag, Judah).

17 One thousand (of Judah) shall flee at the rebuke of one (Assyrian); at the rebuke of five (Assyrians) shall (German: all of you) ye flee: till ye be left as a beacon upon the top of a mountain, and as an ensign on an hill (i.e., lonely, nobody left, scattered).

18 And therefore will the LORD wait (because of your wickedness, the Lord will have to wait), that he may be gracious unto you (at a future time), and therefore will he be exalted, that he may have mercy upon you: for the LORD is a God of judgment (justice): blessed are all they that wait for (German: trust in) him.

19 (Isaiah now describes the ultimate in paradise-like conditions for those who do trust in the Lord.) For the people shall dwell in Zion at Jerusalem: thou shalt weep no more: he will be very gracious unto thee at the voice of thy cry; when he shall hear it, he will answer thee.

20 And though the Lord give you the bread of adversity, and the water of affliction, yet shall not thy teachers (thy teacher, i.e., the Lord) be

* The Savior knows our trials & directs our paths !

52

removed into a corner any more, but thine eyes shall see thy teachers:

21 And thine ears shall hear a word behind thee, saying, This is the way, walk ye in it, when ye turn to the right hand, and when ye turn to the left (i.e., you will be surrounded with truth).

22 Ye shall defile (cease to worship) also the covering of thy graven images of silver (your graven images covered with silver), and the ornament of thy molten images of gold: thou shalt cast them away as a menstruous cloth (they will be totally repulsive to you); thou shalt say unto it, Get thee hence (you will shudder at the thought of idol worship).

23 Then shall he give the rain of thy seed, that thou shalt sow the ground withal; and bread of the increase of the earth, and it shall be fat and plenteous: in that day shall thy cattle feed in large pastures (things will go very will when Israel repents and is gathered).

24 The oxen likewise and the young asses that ear (work the ground in agriculture) the ground shall eat clean provender, which hath been winnowed with the shovel and with the fan.

25 And there shall be upon every high mountain, and upon every high hill, rivers and streams of waters in the day of the great slaughter, when the towers fall (when your enemies have been destroyed).

26 Moreover the light of the moon shall be as the light of the sun, and the light of the sun shall be sevenfold, as the light of seven days (everything will be better than you can imagine), in the day that the LORD bindeth up the breach of his people, and healeth the stroke of their wound (Christ heals when people repent).

27 Behold, the name of the LORD cometh from far, burning with his anger, and the burden thereof is heavy: his lips are full of indignation, and his tongue as a devouring fire (the wicked are destroyed):

28 And his breath, as an overflowing stream (flood), shall reach to the midst of the neck, to sift (German: destroy) the nations with the sieve of vanity (German: until they are all filtered out, i.e., destroyed, gone): and there shall be a bridle in the jaws of the people, causing them to err (they have allowed wickedness to take control of them; that's why they are destroyed).

29 Ye (the righteous survivors) shall have a song, as in the night when a holy solemnity is kept; and gladness of heart, as when one goeth with a pipe (German: flute) to come into the mountain of the LORD, to the mighty One of Israel (the Savior).

30 And the LORD shall cause his glorious voice to be heard, and shall shew the lighting down of his arm (will come crashing down upon the wicked), with the indignation of his anger, and with the flame of a devouring fire, with scattering, and tempest, and hailstones.

31 For through the voice (power) of the LORD shall the Assyrian (the

enemy now threatening Judah) be beaten down, which smote (Israel) with a rod.

32 And in every place where the grounded staff shall pass (every stroke of the rod of punishment), which the LORD shall lay upon him (Assyria), it shall be with tabrets and harps: and in battles of shaking (several "waves" of battle) will he fight with it.

33 For Tophet (the "Place of Burning", i.e., hell) is ordained of old (was planned for in the beginning); yea, for the king (of Assyria) it is prepared; he (God) hath made it deep and large (i.e., there is plenty of room in hell for the Assyrians and all other wicked): the pile thereof is fire and much wood (plenty of fuel to burn them); the breath of the LORD, like a stream of brimstone (fiery molten sulphur), doth kindle it (the Lord is prepared to destroy the wicked).

ISAIAH 31

1 Woe to them (Judah) that go down to Egypt for help; and stay (rely) on horses, and trust in chariots (military might of Egypt), because they (Egyptian soldiers) are many; and in horsemen, because they are very strong; but they look not unto the Holy One of Israel, neither seek the LORD (Judah should turn to the Lord instead of Egypt, for help)!

2 Yet he also is wise, and will bring evil (calamity upon the wicked), and will not call back (retract) his words: but will arise against the house of the evildoers, and against the help (helpers) of them that work iniquity.

3 Now the Egyptians are men, and not God; and their horses flesh, and not spirit. When the LORD shall stretch out his hand, both he that helpeth shall fall, and he that is holpen (helped) shall fall down, and they all shall fail together (Egypt and Judah will both fail).

4 For thus hath the LORD spoken unto me, Like as the lion and the young lion roaring on his prey, when a multitude of shepherds is called forth against him, he will not be afraid of their voice, nor abase himself for the noise of them: so shall the LORD of hosts come down to fight for mount Zion, and for the hill thereof (the Lord will be as unstoppable as a lion among sheep).

5 As birds flying (hovering over their young, protecting them), so will the LORD of hosts defend Jerusalem; defending also he will deliver it; and passing over he will preserve it.

6 Turn ye unto him (the Lord) from whom the children of Israel have deeply revolted (please repent).

7 For in that day every man shall cast away his idols of silver, and his idols of gold, which your own hands have made unto you for a sin (turn away from your idol worship).

8 Then shall the Assyrian fall with the sword, not of a mighty man; and the sword, not of a mean (poor) man,

shall devour him: but he shall flee from the sword, and his young men shall be discomfited (put in slavery; God, not men, will overthrow Assyria).

9 And he shall pass over to his strong hold for fear, and his princes shall be afraid of the ensign, saith the LORD, whose fire is in Zion, and his furnace in Jerusalem.

ISAIAH 32

1 Behold, a king (Jesus) shall reign in righteousness, and princes (his leaders) shall rule in judgment (justice, fairness).

2 And a man (Jesus) shall be as an hiding place from the wind, and a covert (protection) from the tempest; as rivers of water in a dry place, as the shadow of a great rock in a weary land (Jesus will be our refuge and protection).

3 And the eyes of them that see shall not be dim, and the ears of them that hear shall hearken (people will be blessed with understanding and discernment).

4 The heart (mind) also of the rash (impulsive) shall understand knowledge (have good judgement), and the tongue of the stammerers shall be ready to speak plainly (communication will be improved).

5 The vile person (villain) shall be no more called liberal (noble), nor the churl (miser; cruel financier) said to be bountiful (i.e., people will be recognized for what they really are, not what they appear to be).

6 (In verses 6-8, Isaiah describes what the types of people alluded to in verse 5 really are like.) For the vile person will speak villany, and his heart will work iniquity, to practise hypocrisy, and to utter error against the LORD, to make empty the soul of the hungry (oppress the poor and needy), and he will cause the drink of the thirsty to fail.

7 The instruments (devices) also of the churl (wicked money-lenders) are evil: he deviseth wicked devices to destroy the poor with lying words (trickery), even when the needy speaketh right (is in the right).

8 But the liberal (noble) deviseth liberal (honorable, righteous) things; and by liberal things shall he stand (German: he will hold to honorable thoughts and actions).

9 Rise up, ye women (German: proud women) that are at ease (overconfident); hear my voice, ye careless (overconfident, complacent, too secure to change your ways)) daughters; give ear unto my speech (message).

10 Many days and years shall ye be troubled, ye careless women: for the vintage (vineyard) shall fail (not produce), the gathering (harvest) shall not come (famine).

11 Tremble, ye women that are at ease; be troubled, ye careless ones: strip you (of pride), and make you bare, and gird sackcloth upon your

loins (humble yourselves).

12 (In verses 12-14, Isaiah tells of a long period of destruction soon to come upon unsuspecting Israelites) They shall lament for the teats (beat upon the breast in mourning), for the pleasant fields, for the fruitful vine (they will long for the good times).

13 Upon the land of my people shall come up thorns and briers; yea, upon all the houses of joy in the joyous city (rough times are coming because of wickedness):

14 Because the (your) palaces shall be forsaken; the multitude of the city shall be left (deserted); the forts and towers shall be for dens (places of habitation for wild beasts) for ever, a joy of wild asses, a pasture of flocks (you will be scattered and your lands left lonely and desolate);

15 (Isaiah now mentions the peaceful conditions to come upon Israel in a future day of righteousness) Until the spirit be poured upon us from on high, and the wilderness be (become) a fruitful field, and the fruitful field be counted for a forest.

16 Then judgment (justice, fairness) shall dwell in the wilderness, and righteousness remain in the fruitful field.

17 And the work (result) of righteousness shall be peace; and the effect (result) of righteousness quietness (lack of turmoil) and assurance (security) for ever.

18 And my people shall dwell in a peaceable habitation, and in sure (safe) dwellings, and in quiet resting places (German: splendid peace);

19 When it shall hail (destruction upon the wicked), coming down on the forest (wicked people?); and the city (probably the proud and wicked) shall be low in a low place (brought down, humbled).

20 Blessed (happy) are ye (the righteous) that sow beside all waters (German: everywhere), that send forth thither (everywhere) the feet of the ox and the ass (perhaps saying that there will be peace everywhere for the righteous).

ISAIAH 33

1 Woe to thee (probably Sennacherib, king of Assyria, Isa.36:1; symbolic of all wicked who seem to get away with wickedness) that spoilest, and thou wast not spoiled; and dealest treacherously, and they dealt not treacherously with thee! when thou shalt cease to spoil, thou shalt be spoiled; and when thou shalt make an end to deal treacherously, they shall deal treacherously with thee (after the Lord is through using you to punish other wicked nations, you will get your just reward).

2 O LORD, be gracious unto us (Israel); we have waited for thee: be thou their (our) arm every morning, our salvation also in the time of trouble.

3 At the noise of the tumult the

people fled (flee); at the lifting up of thyself (Christ) the nations were (are) scattered.

4 And your spoil (Israel) shall be gathered (by missionaries) like the gathering of the caterpiller: as the running to and fro of locusts (perhaps describing missionaries going everywhere in the last days) shall he (they) run (collect) upon them (Israel).

5 The LORD is exalted; for he dwelleth on high: he hath filled Zion with judgment and righteousness.

6 And wisdom and knowledge shall be the stability of thy times, and strength of salvation: the fear of the LORD is his treasure (results of restoration).

7 (Verses 7-9 refer back to Assyrian attack.) Behold, their (Israel's) valiant ones shall cry without: the ambassadors of peace shall weep bitterly.

8 The highways lie waste, the wayfaring man ceaseth: he hath broken the covenant, he hath despised the cities, he regardeth no man.

9 The earth mourneth and languisheth: Lebanon is ashamed and hewn down: Sharon is like a wilderness; and Bashan and Carmel shake off their fruits.

10 Now will I rise, saith the LORD; now will I be exalted; now will I lift up myself (the time will come when God will take over from the wicked).

11 Ye shall conceive chaff, ye shall bring forth stubble (end result of wicked lifestyles = nothing of value): your breath, as fire, shall devour you (sow evil, harvest misery).

12 And the people shall be as the burnings of lime: as thorns cut up shall they be burned in the fire.

13 Hear, ye that are far off (the whole world), what I have done; and, ye that are near, acknowledge my might (in the future the whole world will know God).

14 The sinners in Zion are afraid; fearfulness hath surprised (seized) the hypocrites. Who among us shall dwell with the devouring fire? who among us shall dwell with everlasting burnings (who will not be burned, destroyed, i.e., who can survive the presence of God)?

15 He that walketh righteously, and speaketh uprightly; he that despiseth the gain of oppressions (unrighteous profit at the expense of others), that shaketh his hands from holding of bribes (refuses bribes), that stoppeth his ears from hearing of blood, and shutteth his eyes from seeing evil (does not participate in evils);

16 He (the righteous) shall dwell on high: his place of defence shall be the munitions (fortress) of rocks: bread shall be given him; his waters shall be sure (reward to the righteous).

17 Thine eyes shall see the king in his beauty: they shall behold the land that is very far off (heaven?).

18 Thine heart shall meditate terror. Where is the scribe (Assyrian tallyman, conqueror)? where is the receiver? where is he that counted the towers (Assyrian army)? (I.e., where

are the wicked now?)

19 Thou shalt not see a fierce people (foreign invaders), a people of a deeper speech than thou canst perceive; of a stammering tongue, that thou canst not understand (enemies who speak foreign languages).

20 Look upon Zion, the city of our solemnities: thine eyes shall see Jerusalem a quiet habitation, a tabernacle that shall not be taken down; not one of the stakes thereof shall ever be removed, neither shall any of the cords thereof be broken (the future has glorious things in store for the righteous).

21 But there the glorious LORD will be unto us a place of broad rivers and streams; wherein shall go no galley (enemy ships) with oars, neither shall gallant ship pass thereby.

22 For the LORD is our judge, the LORD is our lawgiver, the LORD is our king; he will save us.

23 Thy (the wicked's) tacklings (ship's rigging) are loosed; they could not well strengthen their mast, they could not spread the sail (i.e., the wicked will be shut down): then is the prey of a great spoil divided; the lame (the righteous; the wicked have considered the righteous to be lame, weak) take the prey (the wicked).

24 And the inhabitant shall not say, I am sick: the people that dwell therein shall be forgiven their iniquity.

ISAIAH 34

Note: This chapter contains Isaiah's harshest words against the wicked. It is a review of earlier chapters and goes with chapter 35.

1 Come near, ye nations (speaking to the whole world), to hear; and hearken, ye people: let the earth hear, and all that is therein; the world, and all things that come forth of it.

2 For the indignation of the LORD is upon all nations (all the wicked), and his fury upon all their armies: he hath utterly destroyed them, he hath delivered them to the slaughter (Future; ultimate fate of the wicked).

3 Their slain also shall be cast out, and their stink shall come up out of their carcases, and the mountains shall be melted (soaked) with their blood.

4 And all the host (stars?) of heaven shall be dissolved, and the heavens shall be rolled together as a scroll: and all their (starry host?) host shall fall down, as the leaf falleth off from the vine, and as a falling fig from the fig tree (perhaps goes with D&C 133:49 and 88:95; Second Coming).

5 For my sword shall be bathed in heaven (bathed in blood): behold, it shall come down upon Idumea (Edom; the world, see D&C 1:36; connotes the wicked world), and upon the people of my curse, to judgment.

6 The sword of the LORD is filled (bathed) with (in) blood, it is made fat with fatness (covered with fat like a knife used in animal sacrifices), and

with the blood of lambs and goats, with the fat of the kidneys of rams: for the LORD hath a sacrifice in Bozrah (the capital of Edom; see map 9), and a great slaughter in the land of Idumea (the wicked world, ie, the sword of the Lord is going to come crashing down on the wicked of the world).

7 And the unicorns (wild oxen) shall come down with them, and the bullocks (bull calves) with the bulls; and their land shall be soaked with blood, and their dust (land) made fat with fatness (covered with fat trimmed away by sword of justice).

8 For it is the day of the LORD's vengeance, and the year of recompences (deserved rewards) for the controversy (German: avenging) of Zion (i.e., a day of avenging the wrongs done against Zion throughout the history of the world).

9 And the streams thereof (of Edom, i.e., the wicked) shall be turned into pitch (goes up in flames easily), and the dust thereof into brimstone (burning sulphur), and the land thereof shall become burning pitch (i.e., the wicked of the world will be destroyed by fire).

10 It shall not be quenched night nor day (no one can stop the judgements of God); the smoke thereof shall go up for ever: from generation to generation it shall lie waste; none shall pass through it for ever and ever (wickedness will be destroyed completely).

11 (Isaiah often uses the imagery that now follows to emphasize the theme that the wicked will all be gone.) But the cormorant and the bittern (lonely desert creatures) shall possess it; the owl also and the raven shall dwell in it: and he (the Lord) shall stretch out upon it the line (measuring tape) of confusion, and the stones (plumb line) of emptiness (i.e., Edom, the wicked, will not "measure up".).

12 They shall call the nobles thereof to the kingdom, but none shall be there, and all her (Edom's) princes (leaders) shall be nothing (German: they will be people without a kingdom, will have nothing to rule over).

13 And thorns shall come up in her palaces, nettles and brambles in the fortresses thereof: and it shall be an habitation of dragons (jackals), and a court (home) for owls.

14 The wild beasts of the desert shall also meet with the wild beasts (hyenas) of the island, and the satyr (wild goat) shall cry to his fellow; the screech owl also shall rest there, and find for herself a place of rest.

15 There shall the great owl make her nest, and lay, and hatch, and gather under her shadow: there shall the vultures also be gathered, every one with her mate (each of the animals mentioned above were considered unclean by the Israelites).

16 Seek ye out of the book of the LORD, and read: no one of these (unclean creatures) shall fail, none shall want (lack) her mate: for my mouth it hath commanded, and his spirit it hath gathered them.

17 And he hath cast the lot (voted) for them, and his hand hath divided it unto them by line: they shall possess it for ever, from generation to generation shall they dwell therein (If the Lord takes such good care of these "unclean" creatures, think how much more the righteous will get; a transition to chapter 35).

ISAIAH 35

1 The wilderness and the solitary place shall be glad for them (the righteous who return); and the desert shall rejoice, and blossom as the rose (i.e., a paradise awaits the righteous).

2 It shall blossom abundantly, and rejoice even with joy and singing: the glory of Lebanon (the Holy Land; symbolic of anywhere the righteous gather) shall be given unto it, the excellency of Carmel and Sharon, they shall see the glory of the LORD, and the excellency of our God.

3 Strengthen ye the weak (German: tired) hands, and confirm (German: revive) the feeble (German: stumbling) knees.

4 Say to them (the righteous) that are of a fearful (German: discouraged) heart, Be strong, fear not: behold, your God will come with vengeance (upon the wicked), even God with a recompence; he will come and save you (the righteous).

5 Then the eyes of the blind shall be opened, and the ears of the deaf shall be unstopped (the gospel heals).

6 Then shall the lame man leap as an hart (deer), and the tongue of the dumb (people who can't talk; symbolic of those who didn't know gospel) sing: for in the wilderness shall waters (literal; also symbolic of "living water", i.e., the gospel) break out, and streams in the desert.

7 And the parched ground (symbolic of apostate Israel; see Is. 53:2, Mosiah 14:2) shall become a pool, and the thirsty land springs of water (via the restoration of the gospel): in the habitation of dragons (jackals. Isaiah has used this imagery before [see 13:22; 34:13-15] to depict barrenness left when the wicked are destroyed. Here, he depicts the barrenness, apostasy etc. being replaced with lush growth, i.e., restoration of the gospel) where each lay, shall be grass with reeds and rushes (restored productivity).

8 And an highway (perhaps literal highways upon which various groups have returned or will return; symbolically, the path to God, i.e.,the gospel, "strait and narrow" way, temple covenants, baptismal covenants etc.) shall be there, and a way, and it shall be called The way of holiness; the unclean shall not pass over it; but it shall be for those: the wayfaring men, though fools (JST "though they are accounted fools", i.e., though men might consider the righteous to be fools), shall not err therein.

9 No lion shall be there, nor any ravenous beast (enemies of Israel's return; forces of evil) shall go up thereon, it shall not be found there (perhaps looking ahead to millennial

conditions); but the redeemed shall walk there:

10 And the ransomed of the LORD shall return, and come to Zion with songs and everlasting joy upon their heads: they shall obtain joy and gladness, and sorrow and sighing shall flee away (see Rev. 21:4; Rev. 7:17; the final state of the righteous).

ISAIAH 36

1 Now it came to pass in the fourteenth year (about 701 BC) of king Hezekiah (righteous king of Judah), that Sennacherib king of Assyria came up against all the defenced cities of Judah, and took them (perhaps as many as 46 cities).

2 And the king of Assyria sent Rabshakeh (a title meaning "chief of the officers") from Lachish (about 35 miles southwest of Jerusalem—see map 9) to Jerusalem unto king Hezekiah with a great army. And he (Rabshakeh) stood by the conduit of the upper pool in the highway of the fuller's field (where fullers bleached cloth).

3 Then came forth unto him Eliakim (prime minister of Judah), Hilkiah's son, which was over the house, and Shebna the scribe, and Joah, Asaph's son, the recorder.

4 And Rabshakeh said unto them, Say ye now to Hezekiah, Thus saith the great king (sarcastically mimicking "Thus saith the Lord."), the king of Assyria, What confidence is this wherein thou trustest (you are fools to

trust Egypt for protection)?

5 I say, sayest thou, (but they are but vain words) I have counsel (plans with Egypt) and strength for war (Egypt is our ally): now on whom dost thou ((Hezekiah/Judah) trust, that thou rebellest against me (Assyria)?

6 Lo, thou trustest in the staff ("scepter", i.e.,power) of this broken reed ("broken broom straw", Egypt), on Egypt; whereon if a man lean, it will go into his hand, and pierce it ("Egypt is so weak, so thin that if you were to lean on it with your hand it would poke right through!"): so is Pharaoh king of Egypt to all that trust in him (Egypt never could protect anyone).

7 But if thou say to me, We trust in the LORD our God: is it not he (the Lord), whose high places and whose altars (places of worship) Hezekiah hath taken away (King Hezekiah did away with local sites of worship and required the Jews to worship at the temple in Jerusalem), and said to Judah and to Jerusalem, Ye shall worship before this altar (i.e., worship at the temple in Jerusalem)?

8 Now therefore give pledges ("Lets make a bet."), I pray thee, to my master the king of Assyria, and I will give thee two thousand horses, if thou be able on thy part to set riders upon them ("If I give you 2000 horses, I'll bet you can't find 2000 able-bodied soldiers in all of Judah to ride them!").

9 How then wilt thou turn away the

face of one captain of the least of my master's servants, and put thy trust on Egypt for chariots and for horsemen (you'll get no help from puny Egypt!)?

10 And am I now come up without the LORD against this land to destroy it? the LORD said unto me, Go up against this land, and destroy it ("Your God told me to come up and destroy you!" [a lie, but sometimes effective intimidation strategy]).

11 Then said Eliakim and Shebna and Joah unto Rabshakeh, Speak, I (we) pray thee, unto thy servants (us, King Hezekiah's representatives) in the Syrian language; for we understand it: and speak not to us in the Jews' language, in the ears of the people that are on the wall ("Can't we discuss this in a language our citizens don't understand? This is too embarrassing.").

12 But Rabshakeh said, Hath my master sent me to thy master and to thee to speak these words? hath he not sent me to the men that sit upon the wall, that they may eat their own dung, and drink their own piss with you (Before Assyria is through with you, you'll be that bad off!)?

13 Then Rabshakeh stood, and cried with a loud voice in the Jews' language (intentionally so the citizens could easily hear), and said, Hear ye the words of the great king, the king of Assyria.

14 Thus saith the king, Let not Hezekiah deceive you: for he shall not be able to deliver you.

15 Neither let Hezekiah make you trust in the LORD, saying, The LORD will surely deliver us: this city shall not be delivered into the hand of the king of Assyria.

16 Hearken not to Hezekiah: for thus saith the king of Assyria, Make an agreement with me by a present, and come out to me (surrender): and eat ye every one of his vine, and every one of his fig tree, and drink ye every one the waters of his own cistern (stay on your own land for a while, in peace, until I make arrangements to transport you elsewhere);

17 Until I come and take you away to a land like your own land, a land of corn and wine, a land of bread and vineyards (you'll like where I take you).

18 Beware lest Hezekiah persuade you (don't let your foolish king fast-talk you into resisting us Assyrians), saying, The LORD will deliver us. Hath any of the gods of the nations delivered his land out of the hand of the king of Assyria (no other gods in other lands have been able to stop us and yours won't either!)?

19 Where are the gods of Hamath (map 9; part of modern Syria) and Arphad (map 10; part of modern Syria)? where are the gods of Sepharvaim (part of modern Syria)? and have they delivered Samaria out of my hand?

20 Who are they among all the gods of these lands, that have delivered

their land out of my hand, that the LORD should deliver Jerusalem out of my hand?

21 But they (Hezekiah's three men) held their peace, and answered him not a word: for the king's commandment was, saying, Answer him not.

22 Then came Eliakim, the son of Hilkiah, that was over the household, and Shebna the scribe, and Joah, the son of Asaph, the recorder, to Hezekiah with their clothes rent (very distraught), and told him the words of Rabshakeh.

ISAIAH 37

1 And it came to pass, when king Hezekiah heard it, that he rent (tore) his clothes (as a sign of extreme worry), and covered himself with sackcloth, and went into the house of the LORD (the Temple).

2 And he sent Eliakim (his prime minister), who was over the household, and Shebna the (royal) scribe, and the elders (older priests) of the priests covered with sackcloth, unto Isaiah the prophet the son of Amoz.

3 And they said unto him, Thus saith Hezekiah, This day is a day of trouble, and of rebuke (we're in big trouble), and of blasphemy (the Assyrians speak totally disrespectfully of the Lord): for the children are come to the birth, and there is not strength to bring forth (we're doomed, like when a woman is in hard labor, but the baby doesn't come).

4 It may be the LORD thy God will hear (has heard) the words of Rabshakeh (Assyria's representative), whom the king of Assyria his master hath sent to reproach (blaspheme) the living God, and will reprove the words (of Rabshakeh) which the LORD thy God hath heard (hopefully, the Lord will not let them get away with such talk): wherefore lift up thy prayer for the remnant that is left.

5 So the servants of king Hezekiah came to Isaiah.

6 And Isaiah said unto them, Thus shall ye say unto your master, Thus saith the LORD, Be not afraid of the words that thou hast heard, wherewith the servants of the king of Assyria have blasphemed me (the Lord).

7 Behold, I (the Lord) will send a blast upon him (I will change his frame of mind, make him nervous), and he shall hear a rumour (bad news from home), and return to his own land; and I will cause him to fall by the sword in his own land.

8 So Rabshakeh returned, and found the king of Assyria warring against Libnah (southwest of Jerusalem): for he (Rabshakeh) had heard that he (the King of Assyria) was departed from Lachish.

9 And he (the Assyrian King) heard say concerning Tirhakah king of Ethiopia (the Egyptian army), He is come forth to make war with thee. And when he (King of Assyria) heard it, he sent messengers to Hezekiah, saying (the King of Assyria, worried

about approaching Egyptian armies, now presses King Hezekiah for quick surrender),

10 Thus shall ye speak to Hezekiah king of Judah, saying, Let not thy God, in whom thou trustest, deceive thee, saying, Jerusalem shall not be given into the hand of the king of Assyria (your God can't help you; you will be powerless before the Assyrians).

11 Behold, thou hast heard what the kings of Assyria have done to all lands by destroying them utterly; and shalt thou be delivered (what makes you think you'll be different)?

12 Have the gods of the nations delivered them which my fathers have destroyed, as Gozan (Iraq), and Haran (Turkey), and Rezeph (Iraq), and the children of Eden which were in Telassar (Iraq)?

13 Where is the king of Hamath (Syria), and the king of Arphad (Syria), and the king of the city of Sepharvaim (Syria), Hena (unknown), and Ivah (unknown)?

14 And Hezekiah received the letter from the hand of the messengers, and read it: and Hezekiah went up unto the house of the LORD, and spread it before the LORD.

15 And Hezekiah prayed unto the LORD, saying,

16 O LORD of hosts, God of Israel, that dwellest between (German: above) the cherubims, thou art the God, even thou alone, of all the kingdoms of the earth: thou hast made heaven and earth.

17 Incline thine ear, O LORD, and hear; open thine eyes, O LORD, and see: and hear all the words of Sennacherib (King of Assyria), which hath sent to reproach (blaspheme) the living God.

18 Of a truth (it is true), LORD, the kings of Assyria have laid waste all the nations, and their countries (just as the letter in verse 14 says),

19 And have cast their gods into the fire: for they were no gods (weren't real gods), but the work of men's hands, wood and stone: therefore they have destroyed them (that's why Assyria was able to conquer those nations).

20 Now therefore, O LORD our God, save us from his hand, that all the kingdoms of the earth may know that thou art the LORD, even thou only.

21 Then Isaiah the son of Amoz sent unto Hezekiah, saying, Thus saith the LORD God of Israel, Whereas thou hast prayed to me against Sennacherib king of Assyria:

22 This is the word which the LORD hath spoken concerning him; The virgin, the daughter of Zion (the unconquered people of Jerusalem), hath despised thee, and laughed thee to scorn; the daughter of Jerusalem hath shaken her head at thee (not afraid of you Assyrians).

23 Whom hast thou reproached and blasphemed? and against whom hast thou exalted thy voice, and lifted up

thine eyes on high? even against the Holy One of Israel (you chose the wrong one to offend this time; you have mocked the true God).

24 By thy servants hast thou reproached the Lord, and hast said, By the multitude of my chariots am I come up to the height of the mountains, to the sides (west) of Lebanon; and I will (have) cut down the tall cedars thereof, and the choice fir trees thereof: and I will enter (have entered) into the height of his border, and the forest of his Carmel.

25 I have digged (wells), and drunk water (in many a conquered land); and with the sole of my feet have I dried up all the rivers of the besieged places (end of quoting the Assyrian King's boasts).

26 Hast thou (King of Assyria) not heard long ago ("Haven't you heard by now?"), how I (the Lord) have done (allowed) it; and of ancient times, that I have formed it? now have I brought it to pass, that thou shouldest be to lay waste defenced cities into ruinous heaps (I, the Lord allowed you to do these things, otherwise you would never have had such power).

27 Therefore (that is why) their inhabitants were of small power, they were dismayed and confounded: they were as the grass of the field, and as the green herb, as the grass on the housetops, and as corn blasted before it be grown up.

28 But I (the Lord) know thy abode (I know you well), and thy going out, and thy coming in, and thy rage against me.

29 Because thy rage against me, and thy tumult, is come up into mine ears, therefore will I put my hook in thy nose, and my bridle in thy lips (I will control you, King of Assyria), and I will turn thee back by the way (road) by which thou camest (I will stop you cold).

30 And this shall be a sign unto thee (Hezekiah and his people), Ye shall eat this year such as groweth of itself (because of the Assyrian siege, you have not had time to plant crops normally, yet you will harvest some "volunteer" crops from plants that grew from seeds spilled during last years harvest, i.e., you'll be OK food wise); and the second year that which springeth of the same: and in the third year sow ye, and reap, and plant vineyards, and eat the fruit thereof (you'll be back to normal planting and harvesting by the second and third years from now).

31 And the remnant that is escaped of the house of Judah shall again take root downward, and bear fruit upward (a remnant of Judah will flourish again):

32 For out of Jerusalem shall go forth a remnant, and they that escape out of mount Zion: the zeal of the LORD of hosts shall do this (a remnant will flourish again via God's intervention).

33 Therefore thus saith the LORD

concerning the king of Assyria, He shall not come into this city, nor shoot an arrow there nor come before it with shields, nor cast a bank against it (a very definite prophecy).

34 By the way (road) that he came, by the same shall he return (i.e., he will retreat), and shall not come into this city, saith the LORD.

35 For I will defend this city to save it for mine own sake, and for my servant David's sake.

36 Then (after the Assyrian armies had come to the outskirts of Jerusalem and were ready to attack) the angel of the LORD went forth, and smote in the camp of the Assyrians a hundred and fourscore and five thousand: and when they arose early in the morning, behold, they were all dead corpses (185,000 Assyrians were dead the following morning).

37 So Sennacherib king of Assyria departed, and went and returned, and dwelt at Nineveh (his headquarters at home).

38 And it came to pass, as he was worshipping in the house of Nisroch his god, that Adrammelech and Sharezer his sons smote (killed) him with the sword; and they escaped into the land of Armenia: and Esar-haddon his son reigned in his stead (this happened about 20 years after his retreat from Jerusalem).

ISAIAH 38

(Note: Chapters 38 and 39 fit historically before chapters 36 and 37 and could be considered "flashbacks" to 705-703 BC.)

1 In those days (about 705-703 BC) was Hezekiah sick unto death. And Isaiah the prophet the son of Amoz came unto him, and said unto him, Thus saith the LORD, Set thine house in order: for thou shalt die, and not live.

2 Then Hezekiah turned his face toward the wall, and prayed unto the LORD,

3 And said, Remember now, O LORD, I beseech thee, how I have walked before thee in truth and with a perfect heart, and have done that which is good in thy sight. And Hezekiah wept sore (bitterly).

4 Then came the word of the LORD to Isaiah, saying,

5 Go, and say to Hezekiah, Thus saith the LORD, the God of David thy father (ancestor), I have heard thy prayer, I have seen thy tears: behold, I will add unto thy days fifteen years (A major message here is that Heaven pays attention to mighty faith and prayer).

6 And I will deliver thee and this city out of the hand of the king of Assyria: and I will defend this city (This would seem to place Hezekiah's illness sometime during the Assyrian threats to Jerusalem as described in chapters 36 and 37.).

7 And this shall be a sign unto thee from the LORD, that the LORD will do this thing that he hath spoken;

8 Behold, I will bring again the shadow of the degrees, which is gone down in the sun dial of Ahaz, ten degrees backward. So the sun returned ten degrees, by which degrees it was gone down (time was turned backward).

9 (Hezekiah was healed and now gives thanks and praise to the Lord for his miraculous recovery.) The writing (psalm) of Hezekiah king of Judah, when he had been sick, and was recovered of his sickness:

10 I (Hezekiah) said in the cutting off of my days (when I was on my death bed), I shall go to the gates of the grave (I am doomed): I am deprived of the residue (remainder) of my years (I am too young to die).

11 I said, I shall not see the LORD, even the LORD, in the land of the living (I am about to leave this mortal life): I shall behold man no more with the inhabitants of the world (I won't be around anymore to associate with my fellow men).

12 Mine age is departed (German: my time is up), and is removed from me as a shepherd's tent (they are taking my tent down, i.e., I'm "cashing in"): I have (thou hast) cut off like a weaver my life (thou hast "clipped my threads" like a weaver does when the rug is finished): he will cut me off with pining sickness (fatal illness is how the Lord is sending me out of this life): from day even to night wilt thou make an end of me.

13 I reckoned till morning (German: I thought, "If I could just live until morning!"), that, as a lion, so will he break all my bones (I can't stop the Lord if he wants me to die anymore than I could stop a lion): from day even to night wilt thou make an end of me (I'm doomed; my time is short).

14 Like a crane or a swallow, so did I chatter (German: whimper): I did mourn as a dove: mine eyes fail with looking (falter as I look) upward: O LORD, I am oppressed (German: suffering); undertake (German: sooth, moderate my condition) for me (be thou my help, security).

15 What shall I say (How can I express my gratitude)? he hath both spoken unto me, and himself hath done it (JST: "healed me"): I shall go softly (German: in humility) all my years (JST "that I may not walk") in the bitterness of my soul.

16 O Lord, by these things men live, and in all these things is the life of my spirit (JST: "thou who art the life of my spirit, in whom I live;"): so wilt thou recover (heal) me, and make me to live (JST: "and in all these things I will praise thee.").

17 Behold, for peace I had great bitterness (JST: "Behold, I had great bitterness instead of peace"): but thou hast in love to my soul delivered it (JST: "saved me") from the pit of corruption (rotting in the grave): for thou hast cast all my sins behind thy back (Atonement).

18 For the grave cannot praise

(German: Hell does not praise) thee, death can not celebrate thee: they (people in spirit prison) that go down into the pit (hell; see Isaiah 14:15) cannot hope for thy truth (Alma 34:32-34).

19 The living, the living, he shall praise thee, as I do this day (I am very happy to still be alive): the father to the children shall make known thy truth (I will testify to my family and others of your kindness to me).

20 The LORD was ready to save me: therefore we will sing my songs to the stringed instruments (we will put my words of praise to music) all the days of our life in the house of the LORD.

21 For Isaiah had said, Let them take a lump of figs, and lay it for a plaister upon the boil, and he shall recover (perhaps the lump of figs served the same purpose as the lump of clay to heal the blind man in John 9:6 & 7, i.e., faith obedience).

22 Hezekiah also had said, What is the sign that I shall go up to the house of the LORD? (This verse fits after verse 6. See 2 Kings 20:8.)

ISAIAH 39

1 At that time (about 705-703 BC) Merodach-baladan, the son of Baladan, king of Babylon, sent letters and a present to Hezekiah: for he had heard that he had been sick, and was recovered.

2 And Hezekiah was glad of them, and shewed them (the Babylonian delegation who brought the letters and present) the house of his precious things, the silver, and the gold, and the spices, and the precious ointment, and all the house of his armour, and all that was found in his treasures: there was nothing in his house, nor in all his dominion, that Hezekiah shewed them not.

3 Then came Isaiah the prophet unto king Hezekiah, and said unto him, What said these men? and from whence came they unto thee? And Hezekiah said, They are come from a far country unto me, even from Babylon.

4 Then said he, What have they seen in thine house? And Hezekiah answered, All that is in mine house have they seen: there is nothing among my treasures that I have not shewed them.

5 Then said Isaiah to Hezekiah, Hear the word of the LORD of hosts:

6 Behold, the days come, that all that is in thine house, and that which thy fathers have laid up in store until this day, shall be carried to Babylon: nothing shall be left, saith the LORD (prophecy regarding Babylonian captivity, which will take place in about 100 years).

7 And of thy sons that shall issue from thee, which thou shalt beget, shall they take away; and they shall be eunuchs in the palace of the king of Babylon.

8 Then said Hezekiah to Isaiah, Good is the word of the LORD which thou hast spoken. He said moreover,

For there shall be peace and truth in my days. (Some scholars are critical of Hezekiah's response here, but, he remained loyal to God and perhaps he did mourn for his people in the future and it is just not recorded here. See 2 Kings 20:19-20. It is possible to be happy and at peace with God despite others' wickedness. For instance, Mormon in Mormon 2:19 and Lehi in 2 Nephi 1:15.)

ISAIAH 40

1 Comfort ye, comfort ye my people, saith your God.

2 (This verse would seem to refer to the last days and on into the Millennium) Speak ye comfortably (German: in a friendly manner; Hebrew: tenderly) to Jerusalem, and cry unto her, that her warfare (time of service) is accomplished, that her iniquity is pardoned (via repentance and the atonement): for she hath received of the LORD's hand double for all her sins (has paid a heavy penalty for wickedness).

3 The voice of him that crieth in the wilderness, Prepare ye the way of the LORD, make straight in the desert a highway for our God. (This fits John the Baptist as described in Matt. 3:1-3. Other "Eliases" or "preparers", prophets, also fit this passage in the last days as they prepare us for the Second Coming.)

4 Every valley shall be exalted (raised), and every mountain and hill shall be made low: and the crooked shall be made straight, and the rough places (mountains) plain (changes in the earth at the Second Coming; also can be symbolic of wickedness etc. being "straightened out" at the Second Coming):

5 And the glory of the LORD shall be revealed, and all flesh shall see it together (at the same time): for the mouth of the LORD hath spoken it (Second Coming).

6 (This verse is a course in perspective. Man's power is insignificant compared to God. See verse 18) The voice said, Cry (preach). And he said, What shall I cry (preach)? (Answer) All flesh (people) is (are like) grass, and all the goodliness thereof is as the flower of the field (not that we are not significant and important—Christ gave His life for us—but just a reminder that God is way ahead of us and we would be wise to follow and obey Him completely. We are nothing, at this point, compared to Him.):

7 The grass withereth, the flower fadeth: because the spirit of the LORD bloweth upon it: surely the people is grass (man's power and wisdom pale against the Lord's).

8 The grass withereth, the flower fadeth: but the word of our God shall stand for ever (trust in God, not in the "arm of flesh").

9 O Zion, that bringest good tidings (the gospel), get thee up into the high mountain; O Jerusalem, that bringest good tidings, lift up thy voice with

strength; lift it up, be not afraid; say unto the cities of Judah, Behold your God!

10 Behold, the Lord GOD will come with strong hand (German: with power), and his arm (symbolic of power) shall rule for him (He will rule on earth; Second Coming): behold, his reward is with him (He will reward the righteous and the wicked), and his work before him (German: reward precedes Him; 2nd coming, Rev.22:12).

11 He shall feed his flock like a shepherd (He knows each of us by name; millennial reign): he shall gather the lambs with his arm, and carry them in his bosom, and shall gently lead those that are with young (peaceful conditions during the Millennium).

12 (The "course in perspective" continues, leading to verse 18) Who hath measured the waters in the hollow of his hand, and meted out heaven with the span, and comprehended the dust of the earth in a measure, and weighed the mountains in scales, and the hills in a balance? (Who else do you know who can create worlds and design oceans, continents, mountains, heavens etc.?)

13 Who hath directed (taught) the Spirit of the LORD, or being his counseller hath taught him (what mortal could teach God anything!)?

14 With whom took he (God) counsel, and who instructed him, and taught him in the path of judgment,

and taught him knowledge, and shewed to him the way of understanding (the answer, "No one." is implied)?

15 Behold, the nations (of this earth) are as a drop of (in) a bucket (compared to God's domain), and are counted as (like) the small dust of the balance (are about as significant as a small speck of dust on a scale): behold, he taketh up the isles as a very little thing (German: the continents are like the tiniest speck of dust to Him).

16 And Lebanon (sometimes used to represent all of Palestine) is not sufficient to burn, nor the beasts thereof sufficient for a burnt offering (all the wood and all the animals in Lebanon wouldn't even begin to make a sacrifice worthy of who God really is!).

17 All nations before (compared to) him are as nothing; and they are counted (compared) to him less than nothing, and vanity.

18 To whom then will ye liken (compare) God? or what likeness (idol) will ye compare unto him (a transition now to the topic of idols as substitutes for God)?

19 The workman (craftsman) melteth (carves or forms) a graven image, and the goldsmith spreadeth (covers) it over with gold, and casteth (makes) silver chains (i.e., foolish people make idols and then compare them to God).

20 He that is so impoverished that he hath no oblation (German: so poor

that he can give only the smallest offering) chooseth a tree that will not rot (selects wood for an idol); he seeketh unto him a cunning workman to prepare a graven image (idol), that shall not be moved (German: becomes a permanent fixture).

21 Have ye not known (German: Do you not know?)? have ye not heard? hath it not been told you from the beginning? have ye not understood from the foundations of the earth (i.e.,don't you understand!)?

22 It is he (the Lord) that sitteth upon the circle of the earth (is above all), and the inhabitants thereof are as grasshoppers (continues the theme of verse 17); that stretcheth out the heavens as a curtain, and spreadeth them out as a tent to dwell in (the Lord is the creator):

23 That bringeth the princes (leaders) to nothing; he maketh the judges (rulers) of the earth as vanity (nothing).

24 Yea, they (the wicked rulers and leaders) shall not be planted (German: shall be as if they hadn't even been planted); yea, they shall not be sown: yea, their stock shall not take root in the earth: and he shall also blow upon them, and they shall wither, and the whirlwind shall take them away as stubble (they are nothing compared to God).

25 To whom then will ye liken me, or shall I be equal? saith the Holy One (same question as in verse 18).

26 Lift up your eyes on high, and behold (see) who hath created these things (God's creations), that bringeth out their host by number: he calleth them all by names (He knows every one of them) by (because of) the greatness of his might (German: ability), for that he is strong in power; not one faileth (His creations all obey him).

27 Why sayest thou, O Jacob (you Israelites), and speakest, O Israel, My way is hid from the LORD (i.e., I can hide my wickedness from God), and my judgment (cause) is passed over from (disregarded by) my God?

28 Hast thou not known? hast thou not heard (haven't you heard by now), that the everlasting God, the LORD, the Creator of the ends of the earth, fainteth not (German: is not weak), neither is weary? there is no searching of his understanding (you can't comprehend His understanding).

29 He giveth power to the faint; and to them that have no might he increaseth strength (Ether 12:27).

30 Even the youths shall (may grow) faint and be weary, and the young men shall utterly fall (i.e., all mortals have their limitations):

31 But they that wait (base their hopes) upon the LORD shall renew their strength; they shall mount up with wings as eagles (be renewed like molting [lose their old feathers each year, then get new ones] eagles are); they shall run, and not be weary; and they shall walk, and not faint (in pursuing exaltation. See context of

D&C 89:20-21; i.e., the righteous receive extra strength on earth and have a glorious resurrection and receive the strength of the Lord as joint heirs with Christ).

ISAIAH 41

Note: Chapters 41-44 refer mainly to the last days. There are many different opinions among scholars concerning the meaning of some verses in this chapter. In such cases, I have used the Institute of Religion 302 Student Manual as the authority for interpretive notes in parentheses).

1 Keep silence before me (hush, and let me teach you), O islands (all land masses where scattered Israel live); and let the people renew their strength (as mentioned in 40:31): let them come near; then let them speak: let us come near together to judgment. (German: dispute, see who is right, i.e., see who is more powerful, God or your idols; similar to Elijah and priests of Baal in I Kings 18);

2 (Question: "Who is more powerful, your idols or our God?") Who raised up the righteous man from the east (The Savior himself fits this description, coming in from the east wilderness at age 30 to begin his ministry; could also refer to many prophets including Abraham who have come from the "East", i.e., on assignment from the Lord, and assisted in "calling the generations

from the beginning", verse 4), called him to his foot (German: to go forth), gave (him power over) the nations before him, and made him rule over kings? he gave them (kings) as the dust to his sword (they couldn't stop his sword, power, anymore than dust particles could), and as driven stubble to his bow (Nations and kings couldn't stop him).

3 He pursued them, and passed safely; even by the way that he had not gone with his feet (German: without wearying of his errand, assignment; perhaps ties back to 40:31).

4 Who hath wrought and done it (the things referred to above), calling the generations (German: all people) from the beginning? (Answer to the question put in verse 2) I the LORD, the first, and with the last; I am he.

5 The isles (scattered Israel) saw it, and feared (respected it, responded positively); the ends of the earth were afraid, drew near, and came (people from all parts of the earth responded).

6 They helped every one his neighbour; and every one said to his brother, Be of good courage.

7 So (yet, nevertheless) the carpenter encouraged the goldsmith, and he that smootheth with the hammer him that smote the anvil, saying, It is ready for the sodering: and he fastened it with nails, that it should not be moved (yet, many foolishly continued with their worshipping of idols).

8 But thou, Israel, art my servant, Jacob whom I have chosen, the seed of Abraham my friend.

9 Thou whom I have taken (gathered) from the ends of the earth, and called thee from the chief men thereof, and said unto thee, Thou art my servant; I have chosen thee, and not cast thee away (I have not left you).

10 Fear thou not; for I am with thee: be not dismayed; for I am thy God: I will strengthen thee; yea, I will help thee; yea, I will uphold thee with the right hand of my righteousness (The hymn,"How Firm a Foundation", comes from this verse).

11 Behold, all they that were incensed (German: prejudiced; angry) against thee shall be ashamed (shamed) and confounded (German: humiliated): they shall be as nothing; and they that strive with (fight against) thee shall perish (ultimately, your enemies will not succeed against you).

12 Thou shalt seek them (your enemies), and shalt not find them, even them that contended with thee: they that war against thee shall be as nothing, and as a thing of nought (eventually, the wicked will all be gone).

13 For I the LORD thy God will hold thy right hand (covenant hand, i.e., I will strengthen you with covenants), saying unto thee, Fear not; I will help thee.

14 Fear not, thou worm (meek, humble) Jacob, and ye men of Israel; I will help thee, saith the LORD, and thy redeemer, the Holy One of Israel (Jesus).

15 Behold, I will make thee (German: into) a new sharp threshing instrument having teeth (capable of much destruction): thou shalt thresh the mountains (your former strong enemies), and beat them small, and shalt make the hills as chaff (Israel will triumph over her enemies. Perhaps this verse could also remind us that Israel, as a "sharp threshing instrument" will help gather the wheat, scattered Israel, and separate it from the "chaff", i.e., the wicked.)

16 Thou shalt fan (German: scatter; as in the threshing process) them, and the wind shall carry them away, and the whirlwind shall scatter them: and thou shalt rejoice in the LORD, and shalt glory in the Holy One of Israel (Israel will once again become righteous and give glory to God).

17 When the poor and needy seek water, and there is none, and their tongue faileth for thirst, I the LORD will hear them, I the God of Israel will not forsake them (I will help you. I have not left you; see verse 9).

18 I will open rivers in high places, and fountains in the midst of the valleys: I will make the wilderness a pool of water, and the dry land springs of water (geographical changes will help Israel; could also be symbolic of "living water", i.e., the gospel, bringing forth new life in an apostate

wilderness and satisfying the thirst mentioned in verse 17).

19 I will plant in the wilderness the cedar, the shittah (acacia) tree, and the myrtle, and the oil tree; I will set in the desert the fir (cypress) tree, and the pine (ash), and the box tree together (Isaiah often uses trees to represent people, for example, Isa. 2;13; Ezek.31:3; thus various types of trees in this verse could be symbolic of the gospels' going to all races of people in the last days):

20 That they may see, and know, and consider, and understand together, that the hand of the LORD hath done this, and the Holy One of Israel hath created it.

21 Produce your cause (present your case), saith the LORD; bring forth your strong reasons (arguments against the Lord), saith the King of Jacob (Israel).

22 Let them (idol worshippers) bring them (their idols) forth, and shew us what shall happen (predict the future): let them (idols) shew the former things (the past), what they be, that we may consider them, and know the latter end (the final outcome) of them; or declare us things for to come (predict the future).

23 Shew the things that are to come hereafter, that we may know that ye are gods (let's see if your idols can predict the future like God can, i.e., prove your idols are gods): yea, do good, or do evil, that we may be dismayed, and behold it together (just do anything, good or bad, to demon-strate your power to us).

24 Behold, ye (idols) are of nothing, and your work of nought: an abomination is he (the wicked who worship idols) that chooseth you (idols).

25 I have raised up one (perhaps referring back to verse 2) from the north, and he shall come: from the rising of the sun shall he call upon my name: and he shall come upon princes (leaders of nations) as upon morter, and as the potter treadeth clay (he will tread upon the wicked and none will stop him; D&C 133:50-51).

26 Who (which of your idols) hath declared (prophesied this) from the beginning, that we may know? and beforetime, that we may say, He is righteous? yea, there is none that sheweth, yea, there is none that declareth, yea, there is none that heareth your words (none of your idols do a thing!).

27 The first shall say to Zion (the Lord will prophesy it), Behold, behold them: and I (the Lord) will give to Jerusalem one that bringeth good tidings.

28 For I beheld, and there was no man; even among them, and there was no counsellor, that, when I asked of them, could answer a word (idol worship has reduced them to a completely confused people).

29 Behold, they are all vanity (false); their works are nothing: their molten images (idols) are wind and confusion.

ISAIAH 42

1 Behold my servant (Christ, see Matt. 12:18; perhaps in a dual sense could also include the whole house of Israel, see Isaiah 41:8), whom I uphold; mine elect (Christ; those set apart as a chosen people; Israelites; see Noah Webster 1828 dictionary for all three definitions of "elect"), in whom my soul delighteth; I have put my spirit upon him: he shall bring forth judgment to the Gentiles.

2 He shall not cry, nor lift up, nor cause his voice to be heard in the street (Christ was low key, designed his preaching to not make great disturbances, often said to those healed, "tell no one").

3 A bruised reed shall he not break (He came to help the weak, the "bruised", not to crush them more), and the smoking flax (the glowing candle wick which still has a tiny spark of light in it) shall he not quench (i.e., he came to gently fan the spark within into a flame, not to snuff it out): he shall bring forth judgment unto truth (victory, see Matt. 12:20).

4 He shall not fail (falter, stop, quit, see D&C 19:19) nor be discouraged (German: unable to finish), till he have set judgment in the earth: and the isles (all continents, nations) shall wait for (trust in) his law.

5 Thus saith God the LORD, he that created the heavens, and stretched them out; he that spread forth the earth, and that which cometh out of it; he that giveth breath unto the people upon it, and spirit to them that walk therein (i.e., the creator of all):

6 I the LORD have called thee in righteousness, and will hold thine hand, and will keep thee, and give thee for a covenant of the people, for a light of (German: unto) the Gentiles;

7 To open the blind eyes, to bring out the prisoners from the prison, and them that sit in darkness out of the prison house (what Christ and his righteous servants can do).

8 I am the LORD: that is my name: and my glory will I not give to another (you are still my chosen people), neither my praise to graven images (idols).

9 Behold, the former things (truth and keys from former days, i.e., restoration of the gospel) are come to pass, and new things (new knowledge in dispensation of fullness of times) do I declare: before they spring forth I tell you of them (they have been prophesied).

10 Sing unto the LORD a new song, and his praise from the end of the earth (to all the world), ye that go down to the sea, and all that is therein; the isles, and the inhabitants thereof (restored gospel will be preached to all the world).

11 Let the wilderness (dual: literal; apostate Israel) and the cities thereof lift up their voice, the villages that Kedar (nomadic tribe in the wilderness east of Sea of Galilee, see Map 2, D/E 4; Kedar was a grandson of Abraham through Ishmael, see Gen. 25:13) doth inhabit: let the inhabitants

of the rock (Sela, a desert town south of the Dead Sea, see Map 3, D 4) sing, let them shout from the top of the mountains (even remote places like Kedar and Sela will get the gospel and be able to rejoice in it).

12 Let them give glory unto the LORD, and declare his praise in the islands (everybody will hear the gospel in the Last days).

13 The LORD shall go forth as a mighty man, he shall stir up jealousy (with zeal) like a man of war: he shall cry, yea, roar; he shall prevail against his enemies (the Lord will ultimately triumph).

14 I (the Lord) have long time holden my peace (I have been very patient); I have been still, and refrained myself (I have been patient and not shown forth great power): now will I cry like a travailing woman (woman in labor, i.e., delivery time for Israel has come; the restored gospel will go forth with great power that none can stop); I will destroy and devour at once.

15 I will make waste mountains and hills, and dry up all their herbs; and I will make the rivers islands, and I will dry up the pools (after the gospel is restored, there will be great destruction, drought etc. as the Lord preaches "sermons" via the forces of nature etc.).

16 And I will bring the blind (the scattered of Israel) by a way (the restored gospel) that they knew not; I will lead them in paths (truths and covenants of the restored gospel) that

they have not known: I will make darkness light before them, and crooked things straight (effects of the restoration). These things will I do unto them, and not forsake them.

17 They shall be turned back, they shall be greatly ashamed, that trust in graven images, that say to the molten images, Ye are our gods (idol worship will not pay off).

18 Hear, ye deaf; and look, ye blind, that ye may see (open your eyes and ears to the truth).

19 (The Joseph Smith Translation makes many changes in verses 19 through 25, and is used here in place of King James version, verses 19-25.) For I will send my servant unto you who are blind; yea, a messenger to open the eyes of the blind, and unstop the ears of the deaf;

20 And they (those who listen and repent) shall be made perfect (the power of the atonement; 2 Nephi 25:23) notwithstanding their blindness, if they will hearken unto the messenger, the Lord's servant.

21 Thou (Israel) art a people, seeing many things, but thou observest not (you don't obey); opening the ears to hear, but thou hearest not (you don't want to hear the truth).

22 The Lord is not well pleased with such a people, but for his righteousness' sake he will magnify the law and make it honorable.

23 Thou art a people robbed and spoiled; thine enemies, all of them, have snared thee in holes, and they

have hid thee in prison houses; they have taken thee for a prey, and none delivereth; for a spoil, and none saith, Restore (consequences of Israel's wickedness).

24 Who among them (Israel's enemies in verse 23) will give ear unto thee (Israel), or hearken and hear thee for the time to come? and who gave Jacob for a spoil, and Israel to the robbers (who turned Israel over to her enemies)? did not the Lord, he against whom they have sinned (the Lord did, because of Israel's wickedness)?

25 For they (Israel) would not walk in his ways, neither were they obedient unto his law; therefore (that is why) he (the Lord) hath poured upon them the fury of his anger, and the strength of battle; and they (Israel's enemies) have set them (Israel) on fire round about (have caused terrible destruction), yet they (Israel) know not (won't acknowledge that they are being punished), and it burned them, yet they laid it not to heart (refused to repent).

ISAIAH 43

1 But now thus saith the LORD that created thee, O Jacob, and he that formed thee, O Israel (emphasis on the words "created" and "formed" as used in Genesis 1:27 and 2:7, i.e., the true God is your creator as described by Moses; these words will again be repeated for emphasis in verse 7),

Fear not: for I have redeemed thee, I have called thee by thy name; thou art mine (i.e., the Savior will succeed in redeeming a remnant of Israel despite their coming problems as described in 42:22-25).

2 When thou passest through the waters, I will be with thee; and through the rivers, they shall not overflow thee (reflecting back to parting of the Red Sea and Jordan River, i.e., I helped you then and the same power and help is still available to you): when thou walkest through the fire, thou shalt not be burned; neither shall the flame kindle upon thee (Remember how I helped Shadrach, Meshach, and Abed-nego survive the fiery furnace, Daniel 3. I want to protect and bless you too.).

3 For I am the LORD thy God, the Holy One of Israel, thy Saviour: I gave Egypt for thy ransom, Ethiopia and Seba (a people in southern Arabia) for thee (I will ransom you from your enemies, sin, Satan etc. represented by Egypt etc. i.e., I will pay the price that you might go free. Applies literally also, in terms of protection from physical enemy nations, see Isaiah 45:14).

4 Since thou wast (art, are) precious in my sight, thou hast been honourable (honored by me), and I have loved thee: therefore will I give men for thee (prophets' lives have been sacrificed for us, for our benefit), and people for thy life (many have given their lives for the benefit

of others. Most especially, Christ's atonement works for us).

5 Fear not: for I am with thee: I will bring thy (Israel's) seed from the east, and gather thee from the west;

6 I will say to the north, Give up (i.e., give up the Israelites you're holding back from the Lord); and to the south, Keep not back: bring my sons from far, and my daughters from the ends of the earth (the gathering of Israel is world-wide);

7 Even every one that is called by my name: for I have created him for my glory, I have formed him; yea, I have made him (carries the connotation of redemption through the atonement via repentance, i.e., being "born again" as discussed in Alma 5).

8 Bring forth the blind people that have eyes, and the deaf that have ears (spiritually blind and deaf who have ignored prophets' messages).

9 Let all the nations be gathered together, and let the people be assembled: who among them can declare this (the true gospel), and shew us former things (such as premortal life details etc.)? let them bring forth their witnesses (their false gods, sorcerers etc.), that they may be justified (i.e., let's see their false gods, sorcerers etc. do the kinds of things the true God of Israel can do): or let them hear, and say, It (Israel's message as given in verses 11-13) is truth.

10 Ye (Israel) are my witnesses, saith the LORD, and my servant whom I have chosen (to carry the gospel to all the world, see Abraham

2:9): that ye may know and believe me, and understand that I am he: before me there was no God formed, neither shall there be after me.

11 I (Jesus), even I, am the LORD; and beside me there is no saviour. (this is the message!)

12 I have declared, and have saved, and I have shewed, when there was no strange god among you: therefore ye (Israel) are my witnesses (our calling, responsibility), saith the LORD, that I am God.

13 Yea, before the day was I am he (I was God before time began for you and will continue to be God); and there is none that can deliver out of my hand: I will work (perform the atonement), and who shall let (hinder) it?

14 Thus saith the LORD, your redeemer, the Holy One of Israel; For your sake I have sent to (I will triumph over) Babylon (dual: Satan's kingdom; literally Israel's enemies in the nation of Babylon), and have brought (will bring) down all their nobles, and the Chaldeans (inhabitants of Southern Babylon; symbolic of the wicked in all nations), whose cry is in the ships (German: whose shouting will turn to lamenting as I hunt them in their ships, i.e., freedom from your enemies comes through the Savior).

15 I am the LORD, your Holy One, the creator of Israel, your King.

16 Thus saith the LORD, which maketh a way in the sea (parted the Red Sea), and a path in the mighty

waters;

17 Which bringeth forth (German: puts down, dismantles) the chariot and horse, the army and the power; they (your enemies) shall lie down (die) together, they shall not rise: they are extinct, they are quenched as tow (snuffed out like a smoldering candle).

18 Remember ye not the former things, neither consider the things of old (forget the past troubles and oppressions; they are now behind you, referring to the future).

19 Behold, I will do a new thing (the restoration of the gospel, of Israel; the gathering etc.); now it shall spring forth; shall ye not know it (you will see it plainly)? I will even make a way in the wilderness, and rivers in the desert (perhaps dual, referring to physical changes in the earth to help Israel's gathering, also symbolic of effects of "living water", gospel, bringing life to apostate Israel [referred to as "dry ground" in 53:2; 44:3] as water does to the wilderness, desert).

20 The beast of the field shall honour me, the dragons and the owls (jackals and ostriches; i.e., even "unclean" animals and fowls will honor me): because I give waters in the wilderness, and rivers in the desert, to give drink ("living" water also, John 7:37-38) to my people, my chosen.

21 This people have I formed (German: prepared) for myself; they shall shew forth my praise (definite, strong prophecy).

22 But thou hast not called upon me, O Jacob; but thou hast been weary of me, O Israel (you have a poor "track record", a history of disloyalty to me).

23 Thou hast not brought me the small cattle (lambs or young goats) of thy burnt offerings; neither hast thou honoured me with thy sacrifices. I have not caused thee to serve with an offering (German: I have not been pleased with your offerings of the first fruits, Numbers 18:12), nor wearied thee with incense (German: nor taken pleasure in your incense).

24 Thou hast bought me no sweet cane (spices used in making anointing oil for use in the Tabernacle, Exodus 30:23-25) with money, neither hast thou filled (satisfied) me with the fat of thy sacrifices (i.e., your sacrifices are empty ritual): but thou hast made me to serve (burdened me; German: made work for me) with thy sins, thou hast wearied me (German: caused me trouble and pains) with thine iniquities.

25 I (the Savior), even I, am he that blotteth out thy transgressions for mine own sake (i.e., I personally desire very much to forgive you and save you, Moses 1:39, Isaiah 1:18), and will not remember thy sins (if you truly repent, D&C 58:42-43).

26 Put me in remembrance (remember me): let us plead together (German: debate as in a court of law): declare thou (confess your point of view), that thou mayest be justified (go ahead, try to justify your wicked

behavior).

27 Thy first father (ancestors) hath sinned, and thy teachers (priests and ministers) have transgressed against me.

28 Therefore (for this reason) I have profaned (not accepted) the princes (priests and ministers) of the sanctuary, and have given Jacob (Israel) to the curse (German: excommunication, cut off), and Israel to reproaches (German: become the object of scorn).

ISAIAH 44

Note: Verses 1-8 deal mostly with Christ's role in redeeming Israel. Verses 9-20 deal mainly with pagan idol worshipping.

1 Yet now hear, O Jacob my servant; and Israel, whom I have chosen:

2 Thus saith the LORD that made thee, and formed thee from the womb, which will help thee (I have been helping you from the beginning and will continue to do so); Fear not, O Jacob, my servant; and thou, Jesurun (those who are righteous, Deut. 33:26, footnote 26 a), whom I have chosen.

3 For I will pour water (dual: literal; also "living water", 2 N. 9:50) upon him that is thirsty, and floods upon the dry ground (apostate Israel, Isa. 53:2): I will pour my spirit upon thy seed, and my blessing upon thine offspring (similar to the "blessings of Abraham, Isaac, and Jacob", Ab.2:9-11):

4 And they shall spring up as among the grass, as willows by the water courses (i.e., there will be righteous Israelites all over the place!, Isa. 49:21, 1 N. 21-21)

5 One shall say, I am the LORD's; and another shall call himself by the name of Jacob (i.e., they have converted to the Lord and are loyal to him; compare with 19:25); and another shall subscribe with his hand (make covenants) unto the LORD, and surname himself by the name of Israel (take upon himself the name of Christ).

6 Thus saith the LORD the King of Israel, and his (Israel's) redeemer the LORD of (heavenly) hosts; I am the first, and I am the last; and beside me there is no God.

7 And who (what idols; compare with 40:25), as I, shall call, and shall declare it, and set it in order for me, since I appointed (established) the ancient people (my people)? and the things that are coming (i.e., future events), and shall come, let them (your idols, false gods) shew unto them (foretell for you; i.e., this whole verse is a challenge for apostate Israel to have their idols do as well as the Lord in leading them and prophesying the future etc.).

8 Fear ye not, neither be afraid (i.e., trust in me): have not I told thee from that time (from the ancient times, i.e., from the beginning; see verse 7), and have declared it? ye are even my witnesses (Israel's calling, steward-ship). Is there a God beside me? yea, there is no God; I know not any.

9 (Verses 9-20 will now deal

primarily with idol worshipping.) They that make a graven image are all of them vanity (German: vain, conceited, i.e., won't take counsel from God); and their delectable (German: precious) things shall not profit (will do them no good); and they are their own witnesses; they see not, nor know (those who worship idols are as blind and empty-headed as the idols they worship); that they may be ashamed (may be put to shame).

10 Who hath formed a god, or molten a graven image that is profitable for nothing (good for nothing, i.e., who would do such a foolish thing)?

11 Behold, all his fellows (fellow idol worshipers) shall be ashamed: and the workmen, they are of men (are mere mortals): let them all be gathered together, let them stand up; yet they shall fear, and they shall be ashamed together (no matter how many worship idols, it does no good; they will all be put to shame).

12 The smith (blacksmith) with the tongs both worketh in the coals, and fashioneth it (an idol) with hammers, and worketh it with the strength of his arms: yea, he is hungry (i.e., the craftsman is a mere mortal), and his strength faileth: he drinketh no water, and is faint (the craftsmen who make idols for you are mere mortals themselves..How foolish!).

13 The carpenter stretcheth out his rule; he marketh it out with a line; he fitteth it with planes, and he marketh it out with the compass (your craftsmen exercise great care and skill in manufacturing your idols), and maketh it after the figure of a man, according to the beauty of a man; that it may remain in the house (if you were as careful worshipping God as you are in making idols...).

14 He heweth him down cedars, and taketh the cypress and the oak, which he strengtheneth (cultivates and grows) for himself among the trees of the forest: he planteth an ash (tree), and the rain doth nourish it.

15 Then shall it be for a man to burn: for he will take thereof, and warm himself; yea, he kindleth it, and baketh bread; yea, he maketh a god, and worshippeth it (you use most of the tree's wood for normal daily needs, how can you possibly turn around and worship wood from the same tree in the form of idols!); he maketh it a graven image, and falleth down thereto.

16 He burneth part thereof in the fire; with part thereof he eateth flesh; he roasteth roast, and is satisfied: yea, he warmeth himself, and saith, Aha, I am warm, I have seen the fire (i.e., normal uses):

17 And the residue thereof (with the rest of the tree) he maketh a god, even his graven image: he falleth down unto it, and worshippeth it, and prayeth unto it, and saith, Deliver (save) me; for thou art my god (Isaiah is saying how utterly ridiculous it is to assign part of a tree to have powers over yourselves!).

18 They (idol worshipers, see 45:20) have not known (German: know nothing) nor understood (German: understand nothing): for he hath shut their eyes (German: they are blind), that they cannot see; and their hearts, that they cannot understand (i.e., they are as blind and unfeeling, insensitive etc. as the idols they make and worship).

19 And none considereth in his heart (if idol worshipers would just stop and think), neither is there knowledge nor understanding to say, I have burned part of it (the tree spoken of in verse 44) in the fire; yea, also I have baked bread upon the coals thereof; I have roasted flesh, and eaten it: and shall I make the residue thereof an abomination (is it reasonable to make the left over portion into an abominable idol)? shall I fall down to the stock of a tree (is it rational to worship a chunk of wood)?

20 He (the idol worshiper) feedeth on ashes (German: takes pleasure in ashes, perhaps referring to ashes left over from some forms of idol worship): a (German: his own) deceived heart hath turned him aside (German: leads him astray), that he cannot deliver (save) his soul, nor say (wake up and think), Is there not a lie in my right hand (covenant hand, i.e., am I not making covenants with false gods)?

21 Remember these, O Jacob and Israel; for thou art my servant: I have formed thee (the exact opposite of idol worshippers who form their

gods); thou art my servant: O Israel, thou shalt not be forgotten of me.

22 I have blotted out, as a thick cloud, thy transgressions, and, as a cloud, thy sins (the Atonement can still work for you): return unto me; for I have redeemed thee (i.e., please repent).

23 Sing, O ye heavens; for the LORD hath done it: shout, ye lower parts of the earth (German: "o earth below"): break forth into singing, ye mountains, O forest, and every tree therein: for the LORD hath redeemed Jacob, and glorified himself in Israel (speaking of the future).

24 Thus saith the LORD, thy redeemer, and he that formed (German: prepared) thee from the womb, I am the LORD that maketh all things; that stretcheth forth the heavens alone; that spreadeth abroad the earth by myself (I created heaven and earth; no idols helped me!);

25 That frustrateth (causeth to fail) the tokens (signs) of the liars (German: fortune tellers), and maketh diviners mad (German: absurd); that turneth (so-called) wise men backward, and maketh their knowledge (German: business of fortune telling) foolish;

26 (I am the Lord) That confirmeth the word of his servant, and performeth the counsel of his messengers (I support my servants, whereas idols don't support theirs); that saith to Jerusalem, Thou shalt be inhabited; and to the cities of Judah, Ye shall be built, and I will raise up the decayed

places thereof (when I command, things obey; idols can't command and aren't obeyed):

27 (I am the Lord) That saith to the deep, Be dry, and I will dry up thy rivers:

28 That saith of Cyrus (the Persian), He is my shepherd, and shall perform all my pleasure: even saying to Jerusalem, Thou shalt be built; and to the temple, Thy foundation shall be laid (A very specific prophecy! Cyrus conquered Babylon about 538 BC, who had conquered Jerusalem about 50 years earlier in 588 BC. In 537 BC, Cyrus issued a decree to let Jews return home to Palestine. See Bible Dict., p. 640).

ISAIAH 45

1 Thus saith the LORD to his anointed, to Cyrus, whose right hand I have holden (strengthened), to subdue nations before him (The Lord often uses "non-LDS" individuals to help his covenant people. For instance, the British helped the Jews return to their homeland in 1948.); and I will loose the loins of kings (German: take the sword of kings away from them), to open before him the two leaved gates (main city gates); and the gates shall not be shut (the Lord will open the way for Cyrus and none will stop him);

2 I will go before thee, and make the crooked places straight (German: will take out the bumps): I will break in pieces the gates of brass, and cut in sunder (cut through) the bars of iron:

3 And I will give thee the treasures of darkness, and hidden riches of secret places (hidden treasures, probably referring to Babylon, which Cyrus conquers about 538 BC), that thou mayest know that I, the LORD, which call thee (Cyrus) by thy name, am the God of Israel.

4 For Jacob my servant's sake, and Israel mine elect, I have even called thee (Cyrus) by thy name: I have surnamed thee, though thou hast not known me (although you don't know me, I will use you to free the Jews).

5 I am the LORD, and there is none else, there is no God beside me: I girded thee (dressed you for war and strengthened you), though thou hast not known me:

6 That they may know from the rising of the sun, and from the west (from east to west, i.e., everywhere), that there is none beside me. I am the LORD, and there is none else.

7 I form the light, and create darkness: I make peace, and create evil (cause calamity, as in 3 Nephi 9:3-12): I the LORD do all these things.

8 Drop (drip; rain) down, ye heavens, from above, and let the skies pour down righteousness: let the earth open (produce), and let them (heaven and earth) bring forth salvation, and let righteousness spring up together (with it); I the LORD have created it (i.e., let the purposes of creating heaven and earth be wonderfully

fulfilled, i.e., the plan of salvation).

9 Woe unto him that striveth with his Maker! Let the potsherd (vessel of clay; shard, broken piece of pottery) strive with the potsherds of the earth (German: a shard like other mortal shards, i.e., how foolish of a mere mortal to quarrel with his Creator). Shall the clay say to him that fashioneth it, What makest thou? or thy work, He hath no hands (an insolent question, "Who do you think you are, God?"; compare with Isaiah 29:16)?

10 Woe unto him that saith unto his father, What begettest thou? or to the woman (his mother), What hast thou brought forth (i.e., what do you think you're doing; sassy)?

11 Thus saith the LORD, the Holy One of Israel, and his (Israel's) Maker, Ask me of things to come (about the future) concerning my sons, and concerning the work of my hands command (German: acknowledge me as the Creator) ye me (ask me, I'll tell you).

12 I have made the earth, and created man upon it: I, even my hands, have stretched out (created) the heavens, and all their host have I commanded (i.e., I am the Creator).

13 I have raised him (Cyrus) up in righteousness (i.e., I will use him to fulfill my righteous purposes), and I will direct all his ways: he shall build my city (rebuild Jerusalem), and he shall let go my captives (the Jews), not for price nor reward (i.e., the hand of the Lord is in it), saith the LORD of hosts.

14 Thus saith the LORD, The labour of Egypt, and merchandise of Ethiopia and of the Sabeans (a people in southeastern Arabia), men of stature, shall come over unto thee, and they shall be thine: they shall come after thee (behind you); in chains they shall come over, and they shall fall down unto thee, they shall make supplication unto thee, saying, Surely God is in thee; and there is none else, there is no God (all nations will recognize that the Lord is with Cyrus and Israel).

15 Verily thou art a God that hidest thyself (not physically "seeable" on a daily basis like idols are), O God of Israel, the Saviour.

16 They (nations of the world) shall be ashamed (put to shame), and also confounded, all of them: they shall go to confusion together that are makers of idols (results of idol worship).

17 But Israel shall be saved in the LORD with an everlasting salvation: ye shall not be ashamed nor confounded world without end (throughout eternity; results of righteousness).

18 For thus saith the LORD (in answer to the insolent question in verses 9 and 10) that created the heavens; God himself that formed the earth and made it; he hath established it, he created it not in vain, he formed it to be inhabited: I am the LORD; and there is none else.

19 I have not spoken in secret, in a dark place of the earth (I have not hidden from you, played "hard to

get". I have been very open and direct with you.): I said not unto the seed of Jacob, Seek ye me in vain: I the LORD speak righteousness, I declare things that are right.

20 Assemble yourselves and come; draw near together, ye that are escaped (survivors) of the nations: they (idol worshippers, 44:18) have no knowledge (see notes for 44:18) that set up the wood of their graven image, and pray unto a god (idol) that cannot save.

21 Tell ye, and bring them (idol worshippers) near; yea, let them take counsel (plot) together: who hath declared this from ancient time? who hath told it from that time? have not I the LORD? and there is no God else beside me; a just God and a Saviour; there is none beside me (i.e., there is no comparison between idols and the true God!).

22 Look unto me (German: turn to me), and be ye saved, all the ends of the earth (the Atonement applies to all): for I am God, and there is none else.

23 I have sworn (covenanted) by myself, the word is gone out of my mouth in righteousness, and shall not return (D&C 1:38), That unto me every knee shall bow, every tongue shall swear (acknowledge Christ; does not mean that everyone will repent and be righteous; refers to telestials in D&C 76:110).

24 Surely, shall one say, in the LORD have I righteousness and strength: even to him shall men come;

and all that are incensed (angry) against him shall be ashamed (put to shame; disappointed, disconcerted).

25 In the LORD (Christ) shall (can) all the seed of Israel be justified (brought into harmony with God's ways, thus be approved to dwell with God), and shall glory (in the Lord, 1 Corinthians 1:31). (Note: the word "justified" is used in current computer terminology to mean "lined up" as in "justify the right margin". In scripture language, "justified" likewise means "lined up", i.e., "lined up with God's will", or in other words, in harmony with God's commandments and thus worthy to be ratified and approved by the Holy Ghost, the Holy Spirit of Promise, to live with God forever.)

ISAIAH 46

Note: Bel and Nebo were chief gods in Babylon. Ancient cultures such as Babylon believed that each "god" had a territory, and when a city or country was defeated in battle by enemies, it meant that their gods (such as Bel and Nebo) had been defeated by the enemy's gods. Chapter 46 ties in with chapters 13 & 14 concerning Babylon's downfall, and with chapters 40-45 concerning Jehovah's power.

1 Bel boweth down (German: has been defeated), Nebo stoopeth, their idols were upon the beasts, and upon the cattle (i.e., the idols are powerless, can't move by themselves; have to be transported upon beasts of burden):

85

your carriages were heavy loaden; they (the idols) are a burden to the weary beast (The message, by implication, is that Bel and Nebo are burdens to those who "created" them in contrast to the true God of Israel, who lightens the burdens of those he created, who worship him).

2 They (Bel and Nebo) stoop, they bow down together (German: they are both defeated); they could not deliver (German: remove) the burden (i.e., they couldn't do the job), but themselves are gone into captivity (they have failed their worshippers and couldn't even save themselves).

3 Hearken unto me, O house of Jacob, and all the remnant of the house of Israel, which are borne by me (i.e., note that I the Lord carry you, help you, am not a burden) from the belly (from the womb, i.e., from the beginning), which are carried from the womb (i.e., i have carried you from the beginning, contrasted to idolaters' transporting their "gods"):

4 And even to your old age (throughout your entire life) I am he (the true God); and even to hoar (gray) hairs will I carry you: I have made (German: I want to do it), and I will (German: desire to) bear; even I will (German: desire to) carry, and will (German: desire to) deliver you (i.e., I want to help, support and bless you throughout your entire life; I want to be your Redeemer!).

5 To whom will ye liken me, and make me equal, and compare me, that we may be like (who among your

false gods can compare to me)? (Same question as in 40:18, 25)

6 They (idol worshippers) lavish gold out of the bag, and weigh silver in the balance (on the scales; i.e., you pay out much money for your worthless idols), and hire a goldsmith; and he maketh it (an idol) a god: they fall down, yea, they worship.

7 They (idol worshippers) bear him (their idol) upon the shoulder, they carry him, and set him in his place (put the idol in the room or place they want it to stay), and he standeth; from his place shall he not remove (the idol can't even move from the place the people put it): yea, one shall cry unto him (the idol), yet can he (the idol) not answer, nor save him (the idol worshipper) out of his trouble (i.e., idols are totally worthless!).

8 Remember this, and shew yourselves men: bring it again to mind, O ye transgressors (face the issue, you sinners!).

9 Remember the former things of old (the many miracles I performed for you in the past): for I am God, and there is none else; I am God, and there is none like me,

10 Declaring the end from the beginning (prophesying the future), and from ancient times the things that are not yet done (i.e., things that are yet future), saying, My counsel shall stand, and I will do all my pleasure (everything I have said will happen; compare with D&C 1:38):

11 Calling a ravenous bird from the east (a bird of prey, i.e., Cyrus from

Persia), the man that executeth (carries out) my counsel (plans) from a far country (Persia): yea, I have spoken it, I will also bring it to pass; I have purposed (planned) it, I will also do it.

12 Hearken unto me, ye stout-hearted (hardhearted), that are far from righteousness (as mentioned in verse 8):

13 I bring near my righteousness (victory, triumph); it shall not be (German: is not) far off, and my salvation shall not tarry (will not be late): and I will place salvation in Zion for Israel my glory (i.e., I will succeed in bringing salvation and glory to Israel, and you can be a part of it if you repent).

ISAIAH 47

1 Come down (i.e., be humbled), and sit in the dust (a sign of humiliation in eastern cultures; see Isa. 3:26, Lam. 2:10 etc.), O virgin (unconquered) daughter of Babylon (i.e., the Babylonian Empire; see map 11), sit on the ground (humiliation): there is no throne (i.e., Babylon was to be conquered, overthrown; this prophecy was fulfilled literally by Cyrus in 539 BC, and will be fulfilled symbolically as Christ overthrows Satan's kingdom), O daughter of the Chaldeans (inhabitants of Southern Babylonia, part of Babylonian Empire): for thou shalt no more be called tender and delicate (German: desirable).

2 (Emphasizing the imagery of a conquered Babylon, Isaiah now describes conditions and tasks of slaves.) Take the millstones, and grind meal (flour): uncover thy locks (take off your veil, like slaves do), make bare the leg, uncover the thigh (i.e., tie up your skirts and expose your legs so you can get around easily to do the work required of slaves), pass over the rivers (you'll have to wade through canals to get from one field to another as you do the work of slaves).

3 Thy nakedness shall be uncovered (dual: sexual abuses suffered by slaves; also the "true colors", i.e., wickedness of Babylon will be uncovered, exposed), yea, thy shame shall be seen: I (the Lord) will take vengeance, and I will not meet thee (Babylon and all things represented by Babylon) as a man (i.e., you won't be able to stop me because I'm not a mortal man).

4 As for (German: thus doeth) our redeemer, the LORD of hosts is his name, the Holy One of Israel.

5 Sit thou (Babylon) silent, and get thee into darkness, O daughter of the Chaldeans: for thou shalt no more be called, The lady of kingdoms (You've had it!).

6 I (God) was wroth (angry) with my people, I have polluted (German: disowned) mine inheritance (wicked Israel), and given them (prophecy of future) into thine (Babylon's) hand: thou didst shew them (Israel, especially the Jews) no mercy; upon the ancient hast thou very heavily laid thy

yoke (i.e., you abused the power I allowed you to have over Israel; still a prophecy about the future).

7 And thou (Babylon) saidst, I shall be a lady (German: a queen) for ever: so that thou didst not lay these things to thy heart (i.e., you didn't take my warnings seriously), neither didst remember the latter end of it (i.e., you didn't stop to consider the consequences of your behavior).

8 Therefore hear now this, thou (Babylon) that art given to pleasures, that dwellest carelessly, that sayest in thine heart, I am, and none else beside me (I am the most powerful of all!); I shall not sit as a widow (have my kingdom taken away from me), neither shall I know the loss of children (i.e., Babylon boasts she will never be conquered; however, she will be depopulated and her king destroyed):

9 But these two things (the loss of your king and your inhabitants) shall come to thee in a moment in one day, the loss of children, and widowhood: they shall come upon thee in their perfection (in full measure) for (despite) the multitude of thy sorceries, and for (despite) the great abundance of thine enchantments (i.e., the so-called "magic" of your false religions will not save you).

10 For thou hast trusted in (relied on) thy wickedness: thou hast said, None seeth me (i.e., I can get away with it). Thy wisdom and thy knowledge, it hath perverted thee (German: has led you astray); and thou hast said

in thine heart, I am, and none else beside me (I am all-powerful).

11 Therefore (because of the things mentioned above) shall evil come upon thee; thou shalt not know (German: expect it) from whence it riseth: and mischief (ruin) shall fall upon thee; thou shalt not be able to put it off (German: atone for it via sacrifices to false gods; see verse 12): and desolation shall come upon thee suddenly, which thou shalt not know (foresee).

12 Stand now with thine enchantments, and with the multitude of thy sorceries, wherein thou hast laboured from thy youth (like you've done all your lives); if so be thou shalt be able to profit, if so be thou mayest prevail (i.e., go ahead, try to stop this destruction via your false gods, enchantments etc., see if they help or not!).

13 Thou art wearied in the multitude of thy counsels (you have spent many boring hours with your counselors, stargazers etc.). Let now the astrologers, the stargazers, the monthly prognosticators, stand up, and save thee from these things that shall come upon thee (i.e., call their bluff!).

14 Behold, they (your religious leaders as mentioned in verse 13) shall be as stubble; the fire shall burn them; they shall not deliver themselves from the power of the flame: there shall not be a coal to warm at, nor fire to sit before it (i.e., your soothsayers etc. are utterly powerless to save themselves, let alone you!).

15 Thus shall they be unto thee with whom thou hast laboured, even thy merchants (religious leaders), from thy youth: they shall wander every one to his quarter; none shall save thee (the whole message summarized).

ISAIAH 48

1 Hear ye this, O house of Jacob (12 Tribes of Israel), which are called by the name of Israel, and are come forth out of the waters of Judah (waters of baptism, I N. 20:1), which swear (make covenants) by the name of the LORD, and make mention of the God of Israel, but not in truth, nor in righteousness (empty worship is the problem).

2 For they call themselves of the holy city (i.e., they claim to be the Lord's people), and stay themselves upon (pretend to rely upon) the God of Israel; The LORD of hosts is his name.

3 (In the next several verses, Isaiah reminds Israel that there is no lack of obvious evidence that the true God exists.) I have declared the former things from the beginning (i.e., I've had prophets prophesy); and they (their prophecies) went forth out of my mouth, and I shewed them (so you would have solid evidence that I exist); I did them suddenly, and they came to pass (so you can know I am God; 42:9).

4 Because I knew that thou art obstinate, and thy neck is an iron sinew (i.e., won't bend; you are not humble), and thy brow brass (you are thickheaded; can't get things through your skulls);

5 I have even from the beginning declared it (prophecies) to thee; before it (prophesied events) came to pass I shewed it thee: lest thou shouldest say, Mine idol hath done them, and my graven image, and my molten image, hath commanded them (so you couldn't claim your idols, false gods, did it).

6 Thou hast heard, see all this; and will not ye declare it (acknowledge it)? I have shewed thee new things from this time, even hidden things, and thou didst not know them (German: that thou hadst no way of knowing).

7 They (the prophesied events) are created (happening) now, and not from the beginning; even before the day when thou heardest them not (without my prophecies, you couldn't have known in advance); lest thou shouldest say, Behold, I knew them (I set it up this way so you would have obvious evidence that I exist).

8 Yea, thou heardest not; yea, thou knewest not; yea, from that time that thine ear was not opened (you wouldn't listen): for I knew that thou wouldest deal very treacherously (The Lord knew right from the start that it would be hard to "raise" us. Great potential for good inherently has great potential for evil, but it was worth the risk!), and wast called a transgressor from the womb (I've had trouble with

you Israelites right from the start).

9 For my name's sake (because I have a reputation to uphold, i.e., mercy, patience, love, etc.) will I defer mine anger, and for my praise will I refrain for thee, that I cut thee not off (I will not cut you off completely).

10 Behold, I have refined thee, but not with (German: "as") silver ("but not with silver" is deleted in 1 N. 20:10. Perhaps this phrase in the Bible implies that we are not being refined to be "second best" i.e., silver, rather to be gold, the best, celestial. See Rev. 4:4); I have chosen thee (German: I will make you) in the furnace of affliction.

11 For mine own sake, even for mine own sake, will I do it: for how should my name be polluted (German: lest my name be slandered for not keeping my promise)? and I will not give my glory unto another (I will stick with Israel).

12 Hearken unto me, O Jacob and Israel, my called; I am he; I am the first, I also am the last (I am the Savior).

13 Mine hand also hath laid the foundation of the earth (I am the creator), and my right hand (the covenant hand; the hand of power) hath spanned (spread out; created) the heavens: when I call unto them (Israel), they stand up together.

14 All ye, assemble yourselves, and hear; which among them hath declared these things? The LORD hath loved him (Israel): he (God) will do his pleasure on Babylon, and his arm shall be on the Chaldeans (southern Babylon).

15 I, even I, have spoken; yea, I (Jesus speaking for Heavenly Father?) have called him (Jesus?): I have brought him, and he shall make his way prosperous.

16 Come ye near unto me, hear ye this; I have not spoken in secret (I have been open about the gospel etc.) from the beginning; from the time that it was (declared, 1 N. 20:16), there am I (i.e., from the time anything existed, I have spoken): and now the Lord GOD, and his Spirit, hath sent me.

17 Thus saith the LORD, thy Redeemer, the Holy One of Israel (Jesus); I am the LORD thy God which teacheth thee to profit (German: for your profit, benefit), which leadeth thee by the way that thou shouldest go.

18 O that thou (Israel) hadst hearkened to my commandments! then had thy peace been as a river (heading in the right direction), and thy righteousness as the waves of the sea (steady, constant):

19 Thy seed also had been as the sand (your posterity could have been innumerable; exaltation), and the offspring of thy bowels like the gravel thereof (like the sand of the seashore); his name should not have been cut off nor destroyed from before me (i.e., Israel could have had it very good, would not have been conquered).

20 Go ye forth of Babylon (quit wickedness), flee ye from the

Chaldeans, with a voice of singing (be happy in your righteousness) declare ye, tell this, utter it even to the end of the earth; say ye, The LORD hath redeemed his servant Jacob.

21 And they thirsted not when he led them through the deserts (perhaps symbolical of the results of drinking "living water", the gospel, as you follow the Savior through the barren world of the wicked): he caused the waters to flow out of the rock for them: he clave the rock also, and the waters gushed out.

22 There is no peace, saith the LORD, unto the wicked (a major message of Isaiah).

ISAIAH 49

1 Listen, O isles (scattered remnants of Israel throughout the world, 1 N. 21:1), unto me; and hearken, ye people, from far; The LORD hath called me (Israel, see verse 3) from the womb (foreordination); from the bowels of my mother hath he made mention of my name (i.e., Israel has a job to do since the beginning).

2 And he hath made my mouth like a sharp sword (The gospel is hard on the wicked, but helps the righteous by cutting through falsehood); in the shadow (protection) of his hand hath he hid me, and made me a polished shaft; in his quiver hath he hid me (i.e., Israel has been refined and prepared by the Lord to fulfill its calling);

3 And said unto me, Thou art my servant, O Israel, in whom I will be glorified (a prophecy that Israel will yet fulfill its stewardship).

4 (In verses 4-12, Isaiah portrays Israel's loneliness and regrets, as well as the glorious blessings and responsibilities that await her as she repents.) Then I (Israel) said (to myself), I have laboured in vain, I have spent my strength for nought, and in vain (uselessly, in false religions etc.): yet surely my judgment is with the LORD (German: the case against me is in God's hands), and my work (German: my office, my calling) with my God (German: is from God).

5 And now, saith the LORD that formed (foreordained) me (Israel, especially Ephraim) from the womb to be his servant, to bring Jacob (Israel) again to him, Though Israel be not gathered, yet shall I be glorious in the eyes of the LORD, and my God shall be my strength (i.e., those who try valiantly to convert and gather Israel will be blessed, whether or not Israel responds; similar to Nephi with respect to Laman and Lemuel in 1 N. 2:18-21).

6 And he said, It is a light thing (German: not enough of a load) that thou shouldest be my servant to raise up the tribes of Jacob (Israel), and to restore the preserved (remnants or survivors) of Israel: I will also give thee for a light to the Gentiles (quite a prophecy in Isaiah's day when almost any enemy nation could walk all over Israel), that thou mayest be my salvation unto the end of the earth (the

91

responsibility of members of the Church today).

7 Thus saith the LORD, the Redeemer of Israel, and ("and" is deleted in 1 N. 21:7) his (Israel's) Holy One, to him (Israel) whom man despiseth, to him whom the nation abhorreth (German: to the people abhorred by others), to a servant of rulers (I.e., you have been servants and slaves to many nations), Kings shall see (the true gospel as you fulfill your stewardship) and arise (out of respect for God), princes (leaders of nations) also shall worship (German: fall down and worship), because of the LORD that is faithful, and the Holy One of Israel, and he shall choose thee (German: who chose you).

8 Thus saith the LORD, In an acceptable time (beginning with Joseph Smith and the restoration) have I heard thee, and in a day of salvation have I helped thee: and I will preserve thee, and give thee for a covenant of the people, to establish the earth, to cause to inherit the desolate heritages (i.e., the Lord will gather Israel and help Israel fulfill its stewardship as described in verse 6 above);

9 That thou mayest say to the prisoners (including the living and the dead in spiritual darkness), Go forth (Go free); to them that are in darkness, Shew yourselves (German: Come out!). They shall feed in the ways, and their pastures shall be in all high places (i.e., they will have it

good when they repent and follow the true God).

10 They shall not hunger nor thirst; neither shall the heat nor sun smite them: for he (Christ) that hath mercy on them shall lead them, even by the springs of water shall he guide them (benefits of accepting and living the gospel).

11 And I will make all my mountains a way, and my highways shall be exalted.

12 Behold, these (remnants of scattered Israel) shall come from far: and, lo, these from the north and from the west (i.e., the gathering will be from all parts of the world); and these from the land of Sinim (perhaps China, but not certain, see Bible Dict., p.775).

13 Sing, O heavens; and be joyful, O earth; and break forth into singing, O mountains: for the LORD hath comforted his people, and will have mercy upon his afflicted (i.e., the Lord will eventually redeem Israel).

14 But Zion said (Israel hath said), The LORD hath forsaken me, and my Lord hath forgotten me (wicked Israel's complaint. 1 N.21:14 adds "—but he will show that he hath not." to this verse.).

15 Can a woman forget her sucking child, that she should not have compassion on the son of her womb? yea, they (Israel) may forget, yet will I (the Lord) not forget thee (Israel).

16 Behold, I have graven thee upon the palms of my hands (i.e., I will be crucified for you. Just as a workman's hands bear witness of his profession,

his type of work, so shall nail prints in my hands bear witness of my work for you.); thy walls are continually before me (I'll not forget you).

17 Thy children shall make haste; ("haste against", 1 N.21:17) thy destroyers and they that made thee waste shall go forth of (flee) thee (i.e., the tables will be turned).

18 Lift up thine eyes round about, and behold (look into the future): all these (Israelites) gather themselves together, and come to thee (i.e., you thought you had no family left, but look at all your descendants in the future!). As I live (the strongest Hebrew oath or promise possible was to promise by the Living God), saith the LORD, thou shalt surely clothe thee with them all, as with an ornament, and bind them on thee, as a bride doeth (a bride puts on her finest clothing for the occasion, i.e., Israel will have many of her finest descendants in the last days).

19 For thy waste and thy desolate places, and the land of thy destruction (where you've been trodden down for centuries), shall even now be too narrow by reason of the inhabitants (you will have so many Israelites, you'll seem to be running out of room for them all, i.e., latter-day gathering of Israel), and they (your former enemies) that swallowed thee up shall be far away.

20 The children (converts to the true gospel) which thou shalt have, after thou hast lost the other (via apostasy, war etc.), shall say again in thine ears,

The place is too strait for me: give place to me that I may dwell (there is not enough room for us all!).

21 Then shalt thou (Israel) say in thine heart, Who hath begotten me these, seeing I have lost my children ("Where in the world did all these Israelites come from?"), and am desolate, a captive, and removing to and fro (scattered all over)? and who hath brought up these? Behold, I was left alone (I thought I was done for!); these, where had (have) they been?

22 (The Lord now answers the question as to where all these Israelites came from.) Thus saith the Lord GOD, Behold, I will lift up mine hand to the Gentiles, and set up my standard (the true Church, gospel) to the people: and they (the gentiles, i.e., non-Jews) shall bring thy sons in their arms, and thy daughters shall be carried upon their shoulders (i.e., the Lord will open the way and inspire people everywhere to help in gathering Israel).

23 And kings shall be thy nursing fathers, and their queens thy nursing mothers (leaders of nations will help gather Israel; for instance, Great Britain sponsored the return of the Jews to Palestine in 1948): they shall bow down to thee with their face toward the earth, and lick up the dust of thy feet (the tables will be turned and they will show respect for you); and thou shalt know that I am the LORD: for they shall not be ashamed (disappointed) that wait for (trust in) me.

24 Shall the prey be taken from the mighty, or the lawful (the Lord's covenant people) captive delivered (i.e., Israel asks how they can be freed from such powerful enemies)?

25 But thus saith the LORD, Even the captives (Israel) of the mighty (Israel's powerful enemies) shall be taken away (from the enemy), and the prey (victims) of the terrible (tyrants) shall be delivered (set free): for I (the Lord) will contend with him that contendeth with thee, and I will save thy children (the covenant people, 2 N.6:17).

26 And I will feed them that oppress thee with their own flesh (i.e., your enemies will turn on each other and destroy themselves); and they shall be drunken with their own blood, as with sweet wine: and all flesh shall know that I the LORD am thy Saviour and thy Redeemer, the mighty One of Jacob.

ISAIAH 50

Note: This chapter speaks of the future as if it had already happened. Compare with 2 Nephi 7.

1 (The Lord asks "Did I leave you, or did you leave me?") Thus saith the LORD, Where is the bill of your mother's divorcement, whom I have put away (do you think I would divorce you and send you away from me like a man who divorces his wife)? or which of my creditors is it to whom I have sold you (was it I who sold you into slavery)? Behold, for your iniquities have ye sold yourselves (the real cause), and for your transgressions is your mother put away (i.e., you brought it upon yourselves).

2 Wherefore (why), when I (Jesus) came (to save my people), was there no man (who accepted me as Messiah, i.e., why did my people reject me)? when I called, was there none to answer (German: no one answered)? Is my hand shortened at all, that it cannot redeem? or have I no power to deliver (have I lost my power)? behold, at my rebuke (command) I dry up the sea, I make the rivers a wilderness: their fish stinketh, because there is no water, and dieth for thirst (No, I have not lost my power!).

3 I clothe the heavens with blackness, and I make sackcloth (a sign of mourning) their covering (I can cause the sky to be dark during the day, as if it were mourning the dead, which it will do at Christ's death, Matt. 27:45).

4 The Lord GOD (the Father) hath given me (Jesus) the tongue of the learned (i.e., Father taught me well), that I should know how to speak a (strengthening) word in season to him (Israel, 2 N.7:4)) that is weary: he wakeneth morning by morning, he wakeneth mine ear to hear as the learned (German: the Father is constantly communicating with me and I hear as his disciple).

5 The Lord GOD (the Father) hath opened mine ear, and I was not rebel-

lious, neither turned away back (I was obedient and accomplished the Atonement).

6 (Isaiah now prophesies some details surrounding Christ's crucifixion.) I gave my back to the smiters, and my cheeks to them that plucked off the hair (pulled out the whiskers of my beard): I hid not my face from shame and spitting.

7 For the Lord GOD (the Father) will help me; therefore shall I not be confounded (I will not be stopped): therefore have I set my face like a flint (I brace myself for the task), and I know that I shall not be ashamed (I know I will not fail).

8 He (the Father) is near that justifieth me (approves of everything I do); who will (dares to) contend with me? let us (me and those who would dare contend against me) stand together (go to court, as in a court of law, i.e., go ahead and present your arguments against me): who is mine adversary? let him come near to me (face me).

9 Behold, the Lord GOD (the Father) will help me (the Savior); who is he that shall condemn me? lo, they (those who contend against me) all shall wax old as a garment; the moth shall eat them up (the wicked will have their day, then reap the punishment).

10 Who is among you that feareth (respects) the LORD, that obeyeth the voice of his servant, that walketh in darkness, and hath no light? (Answer: No one because the Lord blesses his

true followers with light.) let him trust in the name of the LORD, and stay upon (be supported by) his God.

11 Behold, all ye that kindle a fire, that compass (surround) yourselves about with sparks: walk in the light of your fire (i.e., try to live without God, according to your own philosophies), and in the sparks that ye have kindled (rather than Christ's gospel light). This shall ye have of mine hand (German: you will get what you deserve); ye shall lie down in sorrow (i.e., misery awaits those who try to live without God).

ISAIAH 51

Note: The Lord now speaks to the righteous in Israel. Compare with 2 Nephi 8.

1 Hearken to me, ye that follow after righteousness, ye that seek the LORD: look unto the rock whence (from whence; 2 N. 8:1) ye are hewn (i.e., look at the top quality stone from which you originate), and to the hole of the pit (the rock quarry) whence ye are digged (i.e., consider your origins, you come from the finest stock).

2 Look unto Abraham your father, and unto Sarah (Abraham and Sarah are of equal importance) that bare you (your ancestors, i.e., your heritage is the finest!): for I called him alone, and blessed him (see Ab. 2:9-11), and increased him.

3 For the LORD shall comfort Zion: he will comfort all her waste places;

95

and he will make her wilderness like Eden, and her desert like the garden of the LORD (the Garden of Eden); joy and gladness shall be found therein, thanksgiving, and the voice of melody (wonderful reward for the righteous).

4 Hearken unto me, my people; and give ear unto me, O my nation: for a law shall proceed from me, and I will make my judgment to rest for a light of the people (i.e., my laws will bring light to the nations).

5 My righteousness (triumph; ability to save) is near; my salvation is gone forth, and mine arms shall judge the people (I will personally rule over the nations); the isles (nations of the world) shall wait (trust; rely) upon me, and on mine arm (my power) shall they trust.

6 Lift up your eyes to the heavens, and look upon the earth beneath: for the heavens shall vanish away like smoke, and the earth shall wax old like a garment, and they that dwell therein shall die in like manner: but my salvation (the salvation I bring) shall be for ever (will last forever), and my righteousness (triumph) shall not be abolished (compare D&C 1:38).

7 Hearken unto me, ye that know righteousness (you who are righteous), the people in whose heart is my law (you who have taken my gospel to heart); fear ye not the reproach (insults) of men, neither be ye afraid of their revilings (stinging criticism).

8 For the moth shall eat them (the wicked who revile against the right-eous) up like a garment, and the worm shall eat them like wool (i.e., they are just like moth-eaten clothing that will disintegrate and disappear): but my righteousness (salvation and deliverance) shall be (last) for ever, and my salvation from generation to generation (throughout eternity).

9 (The righteous now reply and invite the Lord's help in their lives.) Awake, awake (German: Now then, come Lord), put on strength, O arm (symbolic of power) of the LORD; awake, as in the ancient days, in the generations of old (i.e., ":Please, Lord, use thy power to save us like you did in olden days."). Art thou not it that hath cut Rahab (German: the proud; i.e., hath trimmed the proud down to size. Rahab can refer to the sea monster, Leviathan, in 27:1, which represents Satan and any who serve him, such as Egypt when Israelites escaped them via the Red Sea.), and wounded the dragon (Satan, see Rev. 12:7-9)?

10 Art thou not it which hath dried the sea, the waters of the great deep; that hath made the depths of the sea a way (a roadway) for the ransomed (the Children of Israel) to pass over (referring to the parting of the Red Sea)?

11 Therefore (because of the Lord's power) the redeemed of the LORD shall return (the gathering), and come with singing unto Zion; and everlasting joy shall be upon their head: they shall obtain gladness and joy; and sorrow and mourning shall flee

away (the results of righteousness).

12 (Now the Lord speaks to righteous Israel reminding them again that he is their God and the one who will help them return.) I, even I, am he that comforteth you: who art thou, that thou shouldest be afraid of a man that shall die (i.e., mortal men), and of the son of man (i.e., mortal men) which shall be made as grass (i.e., short-lived glory of evil mortal men; fear God, not man);

13 And forgettest the LORD thy maker, that hath stretched forth the heavens, and laid the foundations of the earth (how could you forget me, your Creator!); and hast feared continually every day because of the fury of the oppressor, as if he were ready to destroy (why should you live in fear of mortal men)? and where is the fury of the oppressor (the day will come when their fury won't be able to touch you)?

14 The captive exile hasteneth that he may be loosed, and that he should not die in the pit, nor that his bread should fail (the day will come when Israel will be set free, no more to die in captivity, and will have plenty).

15 But I am the LORD thy God, that divided the sea (parted the Red Sea), whose waves roared: The LORD of hosts is his name (is my name, 2 N. 8:15).

16 And I have put my words in thy mouth (I have given you my teachings), and I have covered thee in the shadow (protection) of mine hand, that I may plant the heavens, and lay the foundations of the earth (I created heaven and earth for you), and say unto Zion, Thou art my people (you are my covenant people).

17 Awake, awake, stand up, O Jerusalem, which hast drunk at the hand of the LORD the cup of his fury; thou hast drunken the dregs (the bitter, coarse stuff that settles in the bottom of the cup) of the cup of trembling, and wrung them out (you have "paid through the nose" for your wickedness).

18 There is none to guide her among all the sons whom she (Israel) hath brought forth (i.e., you have spent many years without prophets); neither is there any that taketh her by the hand of all the sons that she hath brought up.

19 These two things are come unto thee; who shall be sorry for thee (2 N. 8:19 changes this line considerably: "These two sons are come unto thee, who shall be sorry for thee—")? desolation, and destruction, and the famine, and the sword: by whom shall I comfort thee? (This verse in the Book of Mormon seems to refer to the two prophets in the last days who will keep the enemies of the Jews from totally destroying them. See Rev. 11)

20 Thy sons (your people) have fainted (German: are on their last leg), (save these two, 2 N. 8:20), they lie at the head of all the streets, as a wild bull in a net (i.e., your wicked people are being brought down like a wild animal by a net of wickedness): they are full of the fury of the LORD (they

are catching the full fury of the Lord), the rebuke of thy God (i.e., the consequences of sin have caught up with them).

21 Therefore hear now this, thou afflicted, and drunken (out of control), but not with wine (rather with wickedness):

22 Thus saith thy Lord the LORD, and thy God that pleadeth the cause of his people (I have not deserted you), Behold, I have taken out of thine hand the cup of trembling (I did the Atonement for you, see D&C 19:15-19), even the dregs of the cup of my fury; thou shalt no more drink it again (Christ will save the Jews in the last days, see 2 N. 9:1-2):

23 But I will put it (the cup of his fury in verse 22) into the hand of them (your enemies) that afflict thee; which have said to thy soul (have said to you), Bow down, that we may go over (lie down so we can walk on you): and thou hast laid thy body as the ground (you did), and as the street, to them that went over (i.e., you have been walked all over, treated like dirt!).

ISAIAH 52

1 Awake, awake; put on thy strength (repent and take Christ's name upon you), O Zion; put on thy beautiful garments (i.e., return to proper use of the priesthood, D&C 113:7&8), O Jerusalem, the holy city: for henceforth there shall no more come into thee the uncircumcised and the unclean (the wicked).

2 Shake thyself from the dust; arise (from being walked on, 51:23), and sit down (in dignity, redeemed at last), O Jerusalem: loose thyself from the bands of thy neck (come forth out of captivity), O captive daughter of Zion.

3 For thus saith the LORD, Ye have sold yourselves for nought (for nothing of value, i.e., apostatized); and ye shall be redeemed without money (i.e., the hand of the Lord is in it).

4 For thus saith the Lord GOD (Jehovah), My people went down aforetime into Egypt to sojourn there; and the Assyrian oppressed them without cause (i.e., were not justified in how they treated Israel; they abused their power as did Babylon, see 47:6).

5 Now therefore, what have I here, saith the LORD, that my people is taken away for nought? they that rule over them make them to howl, saith the LORD; and my name continually every day is blasphemed.

6 Therefore my people shall know my name: therefore they shall know in that day (in the last days) that I am he that doth speak: behold, it is I.

7 ("And then shall they say", 3 N. 20:40, referring to the last days) How beautiful upon the mountains are the feet of him that bringeth good tidings, that publisheth peace; that bringeth good tidings of good, that publisheth salvation; that saith unto Zion, Thy God reigneth (missionary work, gathering etc.)!

8 (Compare with 3 N. 20:32) Thy watchmen (prophets, leaders) shall lift up the voice; with the voice together shall they sing: for they shall see eye to eye, when the LORD shall bring again Zion (the underlined phrase is replaced in 3 N. 20:33 with "Then will the Father gather them together again and give unto them Jerusalem for the land of their inheritance.").

9 (Then shall they, 3 N. 20:34) Break forth into joy, sing together, ye waste places of Jerusalem: for the LORD hath comforted his people, he hath redeemed Jerusalem (will likely occur in the last days, near or at the beginning of the Millennium).

10 The LORD (the Father, 3 N. 20:35) hath made bare his holy arm (shown forth his power) in the eyes of all the nations; and all the ends of the earth shall see the salvation (the power to save and redeem) of our God (of the Father; and the Father and I are one. 3 N. 20:35).

11 ("And then shall a cry go forth," 3 N. 20:41; i.e., referring to the last days) Depart ye, depart ye, go ye out from thence (from among the wicked, D&C 38:42), touch no unclean thing; go ye out of the midst of her (Babylon, i.e., wickedness); be ye clean, that bear the vessels of the LORD (a major message of Isaiah).

12 For ye shall not go out with haste, nor go by flight (the gospel brings calmness): for the LORD will go before you; and the God of Israel will be your rereward (rearward, i.e., protection, see D&C 49:27).

13 Behold, my servant (could be Joseph Smith Jr., 3 N. 21:10-11, p. 428 of Rel. 121 B.of M. Student Manual; or Christ; or modern servants, prophets of God; or all of the above working together to fulfill verse 15) shall deal prudently, he shall be exalted and extolled, and be very high.

14 As many were astonied (astonished) at thee; his visage was so marred more than any man (the Savior as well as most prophets are highly praised by some, see verse 13, and much maligned by others), and his form more than the sons of men:

15 So shall he sprinkle (JST: gather) many nations; the kings shall shut their mouths at him: for that which had not been told them shall they see; and that which they had not heard shall they consider (see 3 N. 21:8; kings, i.e., powerful leaders will not be able to stop the Lord's work in the last days).

ISAIAH 53

1 Who hath believed our report (German: Who listens to us prophets anyway)? and to whom is the arm of the LORD revealed (who sees God's hand in things)?

2 For he (Jesus) shall grow up before him (possibly referring to the Father, but could also refer to mankind as implied in verse 1) as a tender plant (a new plant, i.e., a restoration of truth), and as a root out

of a dry ground (apostate Judaism): he (Jesus) hath no (special) form nor comeliness (attractiveness); and when we shall see him, there is no beauty that we should desire him (i.e., normal people couldn't tell he was the Son of God just by looking at him).

3 He (Jesus) is despised and rejected of men; a man of sorrows, and acquainted with grief (he endured much suffering and pain): and we hid as it were our faces from him (wouldn't even look at him); he was despised, and we (people in general) esteemed him not (German: paid no attention to him; even his own brothers rejected him at first, John 7:5).

4 Surely he hath borne our griefs, and carried our sorrows (the Atonement): yet we did esteem him stricken, smitten of God, and afflicted (we didn't recognize him as the Great Atoner, rather thought he was just another criminal receiving just punishment from God).

5 But he was wounded for our transgressions, he was bruised for our iniquities: the chastisement of our peace (required for peace) was upon him (he was punished so that we could have peace); and with his stripes (wounds and punishments) we are healed (from our sins, upon repentance).

6 All we like sheep have gone astray; we have turned every one to his own way (every one of us has sinned; we all need the Atonement);

and the LORD (the Father) hath laid on him (the Savior) the iniquity of us all (2 N. 9:21).

7 (Isaiah continues to speak prophetically as if the future events he is foretelling have already taken place, thus emphasizing the fact that they will take place.) He (Christ) was oppressed, and he was afflicted, yet he opened not his mouth (for instance, he wouldn't even speak to Pilate, Mark 15:3): he is brought as a lamb to the slaughter, and as a sheep before her shearers is dumb (won't speak), so he openeth not his mouth.

8 He was taken from prison and from judgment (he was refused fair treatment): and who shall declare his generation? for he was cut off out of the land of the living: for the transgression of my people was he stricken (he was punished for our sins).

9 And he made his grave with the wicked (he died with convicted criminals), and with the rich in his death (a rich man donated his tomb, John 19:38-42); because he had done no violence (German: wrong), neither was any deceit in his mouth (Christ was perfect).

10 Yet it pleased the LORD to bruise him (i.e., it was the Father's will to allow the Atonement performed by his Son); he hath put him to grief: when thou (he, i.e., Christ) shalt make (makes) his soul (German: life) an offering for sin, he shall see his seed (his loyal followers, i.e., success, Mosiah 15:10-12), he

shall prolong his days, and the pleasure of the LORD shall prosper in his hand.

11 He shall see (the results) of the travail (suffering) of his soul, and shall be satisfied (shall have joy, i.e., the Atonement will bear fruit): by his knowledge (by the knowledge he brings) shall my righteous servant justify (save; prepare them to be approved by the Holy Ghost, i.e., sealed by the Holy Spirit of Promise) many; for he shall bear their iniquities.

12 Therefore will I divide him a portion with the great (he will receive his reward), and he shall divide the spoil with the strong (the righteous); because he hath poured out his soul unto death (laid down his life): and he was numbered with the transgressors; and he bare the sin of many, and made intercession for the transgressors.

ISAIAH 54

Note: This chapter deals with the last days and compares with 3 Nephi 22. A major message of this chapter is that in the last days, Israel will finally be righteous and successful.

1 Sing, O barren (one who has not produced children, i.e., Israel who has not produced righteous children), thou that didst not bear; break forth into singing, and cry aloud, thou that didst not travail (go into labor) with child (i.e., in former days, you did not succeed in bringing forth righteous

children, loyal to Christ): for more are the children (righteous converts) of the desolate (perhaps meaning scattered Israel) than the children of the married wife (perhaps meaning Israelites who remained in the Holy Land, i.e., now, in the last days, you've got more righteous Israelites than you ever thought possible, almost all the converts coming from outside the land of Israel), saith the LORD.

2 Enlarge the place of thy tent (make more room!), and let them stretch forth the curtains of thine habitations: spare not, lengthen thy cords, and strengthen thy stakes (the Church will greatly expand in the last days as righteous Israel is gathered);

3 For thou shalt break forth on the right hand and on the left (righteous Israel will show up everywhere); and thy seed shall inherit the Gentiles, and make the desolate cities (cities without the true gospel) to be inhabited (Church membership will grow throughout the world).

4 Fear not; for thou shalt not be ashamed (you will not fail in the last days): neither be thou confounded; for thou shalt not be put to shame: for thou shalt forget the shame of thy youth, and shalt not remember the reproach of thy widowhood any more (i.e., you can forget the failures of the past when Israel was apostate; the once "barren" church is going to bear much fruit in the last days).

5 For thy Maker is thine husband

(you have returned to your creator in the last days); the LORD of hosts is his name; and thy Redeemer the Holy One of Israel; The God of the whole earth shall he be called.

6 For the LORD hath called thee as a woman forsaken and grieved in spirit (Israel has been through some very rough times), and a wife of youth, when thou wast refused (when you didn't bear righteous children), saith thy God.

7 For a small moment have I forsaken thee (because you apostatized); but with great mercies will I gather thee (in the last days).

8 In a little wrath I hid my face from thee for a moment (when you rejected me); but with everlasting kindness will I have mercy on thee, saith the LORD thy Redeemer.

9 For this (your situation) is as the waters of Noah unto me: for as I have sworn (promised) that the waters of Noah should no more go over the earth; so have I sworn that I would not be wroth with thee, nor rebuke thee (just as I promised not to flood the earth again, so I have promised to accept you back as you return to me in the last days).

10 For the mountains shall depart, and the hills be removed; but my kindness shall not depart from thee, neither shall the covenant of my peace be removed, saith the LORD that hath mercy on thee (Isaiah reminds us here of the true nature of God, a very kind and merciful God indeed!

Unfortunately, many people have not been correctly taught this truth.).

11 O thou (Israel) afflicted, tossed with tempest, and not comforted (you have been through some very rough times), behold, I will lay thy stones with fair colours (i.e., I will use the finest "materials" to build your "celestial homes"), and lay thy foundations with sapphires (precious gem stones).

12 And I will make thy windows (German: battlements) of agates (gem stones), and thy gates of carbuncles (bright, glittering gem stone), and all thy borders of pleasant stones (similar to the description of the celestial city in Revelation 21, i.e., you Israelites will have it very good, even better than you can imagine, when you repent and return unto me to dwell).

13 And all thy children shall be taught of the LORD; and great shall be the peace of thy children (likely referring to the Millennium; see D&C 45:58-59).

14 In righteousness shalt thou be established: thou shalt be far from oppression; for thou shalt not fear: and from terror; for it shall not come near thee (seems to refer to millennial conditions).

15 Behold, they (enemies of righteousness) shall surely gather together, but not by me: whosoever shall gather together against thee shall fall for thy sake (I will protect you, you will finally have peace).

16 Behold, I have created the smith

that bloweth the coals in the fire, and that bringeth forth an instrument for his work; and I have created the waster (German: the Destroyer) to destroy (i.e., I created all things and can control all things; you are safe with me).

17 No weapon that is formed against thee shall prosper; and every tongue that shall rise against thee in judgment thou shalt condemn. This is the heritage of the servants of the LORD, and their righteousness is of me, saith the LORD (there is safety for the righteous with me).

ISAIAH 55

Note: The Lord here invites all to come partake of the bounties of the gospel (which are equally available to all, either here on earth or afterward in the spirit world).

1 Ho (German: come now!), every one that thirsteth, come ye to the waters (the Living Water, i.e., Christ; see John 4:14, 7:37-38), and he that hath no money; come ye, buy (with your good works, keeping the commandments etc.), and eat; yea, come, buy wine and milk without money and without price (i.e., the gospel is available to all without regard to economic status).

2 Wherefore (why) do ye spend money for that which is not bread (i.e., not of true value)? and your labour for that which satisfieth not

(i.e., why are you so materialistic)? hearken diligently unto me (the Lord), and eat ye that which is good (that which comes of Christ), and let your soul delight itself in fatness (the richness of the gospel).

3 Incline your ear (listen carefully), and come unto me (Christ): hear, and your soul shall live (you will receive salvation); and I will make an everlasting covenant (i.e., the fullness of the gospel, see D&C 66:2) with you, even the sure mercies of David (German: the mercies and pardons of Christ spoken of by David. David himself couldn't be completely forgiven, D&C 132:39. "David" is often used symbolically for Christ, Isaiah 22:22; hence, "sure mercies of David" can mean the "sure mercies of Christ").

4 Behold, I have given him (Christ) for a witness to the people, a leader and commander to the people.

5 (There could be many different interpretations of this verse. One possibility is presented here.) Behold, thou (Christ) shalt call a nation that thou (Israel) knowest not, and nations (the true Church in the last days) that knew not thee (weren't personally acquainted with ancient Israel) shall run unto thee (shall gather Israel) because of the LORD thy God (under the direction of the Lord), and for the Holy One of Israel; for he (Israel) hath glorified thee (God). (I.e., in the last days, Israel will be gathered, will return to God and be saved.)

6 Seek ye the LORD while he may be found, call ye upon him while he is near (vs. 6 & 7 are an invitation to repent and return to a kind, merciful God):

7 Let the wicked forsake his way, and the unrighteous man his thoughts: and let him return unto the LORD, and he (the Lord) will have mercy upon him; and to our God, for he will abundantly pardon.

8 For my thoughts (chiasmus A) are not your thoughts, neither are your ways (chiasmus B) my ways, saith the LORD.

9 For as the heavens (chiasmus C) are higher than the earth (chiasmus C'), so are my ways (chiasmus B') higher than your ways, and my thoughts (chiasmus A') than your thoughts (i.e., come unto me and live as I do, which way of life is much more satisfying than you can possibly comprehend).

10 For as the rain cometh down, and the snow from heaven, and returneth not thither, but watereth the earth, and maketh it bring forth and bud, that it may give seed to the sower, and bread to the eater:

11 So shall my word be (i.e., designed to bring forth exaltation) that goeth forth out of my mouth: it shall not return unto me void, but it shall accomplish that which I please, and it shall prosper in the thing whereto I sent it (my gospel will ultimately succeed).

12 For ye shall go out (from premortality to earth) with joy, and be led forth (to return home to God) with peace: the mountains and the hills shall break forth before you into singing, and all the trees of the field shall clap their hands (God's creations rejoice as their role in helping man achieve exaltation is fulfilled).

13 Instead of the thorn shall come up the fir tree, and instead of the brier shall come up the myrtle tree (the earth will eventually be celestialized, see D&C 130:9): and it (the earth and many of its inhabitants' achieving celestial glory) shall be to the LORD for a name (will increase God's glory and dominion), for an everlasting sign (that God's promises are fulfilled and that man can achieve exaltation) that shall not be cut off (that will never end).

ISAIAH 56

Note: Verses 1-8 extend the invitation to exaltation to all, including gentiles.

1 Thus saith the LORD, Keep ye judgment, and do justice (i.e., be righteous): for my salvation is near to come, and my righteousness to be revealed.

2 Blessed is the man that doeth this (good), and the son of man that layeth hold on it (that follows my counsel to live righteously); that keepeth the Sabbath from polluting it, and keepeth his hand from doing any evil.

3 Neither let the son of the stranger (i.e., the gentiles), that hath joined

himself to the LORD (that has joined the Church, i.e., accepted and follows Christ), speak, saying, The LORD hath utterly separated me from his people ("The Lord has made me a second class citizen forever."): neither let the eunuch (see Bible Dict., page 667) say, Behold, I am a dry tree (i.e., can't have children; eunuchs were not allowed into the congregation of Israel, Deut. 23:1).

4 For thus saith the LORD unto the eunuchs (symbolically represent a class of people that the Israelites despised and would never consider to be potential citizens of heaven) that keep my sabbaths, and choose the things that please me (keep my commandments), and take hold of my covenant (make and keep covenants with me);

5 Even unto them will I give in mine house (temple; Cel. Kingdom) and within my walls (perhaps dual, meaning temples or heavenly home) a place and a name (King Benjamin promised his people a "name", Mosiah 1:11, i.e., the name of Christ, Mosiah 5:8) better than of sons and of daughters (i.e., they will have more honor and glory in exaltation than they would have had from having sons and daughters on earth): I will give them an everlasting name, that shall not be cut off (i.e., eunuchs and all "outsiders" can be exalted too!).

6 Also the sons of the stranger (gentiles), that join themselves to the LORD (make covenants), to serve him,

and to love the name of the LORD, to be his servants, every one that keepeth the Sabbath from polluting it, and taketh hold of my covenant (i.e., all gentiles can receive exaltation, if they keep the commandments);

7 Even them will I bring to my holy mountain (God's Kingdom), and make them joyful in my house of prayer: their burnt offerings and their sacrifices shall be accepted upon mine altar; for mine house shall be called an house of prayer for all people (i.e., celestial exaltation is available for all people who make covenants with the Lord and keep his commandments).

8 The Lord GOD which gathereth the outcasts of Israel (scattered Israel) saith, Yet will I gather others (gentiles) to him (Israel), beside those (Israelites) that are gathered unto him (Israel).

9 (Isaiah switches topics now to the gentile "beasts" who will come to "devour" the wicked of Israel.) All ye beasts (gentile armies) of the field, come to devour (come to devour Israel), yea, all ye beasts in the forest.

10 His watchmen (Israel's wicked leaders) are blind: they are all ignorant (of the dangers of wickedness), they are all dumb dogs (not doing their job of warning the people of danger), they cannot bark (they won't sound the alarm); sleeping, lying down, loving to slumber (they are asleep on the job).

11 Yea, they are greedy dogs which can never have enough (are never satisfied), and they are shepherds that cannot understand (leaders who don't

understand the seriousness of the situation): they all look to their own way (look only after their own interests), every one for his gain, from his quarter.

12 Come ye, say they, I will fetch wine, and we will fill ourselves with strong drink ("Let's party!"); and to morrow shall be as this day, and much more abundant ("And tomorrow we will have even a bigger and better party!").

ISAIAH 57

1 (Isaiah gives counsel and comfort to the righteous in the next two verses.) The righteous perisheth (the righteous suffer when the wicked rule, D&C 98:7), and no man layeth it to heart (no one seems to care): and merciful men are taken away, none considering that the righteous is taken away from the evil to come.

2 He (the righteous) shall enter into peace: they shall rest in their beds (or on their couches), each one walking in his uprightness (i.e., personal righteousness leads to inner peace here and peace in eternity).

3 (Isaiah now addresses the wicked.) But draw near hither, ye sons of (followers of) the sorceress (i.e., people who live wickedly), the seed of (followers of) the adulterer and the whore (i.e., gross wickedness; used in 1 N.22:14 to represent Satan's kingdoms).

4 Against whom do ye sport yourselves (whom are you mocking)?

against whom make ye a wide mouth (making faces), and draw out the tongue (sticking your tongues out)? are ye not children of transgression (totally caught up in sin), a seed of falsehood (a bunch of liars),

5 Enflaming yourselves (sexually arousing yourselves) with idols under every green tree (German: You run to your gods with sexual arousal [referring to religious prostitution used as part of pagan worship].), slaying the (your) children in the valleys under the clifts of the rocks (killing your children as human sacrifices)?

6 Among the smooth stones of the stream (used for building altars etc. for idol worship) is thy portion (German: You base your whole existence on your false gods, idols!); they, they are thy lot (i.e., you have chosen them over me, therefore, you will have to depend on them for your reward): even to them hast thou poured a drink offering (part of idol worship that was originally for worship of the true God, Ex. 29:40; i.e., they have perverted proper worship ceremonies over to their idol worship), thou hast offered a meat offering (to your idols; Ex. 29:41). Should I receive comfort in these (Do you expect me to be happy about such perversions of true worship)?

7 (In verses 7 and 8, the Lord chastises Israel for breaking the 7th commandment literally by having sexual intercourse with temple prostitutes as part of pagan worship services.) Upon a lofty and high

mountain hast thou set thy bed: even thither wentest thou up to offer sacrifice.

8 Behind the doors also and the posts hast thou set up thy remembrance (German: statue): for thou hast discovered (uncovered, exposed, undressed) thyself to another than me (i.e., you have "stepped out on me", been unfaithful to me), and art gone up; thou hast enlarged thy bed (made room for many false gods in your life), and made thee a covenant with them (you have given your loyalty to many false gods); thou lovedst their bed where thou sawest it.

9 And thou wentest to the king (Molech, a large, brass idol with a hollow fire-pit stomach, used for sacrificing children) with ointment, and didst increase thy perfumes (i.e., you have worshipped the idol, Molech, with ointment and perfumes), and didst send thy messengers far off, and didst debase thyself even unto hell (i.e., "You have travelled all the way to hell to find new and worse ways to commit sin!"; Implies that they have made covenants with Satan himself).

10 Thou art wearied in the greatness of thy way (you got tired trying to find worse ways to sin); yet saidst thou not, There is no hope (but you didn't give up, rather, said to yourself "There has got to be something more wicked we can do!"): thou hast found the life of thine hand (renewal of strength); therefore thou wast not grieved (you kept striving for worse

wickedness against all odds).

11 And of whom hast thou been afraid or feared, that thou hast lied (Why have you respected false gods instead of me?), and hast not remembered me, nor laid it to thy heart (You don't even seem to be aware of me)? have not I held my peace even of old, and thou fearest me not (Have I been too kind and gentle with you)?

12 I will declare (German: point out) thy (so-called) righteousness, and thy works; for they shall not profit thee (i.e., I will expose your so-called righteousness and good works; they won't save you).

13 When thou criest (cry out for help when you are in trouble), let thy companies (of idols) deliver (save) thee; but the wind shall carry them all away (i.e., your idols and false gods are no more secure and stable than a tumbleweed in the wind); vanity shall take them (a puff of breath will blow them away): but he that putteth his trust in me shall possess the land, and shall inherit my holy mountain (I do have power to save you and can give you great blessings);

14 And (I, the Lord) shall say, Cast ye up, cast ye up (German: make a highway, make a highway), prepare the way (clear the way), take up the stumbling block out of the way of my people (i.e., prepare the way for the return of my people, certainly foreshadowing the restoration).

15 For thus saith the high and lofty One (the Lord) that inhabiteth eternity, whose name is Holy; I dwell in

the high and holy place, with him also that is of a contrite and humble spirit (the contrite and humble will find safety and security with me), to revive (German: refresh) the spirit of the humble, and to revive the heart of (give new courage to) the contrite ones.

16 For I will not contend (against you) for ever, neither will I be always wroth (angry): for the spirit should fail before me (i.e., if I did, all mankind would perish), and the souls (people) which I have made (no one would survive).

17 For the iniquity (because of the wickedness) of his (Israel's) covetousness (wicked greediness) was I wroth, and smote him: I hid me (I withdrew my spirit), and was wroth, and he (Israel) went on frowardly in the way of his heart (kept right on in his wicked ways).

18 I have seen his ways (probably referring to Israelites who repent with a contrite and humble spirit as mentioned in verse 15), and will heal him: I will lead him also, and restore comforts (comfort him) unto him and to his mourners (those Israelites who mourn for their sins, i.e., who repent).

19 I create the fruit of the lips (i.e., speech; German: I will create fruit of the lips that preaches:); Peace, peace to him (the righteous) that is far off, and to him that is near, saith the LORD; and I will heal him (the repentant, anywhere he is found).

20 But the wicked are like the troubled sea, when it cannot rest, whose waters cast up mire and dirt.

21 There is no peace, saith my God, to the wicked (a major message from the Lord through Isaiah).

ISAIAH 58

Note: Verses 1-3 seem to imply that the people have been complaining about not getting the blessings they want from the Lord even though they keep the letter-of-the-law ordinances.

1 Cry aloud, spare not, lift up thy voice like a trumpet, and shew my people their transgression, and the house of Jacob their sins (i.e., Go ahead, Isaiah. Tell the people why they aren't getting the desired blessings. Tell them of their sins!).

2 Yet they seek me daily (are going through the motions, doing all the rituals), and (appear to) delight to know my ways, as a nation that did righteousness (German: as if they were a nation who had not forsaken the ordinances of their God), and forsook not the ordinance of their God: they ask of me the ordinances of justice (German: they demand their rights); they take delight in approaching to God (German: want to debate with God and demand their rightful blessings).

3 Wherefore (why) have we fasted, say they, and thou seest not (you don't seem to notice)? wherefore have we afflicted our soul (why do we put our bodies through this pain), and thou takest no knowledge (you ignore it)?

(God now answers their question.) Behold, in the day of your fast ye find pleasure (German: you do what you desire), and exact all your labours (German: make your employees work).

4 Behold, ye fast for strife and debate (your way of fasting causes contention), and to smite with the fist of wickedness: ye shall not fast as ye do this day, to make your voice to be heard on high (i.e., you cannot expect the Lord to bless you for such hypocritical fasting!).

5 Is it such a fast that I have chosen (Do you really think such fasting pleases me)? a day for a man to afflict his soul (German: do evil to his body)? is it to bow down his head as a bulrush, and to spread sackcloth and ashes under him? wilt thou call this a fast, and an acceptable day to the LORD (i.e., do you really think outward appearance is everything)?

6 Is not this the fast that I have chosen (i.e., let me tell you the real purpose of the fast)? to loose the bands of wickedness (i.e., to help you grow in righteousness), to undo the heavy burdens (that are brought on by sin), and to let the oppressed (by sin) go free, and that ye break every yoke (break loose from every kind of sin)?

7 Is it not to deal thy bread to the hungry (to feed the hungry), and that thou bring the poor that are cast out to thy house (to take care of the homeless)? when thou seest the naked, that thou cover him (to clothe the naked); and that thou hide not thyself from

thine own flesh (to help your own family and relatives)?

8 Then (when you do the above) shall thy light break forth as the morning, and thine health shall spring forth speedily: and thy righteousness shall go before thee; the glory of the LORD shall be thy rereward (rear guard; protection).

9 Then shalt thou call, and the LORD shall answer; thou shalt cry (pray), and he shall say, Here I am. If thou take away from the midst of thee the yoke (root out the evils from among you), the putting forth of the finger (pointing in a gesture of scorn), and speaking vanity (maliciously);

10 And if thou draw out thy soul (German: heart) to the hungry (help the hungry), and satisfy the afflicted soul (help the afflicted); then shall thy light rise in obscurity (shine in the darkness), and thy darkness be as the noonday (instead of darkness, you will have light):

11 And the LORD shall guide thee continually, and satisfy thy soul in drought, and make fat thy bones (strengthen you): and thou shalt be like a watered garden, and like a spring of water, whose waters fail not (never cease).

12 And they that shall be of thee shall build the old waste places (German: and through you shall the old waste places be built): thou shalt raise up the foundations of many generations; and thou shalt be called, The repairer of the breach, The restorer of paths to dwell in (perhaps

indicating that as Israel returns to the Lord and does the things prescribed in verses 6 and 7, then they will be the means of restoring the Church).

13 (The Lord now reminds them of the importance of keeping the Sabbath holy.) If thou turn away thy foot from the Sabbath, from doing thy pleasure on my holy day (i.e., if you will do my will rather than your will on the Sabbath); and call the Sabbath a delight (i.e., have a good attitude about the Sabbath), the holy of the LORD, honourable; and shalt honour him (the Lord), not doing thine own ways, nor finding thine own pleasure, nor speaking thine own words:

14 Then shalt thou delight thyself in the LORD (you will have joy in the Lord); and I will cause thee to ride upon the high places of the earth, and feed thee with the heritage of Jacob thy father (i.e., you will receive the Lord's choicest blessings): for the mouth of the LORD hath spoken it (this is a promise!).

ISAIAH 59

1 (Verses 1-8 explain that the Israelites have put distance between themselves and the Lord by their wicked behaviors.) Behold, the LORD's hand is not shortened, that it cannot save; neither his ear heavy, that it cannot hear (i.e., the Lord has not lost his power, perhaps referring back to the peoples' questions in 58:3):

2 But your iniquities have separated

between you and your God, and your sins have hid his face from you, that he will not hear (i.e., your wickedness has separated you from God).

3 For your hands are defiled with blood (perhaps referring to their killing the prophets and others as implied in verse 7, "shed innocent blood"), and your fingers with iniquity (you've got your hands on all kinds of wickedness); your lips have spoken lies (you are dishonest), your tongue hath muttered perverseness (German: unrighteousness; i.e., you are wicked through and through!).

4 None calleth (seeks) for justice, nor any pleadeth for (desires) truth: they trust in vanity (man rather than God), and speak lies (are dishonest); they conceive mischief (they are constantly dreaming up more ways to sin), and bring forth iniquity (i.e., their desires are to do evil continually).

5 They hatch cockatrice' ("adder"; very poisonous snake) eggs (i.e., they "hatch" all kinds of wickedness), and weave the spider's web (design entanglements in sin): he that eateth of their eggs dieth, and that which is crushed breaketh out into a viper (they are creating a menu for spiritual death and going from bad to worse).

6 Their webs (i.e., the things they've surrounded themselves with) shall not become garments, neither shall they cover themselves ("insulate" themselves) with their works (i.e., they will not "insulate" themselves from consequences of wickedness; they can't get

completely comfortable in wickedness, see 28:20): their works are works of iniquity, and the act of violence is in their hands.

7 Their feet run to evil (they are anxious to sin), and they make haste to shed innocent blood: their thoughts are thoughts of iniquity (evil desires are constantly on their minds); wasting and destruction are in their paths (i.e., they are wasting away their lives, heading for disaster).

8 The way of peace they know not; and there is no judgment (justice) in their goings: they have made them (for themselves) crooked paths (i.e., they have created a very wicked and perverse lifestyle for themselves): whosoever goeth therein shall not know peace (there is no peace for the wicked, 57:21).

9 (In verses 9-15, Israel admits guilt and faces the issue that they are behaving wickedly, like Alma the Younger did as described in Alma 36:13-14.) Therefore (for this reason) is judgment far from us, neither doth justice (charity, righteousness) overtake us: we wait for (look forward to) light, but behold obscurity; for brightness, but we walk in darkness (because of our wickedness).

10 We grope for the wall like the blind, and we grope as if we had no eyes (we are stumbling around in the dark): we stumble at noonday as in the night; we are in desolate places as dead men (we are as good as dead, we've about had it).

11 We roar all like bears, and mourn sore like doves: we look for judgment (pleasant treatment), but there is none; for salvation, but it is far off from us (we are a long way away from God).

12 For (because we are so wicked) our transgressions are multiplied before thee, and our sins testify against us: for our transgressions are with us (we are dragging our sins around with us); and as for our iniquities, we know (German: feel) them (i.e., we are aware of and acknowledge our sins);

13 In transgressing and lying against the LORD, and departing away from our God, speaking oppression and revolt, conceiving and uttering from the heart words of falsehood (i.e., our hearts have not been right before God).

14 And judgment is turned away backward, and justice standeth afar off: for truth is fallen in the street (i.e., our lifestyle is completely out of line), and equity (honesty) cannot enter.

15 Yea, truth faileth (is lacking); and he that departeth from evil maketh himself a prey (i.e., when a person repents and turns from evil, he is mocked and becomes a victim in a wicked society. From here to the end of verse 21, Isaiah says that the Lord can now start redeeming Israel, because they have faced guilt, verses 9-15, and are turning from transgression, verse 20): and the LORD saw it, and it displeased him that there was no judgment.

16 And he saw that there was no man (i.e., no one besides Christ could

do the job of redeeming Israel; similar to Rev. 5:3-4), and wondered that there was no intercessor: therefore his (the Lord's) arm brought salvation unto him (German: himself, i.e., Christ had the power within himself, see 63:5); and his (Christ's personal) righteousness, it sustained him (Christ).

17 For he (Christ) put on righteousness as a breastplate, and an helmet of salvation upon his head (breastplate and helmet are armor and imply intense attacks by the enemies of righteousness); and he put on the garments of vengeance for clothing (i.e., Christ can save us via His righteousness and power of salvation or punish us, depending on our deeds as stated in verse 18), and was clad with zeal as a cloke (i.e., Christ is completely able to be the intercessor desired in verse 16).

18 According to their deeds, accordingly he will repay, fury to his (Christ's) adversaries, recompence (Alma 41:4) to his enemies; to the islands (all continents, nations) he will repay recompence (emphasis is on "recompence", i.e., giving them what they have earned).

19 So shall they fear (respect, reverence) the name of the LORD from the west, and his glory from the rising of the sun (from east to west, i.e., everywhere). When the enemy (German: the Lord) shall come in like a flood (i.e., the judgements of God will come quickly to the whole earth, "islands",

verse 18), the Spirit of the LORD shall lift up a standard against him (the enemies; wicked in verse 18).

20 And the Redeemer shall come to Zion, and unto them that turn from transgression in Jacob (among the House of Israel), saith the LORD (the righteous will live with Christ; implies Millennium).

21 As for me (the Lord), this is my covenant with them (those who have turned away from sin, verse 20), saith the LORD; My spirit that is upon thee, and my words (the fullness of the gospel) which I have put in thy mouth, shall not depart out of thy mouth, nor out of the mouth of thy seed, nor out of the mouth of thy seed's seed, saith the LORD, from henceforth and for ever (i.e., an everlasting covenant which will see ultimate fulfillment with those of the Celestial Kingdom).

ISAIAH 60

1 (Isaiah now prophesies that in the last days the Church of Jesus Christ will arise, shine forth and be a light to the nations as mentioned in Isa. 5:26 etc.) Arise, shine; for thy light is come, and the glory of the LORD is risen upon thee.

2 For, behold, the darkness (spiritual darkness in the last days, see Teachings of the Prophet Joseph Smith, p. 47) shall cover the earth, and gross darkness the people: but the LORD shall arise upon thee, and his

glory shall be seen upon thee (the restored Church, i.e., Zion in the last days).

3 And the Gentiles shall come to (German: walk in) thy light, and kings to the brightness of thy rising (German: to the brightness that has come upon you).

4 Lift up thine eyes round about, and see: all they gather themselves together, they come to thee (Israel, Zion): thy sons (converts) shall come from far, and thy daughters (converts) shall be nursed at thy side (i.e., people will gathered to Zion from far and near).

5 Then thou shalt see, and flow together (be radiant, be very happy), and thine heart shall fear (German: be surprised, thrill), and be enlarged (swell; rejoice); because the abundance of the sea (multitude) shall be converted unto thee (Zion), the forces (wealth) of the Gentiles shall come unto thee.

6 The multitude of camels shall cover thee, the dromedaries (young camels) of Midian and Ephah (see map 3, parts of Jordan and Saudi Arabia); all they from Sheba (part of Saudi Arabia) shall come: they shall bring gold and incense (similar to when the Wise Men came to Christ; perhaps symbolic of when people come to Christ); and they shall shew forth the praises of the LORD (i.e., people from these Arabic countries will come unto Christ; symbolic of people from all nations coming to

Christ in the last days).

7 All the flocks (perhaps symbolic of converts) of Kedar (Syria, map 2) shall be gathered together unto thee, the rams (strong men, leaders, chiefs) of Nebaioth shall minister unto thee (Israel in the last days): they (people out of all nations) shall come up with acceptance on mine altar (shall become acceptable to me), and I will glorify the house of my glory.

8 Who are these that fly as a cloud, and as the doves to their windows (i.e., "Who are these people who flock in over the sea?", i.e., the gathering)?

9 Surely the isles (nations) shall wait (German: trust in; look forward eagerly) for me, and the ships of Tarshish first, to bring thy sons (converts) from far, their silver and their gold with them, unto the name of the LORD thy God, and to the Holy One of Israel, because he hath glorified thee (Israel; the True Church).

10 And the sons of strangers (foreigners) shall build up thy walls (will help build up Zion), and their kings shall minister unto thee: for in my wrath I smote thee (in times past, I've had to severely discipline you), but in my favour have I had mercy on thee (but in the last days as you return to me, you will partake of my mercy).

11 Therefore thy gates shall be open continually (you will not fear attack by enemies); they shall not be shut day nor night; that men may bring unto thee the forces (wealth) of the Gentiles, and that their kings may be

brought (German: that their kings may be brought to you also).

12 For the nation and kingdom that will not serve thee shall perish; yea, those nations shall be utterly wasted.

13 The glory (the best of) of Lebanon (the Holy Land) shall come unto thee, the fir tree, the pine tree, and the box together, to beautify the place of my sanctuary (temple); and I will make the place of my feet (i.e., footstool, earth, temple) glorious.

14 The sons also of them (your former enemies) that afflicted thee shall come bending unto thee; and all they that despised thee shall bow themselves down at the soles of thy feet (i.e., your former enemies and oppressors will humbly respect you); and they shall call (acknowledge) thee, The city of the LORD, The Zion of the Holy One of Israel.

15 Whereas thou hast been forsaken and hated (in the past), so that no man went through thee (people hated you and avoided you), I will make thee an eternal excellency, a joy of many generations.

16 Thou shalt also suck the milk of (be nourished and assisted by) the Gentiles, and shalt suck the breast of (be nourished and assisted by) kings: and thou shalt know that I the LORD am thy Saviour and thy Redeemer, the mighty One of Jacob.

17 For (instead of) brass I will bring gold, and for (instead of) iron I will bring silver, and for (instead of) wood brass, and for (instead of) stones iron

(i.e., you will prosper): I will also make thy officers (leaders) peace, and thine exactors (rulers) righteousness.

18 Violence shall no more be heard in thy land, wasting nor destruction within thy borders (i.e., wonderful peace awaits the righteous); but thou shalt call thy walls Salvation (you will be surrounded with peace and salvation), and thy gates Praise.

19 The sun shall be no more thy light by day; neither for brightness shall the moon give light unto thee: but the LORD shall be unto thee an everlasting light, and thy God thy glory (some conditions in New Jerusalem will be similar to conditions in the Celestial glory as described in Rev. 21:23; 22:5).

20 Thy sun shall no more go down; neither shall thy moon withdraw itself: for the LORD shall be thine everlasting light, and the days of thy mourning shall be ended (your earthly sorrows will be over).

21 Thy people also shall be all righteous: they shall inherit the land (earth) for ever (D&C 88:17-20; 130:9), the branch of my planting, the work of my hands (i.e., the righteous), that I may be glorified.

22 A little one (a seemingly unimportant, insignificant person) shall become a thousand, and a small (insignificant) one a strong nation (perhaps referring to "a continuation of the seeds [children] forever", D&C 132:19, i.e., eternal posterity): I the LORD will hasten (act quickly) it in

his (my) time (i.e., the Lord will act quickly to bestow these blessings, when the time is right).

ISAIAH 61

1 (Isaiah here describes Christ's authority, power and purposes for his earthly ministry. The Savior quoted verse 1 and the first phrase of verse 2 in Luke 4:18-19 as he identified himself as the Messiah.) The Spirit of the Lord GOD (Jehovah) is upon me; because the LORD hath anointed me (ie. my missionary calling is) to preach good tidings (the gospel) unto the meek; he hath sent me to bind up (apply first aid; to heal) the broken-hearted, to proclaim liberty to the captives (those in spiritual bondage here and in spirit prison), and the opening of the prison (spirit prison) to them that are bound;

2 To proclaim the acceptable year (the time designated by the Father for me to perform my earthly mission. DNTC, Vol. I, p. 161) of the LORD, and the day of vengeance of our God; (this phrase refers to destruction of wicked at 2nd Coming) to comfort all that mourn;

3 To appoint (extend compassion) unto them that mourn in Zion, to give unto them beauty for ashes, the oil of joy for mourning, the garment of praise for (ie. give beautiful clothing, life instead of) the spirit of heaviness (depression); that they might be called trees of righteousness, (ie. righteous

people in the Lords garden) the planting of the LORD, that he might be glorified.

4 And they shall build the old wastes, they shall raise up the former desolations, and they shall repair the waste cities, the desolations of many generations (ie. in last days Zion will be built up).

5 And strangers (foreigners, your former enemies) shall stand and feed your flocks, and the sons of the alien (foreigner) shall be your plowmen and your vinedressers (i.e., tables are turned, former enemies will be your servants now).

6 But ye shall be named the Priests of the LORD: (make covenants leading to exaltation) men shall call you the Ministers of our God: (you will have priesthood authority) ye shall eat the riches of the Gentiles, and in their glory (wealth) shall ye boast (German: enjoy) yourselves.

7 For (in return for) your shame (German: humiliation in times past; ye shall have double (birthright blessing; D&C 132:20); and for confusion they (righteous Israel in the last days and beyond) shall rejoice in their portion: therefore in their land they shall possess the double (i.e., birthright blessing, Deut. 21:17): everlasting joy shall be unto them.

8 For I the LORD love judgment (justice, righteousness), I hate robbery (plundering) for (with) burnt offering (i.e., I hate hypocrisy, evil lifestyles combined with empty rituals); and I

will direct their work in truth, and I will make an everlasting covenant with them.

9 And their seed (the righteous) shall be known among the Gentiles (i.e., the gospel will spread to all nations), and their offspring among the people: all that see them shall acknowledge them, that they are the seed which the LORD hath blessed (ie: those who receive the blessings of Abraham 2:8-11).

10 (Isaiah now rejoices and sings songs of praise to the Lord.) I (Isaiah or Zion) will greatly rejoice in the Lord, my soul shall be joyful in my God; for he hath clothed me with the garments of salvation (2 Ne 4:33-35, similar to Nephi's rejoicing in the Lord), he hath covered me with the robe of righteousness, as a bridegroom decketh himself with ornaments (German: priestly clothing; Hebrew: mitre or cap in Exodus 39:28, footnote b), and as a bride adorneth herself with her jewels. (Reference to garments, robes, priestly "ornaments" or cap in this verse points one's mind to ordinances of exaltation in temples today.)

11 For as the earth bringeth forth her bud, and as the garden causeth the things that are sown in it to spring forth; so the Lord GOD will cause righteousness (victory of Zion) and praise (of Zion, Israel) to spring forth before (among) all the nations (i.e.,the Lord will restore Israel and will again make available the blessings of exaltation in the last days).

ISAIAH 62

1 For Zion's sake will I not hold my peace (remain silent), and for Jerusalem's sake I will not rest (remain silent), until the righteousness thereof (victory of Zion) go forth as brightness (very noticeable, beautifully conspicuous), and the salvation thereof as a lamp that burneth (flaming torch).

2 And the Gentiles shall see thy righteousness, and all kings thy glory: and thou shalt be called by a new name (symbolic of life in celestial glory, D&C 130:11; Rev. 2:17), which the mouth of the LORD shall name.

3 Thou shalt also be a crown of glory (symbolic of exaltation, Rev 4:4; 2 Tim 4:8) in the hand of the LORD, and a royal diadem (crown, symbolic of royal power and authority) in the hand of thy God.

4 Thou shalt no more be termed Forsaken (ie, you will never again be forsaken); neither shall thy land any more be termed Desolate: but thou shalt be called Hephzi-bah (JST: delightful), and thy land Beulah (the married wife, i.e., you will belong to the Lord and Lord to you): for the LORD delighteth in thee, and thy land shall be married (ie, you will belong to the Lord).

5 For as a young man marrieth a virgin, so shall thy sons (JST: God) marry thee: and as the bridegroom rejoiceth over the bride, so shall thy God rejoice over thee.

6 I have set watchmen (prophets)

upon thy walls, O Jerusalem, which shall never hold their peace (remain silent) day nor night: ye that make mention of the LORD (prayer and worship the Lord), keep not silence,

7 And give him (the Lord) no rest (don't stop praying), till he (the Lord) establish, and till he (the Lord) make Jerusalem (Zion) a praise in the earth (highly respected throughout the earth).

8 The LORD hath sworn by his right hand (has covenanted), and by the arm of his strength, Surely I will no more give thy corn (crops) to be meat (food) for thine enemies; and the sons of the stranger (foreigners, gentiles) shall not drink thy wine, for the which thou hast laboured (ie: you will live in peace with me)

9 But they that have gathered (harvested) it shall eat it, and praise (give thanks to) the LORD; and they that have brought it (made it) together shall drink it in the courts of my holiness (ie: you will enjoy the fruits of your labors in peace in my holy courts).

10 Go through, go through the gates (come to Zion, via the gates, i.e., gospel ordinances, coupled with righteous living); prepare ye the way of the people; cast up, cast up the highway (the highway to Zion, God, will be built up); gather out the stones (remove the stumbling blocks); lift up a standard (ensign i.e., gospel of Jesus Christ) for the people.

11 Behold, the LORD hath proclaimed unto the end of the (all of the) world, Say ye to the daughter of Zion (Jerusalem, ie: the righteous), Behold, thy salvation (your Deliverer) cometh; behold, his (Christ's) reward (i.e., He brings your reward with Him when He comes) is with him, and his work before him.

12 And they shall call them (the righteous will be referred to as), The holy people, The redeemed of the LORD: and thou (righteous Israel) shalt be called, Sought out, A city not forsaken (i.e., chosen by the Lord to be blessed).

ISAIAH 63

Isaiah now refers to the Second Coming and destruction of the wicked, verses 1-6.

1 Who is this (Christ) that cometh (the Second Coming) from Edom (travelers from East to Jerusalem usually came north past the Dead Sea then west to Jerusalem. From Edom could also mean from the East, or heaven, D&C 133:46), with dyed (red - see vs 2) garments from Bozrah (the capital city of Edom)? this that is glorious in his apparel (Christ comes in glory), travelling in the greatness of his strength (Christ comes in great power at Second Coming)? I (Christ; i.e., "It is I", the Savior) that speak in righteousness, mighty to save (the repentant).

2 Wherefore (why) art thou red in thine apparel (what is the red spattered all over your clothing?), and thy garments like him that treadeth in the

winefat (Hebrew: press, ie. the wine press and the vat for collecting the juice of the grapes)?

3 I have trodden the winepress alone (I was the only one capable of doing the atonement); and of the people there was none with me (I had to do it alone): for I will tread them (the wicked) in mine anger, and trample them in my fury; and their blood (the blood of the wicked, D&C 133:51) shall be sprinkled upon my garments, and I will stain all my raiment (i.e., judgement will be thorough).

4 For the day of vengeance is in mine heart (German: is part of my task, my responsibility), and the year of my redeemed is come (the time has come for the righteous to be set free from the cares of a wicked world, perhaps referring to Millennium).

5 And I looked, and there was none to help (no mortal, i.e., no one could help me do the Atonement); and I wondered that there was none to uphold (I did it alone): therefore mine own arm (the power was within me) brought salvation unto me; and my fury (my own divine strength), it upheld me.

6 And I will tread down the people (the wicked) in mine anger, and make them drunk in my fury (i.e., judgement will fall upon the wicked), and I will bring down their strength to the earth (I will humble the wicked).

7 I will mention the lovingkindnesses (Isaiah now turns to the kindness and blessings of the Lord to the righteous) of the LORD, and the praises of the LORD, according to all that the LORD hath bestowed on us, and the great goodness toward the house of Israel, which he hath bestowed on them according to his mercies, and according to the multitude of his lovingkindnesses.

8 For he said, Surely they are my people, children that will not lie (German: people of integrity): so (German: for that reason) he was their Saviour.

9 In all their affliction he was afflicted (He suffered and paid for their sins, D&C 133:53-55), and the angel of his presence saved them (the Lord rescued the children of Israel from Egypt): in his love and in his pity he redeemed them; and he bare them, and carried them all the days of old (See D&C 133:53-55, referring to righteous).

10 But they (the children of Israel) rebelled, and vexed his holy Spirit: therefore he was turned to be their enemy, and he fought against them. (i.e., He had to discipline them severely)

11 Then he remembered, (His people remembered) the days of old, Moses, and his people, saying, Where is he that brought them (us) up out of the sea (parting of the Red Sea) with the shepherd (leaders) of his flock? where is he that put his holy Spirit within him? (within them; Isaiah reminds the people that they had been greatly blessed by the Lord in times past, verses 11-14, in contrast to wicked Israel's punishments in

Isaiah's day and for centuries since then.)

12 That led them by the right hand of Moses with his glorious arm, dividing the water (parting the Red Sea) before them, to make himself an everlasting name?

13 That led them (Children of Israel) through the deep (Red Sea), as (easily as a) an horse in the wilderness (walks along in the desert), that they should not stumble?

14 As a beast goeth (as cattle walk easily) down into the valley, the Spirit of the LORD caused him (them, ie. Israelites) to rest: so didst thou lead thy people, to make thyself a glorious name (you lead your people and became very famous as a result).

15 (Isaiah pleads with the Lord to bless Israel) Look down from heaven, and behold from the habitation of thy holiness (German: from your heavenly home) and of thy glory: where is thy zeal and thy strength, the sounding of thy bowels (thy tenderness) and of thy mercies toward me? are they restrained?

16 Doubtless thou art our father, though Abraham be ignorant of us, and Israel acknowledge us not (Abraham is long since dead, can't help us. Jacob is long since dead, can't help us): thou, O LORD, art our father, our redeemer; thy name is from everlasting (German: you have been our Redeemer since the beginning).

17 O LORD, why hast thou made (JST: suffered, i.e., allowed; German:

allowed) us to err from thy ways, and hardened (allowed us to harden) our heart from thy fear (German: to the point that we no longer feared you)? Return for thy servants' sake, the tribes of thine inheritance (i.e., let us be thy people again).

18 The people of thy holiness have possessed it (the temple) but a little while: our adversaries have trodden down thy sanctuary (the temple, D&C 64:11, ie. enemies have possessed the temple more than we have through the ages).

19 We are thine: thou never barest rule over them (German: we have become just like people over whom you have never ruled); they were not called by thy name (Like people who are not your covenant people, not bearing your name.).

ISAIAH 64

Isaiah continues the theme of 63:15, desiring that the Lord would come down now and rule over Israel.

1 Oh that thou wouldest rend the heavens, that thou wouldest come down, that the mountains might flow down at thy presence,

2 As when the melting fire burneth, the fire causeth the waters to boil, to make thy name known to thine adversaries, that the nations may tremble at thy presence!

3 When thou didst terrible things (German: because of the miracles you

do) which we looked not for (German: which we didn't expect), thou camest down, the mountains flowed down at thy presence.

4 For since the beginning of the world men have not heard, nor perceived by the ear, neither hath the eye seen, O God, beside thee, what he hath prepared for him that waiteth for him (trusts in Him; i.e., no one can even imagine the blessings the Lord has in store for the righteous).

5 Thou meetest (you guide) him that rejoiceth and worketh righteousness, those that remember thee in thy ways: behold, thou art wroth; for we have sinned: in those is continuance, and we shall be saved.

6 But (JST: we have sinned:) we are all as an unclean thing, and all our righteousnesses are as filthy rags (the few things we do right are of little value because of our gross wickedness); and we all do fade as a leaf (we are fading away because of wickedness); and our iniquities, like the wind, have taken us away (i.e., our wickedness has separated us from thee).

7 And there is none that calleth upon thy name (no one turns to the Lord), that stirreth up himself to take hold of thee: for thou hast hid thy face from us, and hast consumed us, because of our iniquities (i.e., we have separated ourselves from you).

8 But now ("And yet"), O LORD, thou art our father; we are the clay, and thou our potter (our maker); and we all are the work of thy hand.

9 Be not wroth very sore (please don't be too angry with us), O LORD, neither remember (our) iniquity for ever: behold, see, we beseech thee, we are all thy people.

10 Thy holy cities are a wilderness, Zion is a wilderness, Jerusalem a desolation (i.e., much destruction has come to us already because of our wickedness).

11 Our holy and our beautiful house (temple), where our fathers praised thee, is burned up with fire: and all our pleasant (German: beautiful-to-look-at) things are laid waste.

12 Wilt thou refrain thyself for these things (continue to withhold blessings despite our pleas), O LORD? wilt thou hold thy peace (keep silent), and afflict us very sore (continue to punish us severely i.e., please have mercy on us!)?

ISAIAH 65

1 (Note: JST, verse one, seems to answer the question in 64:12, "How long will you remain silent and keep punishing us?") I am sought of them that asked not for me (JST: I am found of them who seek after me. I give unto all them that ask of me;); I am (JST: I am not) found of them that sought me not (JST: or that inquireth not after me): I said (JST: unto my servant [probably meaning Isaiah]), Behold me, behold me (JST: look unto me), (JST: I will send you) unto a nation that was (JST: is) not called by my name (i.e., that has not taken upon

them my name).

2 I have spread out my hands (i.e., invited them to come unto me) all the day (constantly) unto a rebellious people, which walketh in a way that was not good, after their own thoughts (i.e., they are rebellious and wicked);

3 A people that provoketh me to anger continually to my face; that sacrificeth in gardens, and burneth incense upon altars of brick (Ex. 20:25 commanded them to use unhewn [uncut] stones in making altars; i.e., they just won't obey God!);

4 Which remain (German: sit) among the graves (implies that they were breaking the commandment in Lev. 19:31, i.e., were attempting to commune with spirits of the dead), and lodge in the monuments (German: hang around the graveyards overnight), which eat swine's flesh (strictly forbidden by Mosaic law), and broth of abominable (unclean) things is in their vessels (i.e., they are breaking every rule in the book!);

5 Which say, Stand by thyself ("stay away from me"), come not near to me; for I am holier than thou. These are a smoke in my nose (i.e., such hypocrites are a constant source of irritation to God), a fire that burneth all the day.

6 Behold, it is written before me: I will not keep silence, but will recompense (pay back, reward), even recompense into their bosom (i.e., drop their sins right back into their own laps; they will be held account-

able for their wickedness),

7 Your iniquities, and the iniquities of your fathers together (along with), saith the LORD, which have burned incense upon the mountains, and blasphemed me upon the hills (i.e., your ancestors also rebelled): therefore will I measure their former work into their bosom (I will drop their sins right back into their laps).

8 Thus saith the LORD, As the new wine (fresh grape juice) is found in the cluster (of grapes, i.e., there is still potential for good in Israel), and one saith, Destroy it not; for a blessing is in it (i.e., Israel still has potential): so will I do for my servants' sakes, that I may not destroy them all (a remnant of Israel will remain).

9 And I will bring forth a seed (descendants) out of Jacob (Israel), and out of Judah an inheritor of my mountains (God's kingdom and blessings): and mine elect shall inherit it, and my servants shall dwell there.

10 And Sharon shall be a fold of flocks, and the valley of Achor a place for the herds to lie down in, for my people that have sought me (i.e., the righteous will receive wonderful blessings).

11 But ye are they that forsake the LORD, that forget my holy mountain (the gospel etc.), that prepare a table for that troop (Gad, an idol of fortune), and that furnish the drink offering unto that number (Meni, an idol of fate or destiny).

12 Therefore (because of your wickedness) will I number (destine)

you to the sword, and ye shall all bow down to the slaughter (i.e., great destruction will come upon you): because when I called, ye did not answer; when I spake, ye did not hear; but did evil before mine eyes, and did choose that (wickedness) wherein I delighted not.

13 (Isaiah now contrasts rewards for the righteous with punishments for the wicked) Therefore thus saith the Lord GOD, Behold, my servants (the righteous) shall eat, but ye (the wicked) shall be hungry: behold, my servants shall drink, but ye shall be thirsty: behold, my servants shall rejoice, but ye shall be ashamed (put to shame, devastated):

14 Behold, my servants shall sing for joy of heart, but ye shall cry for sorrow of heart, and shall howl for vexation of spirit.

15 And ye (the wicked) shall leave your name for a curse unto my chosen (i.e., it is you, the wicked, who will be cursed): for the Lord GOD shall slay thee (you will be destroyed), and call his servants by another name (i.e., a new name, Isa. 62:2; symbolic of Celestial glory, D&C 130:11):

16 That he who blesseth himself (asks for blessings from the Lord) in the earth shall bless himself in the God of truth (i.e., will pray to God, not idols); and he that sweareth (makes covenants) in the earth shall swear by the God of truth (rather than idols); because the former (past) troubles are forgotten (over), and because

they are hid from mine eyes (i.e., your troubles will then be over, gone).

17 For, behold, I create new heavens and a new earth (paradisiacal conditions during the Millennium): and the former shall not be remembered, nor come into mind (because past troubles will be completely overshadowed by the beauties of millennial life).

18 But be ye glad and rejoice for ever in that which I create: for, behold, I create Jerusalem a rejoicing, and her people a joy.

19 And I will rejoice in Jerusalem, and joy in my people: and the voice of weeping shall be no more heard in her, nor the voice of crying (millennial conditions).

20 There shall be no more thence (during the Millennium) an infant of days. (German: an infant who lives just a few days), nor an old man that hath not filled his days (lived out his years completely): for the child shall die (JST: live to be) an hundred years old; but the sinner being an hundred years old shall be accursed.

21 And they shall build houses, and inhabit them; and they shall plant vineyards, and eat the fruit of them (i.e., no one will attack and take things away during the Millennium).

22 They shall not build, and another inhabit; they shall not plant, and another eat: for as the days (age, D&C 101:30) of a tree (i.e., 100 years, Isa. 65:20) are the days of my people, and mine elect shall long enjoy the work of their hands.

(Conditions during the Millennium)

23 They shall not labour in vain, nor bring forth (German: bear children) for trouble (into a world of trouble); for they (the children you bring forth during the Millennium) are the seed (children) of the blessed (you, the righteous) of the LORD, and their offspring (descendants) with them.

24 And it shall come to pass, that before they call, I will answer; and while they are yet speaking, I will hear (i.e., conditions during the Millennium will be even better than you can imagine!).

25 The wolf and the lamb shall feed together, and the lion shall eat straw like the bullock: and dust shall be the serpent's meat (food). They shall not hurt nor destroy in all my holy mountain, saith the LORD (peace will abound during the Millennium).

ISAIAH 66

1 (The Lord now says that everything he has created is designed for the purpose of developing humble, righteous people.) Thus saith the LORD, The heaven is my throne, and the earth is my footstool: where is the house that ye build unto me? and where is the place of my rest?

2 For all those things hath mine hand made, and those things (everything I have created) have been (created), saith the LORD: but to this man (the humble, righteous person) will I look (i.e., with this type of person I am pleased), even to him that

is poor (humble) and of a contrite spirit, and trembleth at my word (i.e., takes God's word seriously).

3 (Isaiah now switches topics and speaks of Hypocrites.) He (the type of person who wants to look good by offering sacrifices to God, yet intentionally lives in sin) that killeth an ox is as if he slew a man (is like a murderer); he that sacrificeth a lamb, as if he cut off (German: broke) a dog's neck (Ex. 13:13, i.e., his efforts are useless, just as an animal with a broken neck is useless); he that offereth an oblation (a grain offering), as if he offered swine's blood; he that burneth incense, as if he blessed (worshipped) an idol. Yea, they have chosen (i.e., they have their agency) their own ways, and their soul delighteth in their abominations (i.e., they are wicked and like to be so!).

4 I also will choose (i.e., they have "chosen" to have the Lord "choose" to punish them) their delusions (punishments), and will bring their fears (German: that which they dread) upon them; because when I called, none did answer; when I spake, they did not hear (i.e., they have been intentionally disobedient): but they did evil before mine eyes, and chose that in which I delighted not (i.e., they chose wickedness).

5 Hear the word of the LORD, ye (the righteous) that tremble at his word (that take his word seriously); your brethren (i.e., your own people) that hated you, that cast you out for

my name's sake (that persecuted you because you obeyed me), said, Let the LORD be glorified (i.e., let the Lord come and show his power…we're not afraid!; the haughty attitude of the wicked): but he (the Lord) shall appear to your (the righteous) joy, and they (the wicked) shall be ashamed (put to shame, devastated).

6 A voice of noise from the city, a voice from the temple, a voice of the LORD that rendereth recompence to his enemies (i.e., the punishments spoken of will surely come upon the wicked).

7 (Verses 7 and 8 seem to parallel 49:21, "Who hath begotten me these…?" i.e., "Where in the world did all these Israelites come from?". Isaiah is describing the very rapid growth of Zion as the earth is prepared for the Millennium, verse 22.) Before she travailed (went into labor), she brought forth (her child was born); before her pain (labor pains) came, she (perhaps the Church of God, JST: Rev. 12:7, i.e., the Church brings forth the Kingdom of God very rapidly upon the earth) was delivered of a man child (the kingdom of God, JST: Rev. 12:7; i.e., the Kingdom of God will grow much faster than expected).

8 Who hath heard such a thing? who hath seen such things? Shall the earth be made to bring forth in one day (i.e., it will seem to happen overnight!)? or shall a nation (righteous Israel) be born at once? for as soon as Zion

travailed, she brought forth her children (can refer to rapid progress of the work in the last days, or the Second Coming's bringing righteousness or both).

9 Shall I bring to the birth, and not cause to bring forth (i.e., get everything ready and then not follow through with what I have had prophesied)? saith the LORD: shall I cause to bring forth, and shut the womb (stop it at the last moment)? saith thy God.

10 Rejoice ye with Jerusalem (i.e., the Lord's people), and be glad with her, all ye that love her (the Lord's Kingdom): rejoice for joy with her, all ye that mourn for her (i.e., the day will come when joy and peace will reign supreme):

11 (Isaiah now describes wonderful blessings that will come to those who join Zion and seek nourishment from the Lord therein.) That ye may suck, and be satisfied with the breasts of her consolations; that ye may milk out, and be delighted with the abundance of her glory.

12 For thus saith the LORD, Behold, I will extend peace to her (Zion and the righteous) like a river (i.e., a constant supply), and the glory (wealth) of the Gentiles like a flowing stream: then shall ye (the righteous) suck, ye shall be borne upon her sides (German: in her arms), and be dandled (German: held happily) upon her knees.

13 As one whom his mother

comforteth, so will I comfort you (i.e., the righteous will feel right at home with me; millennial conditions); and ye shall be comforted in Jerusalem (God's kingdom).

14 And when ye (the righteous) see this, your heart shall rejoice, and your bones shall flourish like an herb (German: you will green up like lush grass): and the hand of the LORD shall be known toward his servants (i.e., great blessings will come to the righteous), and his indignation toward his enemies (but the wicked will be punished).

15 For, behold, the LORD will come with fire, and with his chariots like a whirlwind, to render his anger with fury, and his rebuke with flames of fire (Second Coming).

16 For by fire and by his sword will the LORD plead with all flesh (judge all people): and the slain of the LORD shall be many (i.e., there will be large numbers of wicked at the Second Coming, and they will be destroyed at his coming).

17 (Isaiah now refers again to forbidden practices among the wicked of Israel, as already mentioned in verse 3.) They (the wicked) that sanctify themselves, and purify themselves in the gardens behind one tree in the midst (i.e., attempting to make themselves holy via false gods etc.), eating swine's flesh (strictly forbidden), and the abomination, and the mouse (a forbidden food, Lev. 11:29), shall be consumed together (at the same time at the Second Coming), saith the LORD.

18 For I know their (the wicked) works and their thoughts (and that is why they will be destroyed): (Isaiah begins a new topic now, the gathering) it shall come, that I will gather all nations and tongues; and they shall come, and see my glory.

19 And I will set a sign (see Isa. 5:26, "ensign", i.e., the true gospel, certainly including the Book of Mormon as explained in 3 N. 21:1-7) among them (the remnant of Israel), and I will send those that escape of them (a righteous remnant, Isa. 37:32, of Israel; missionary work) unto the nations, to Tarshish (Spain?), Pul (Lybia), and Lud, that draw the bow (i.e., famous for skilled archers), to Tubal (Turkey), and Javan (Greece; Isaiah has thus described basically all the commonly known world in his day), to the isles afar off (to all nations), that have not heard my fame, neither have seen my glory; and they shall declare my glory among the Gentiles (i.e., the gospel will be preached to all nations).

20 And they (the missionaries; the true Church) shall bring all your brethren (Israelites; i.e., the gathering) for an offering (righteous lives; see I Samuel 15:22) unto the LORD out of all nations upon horses, and in chariots (Jeremiah 23:3), and in litters, and upon mules, and upon swift beasts, to my holy mountain Jerusalem (i.e., to the true gospel),

saith the LORD, as the children of Israel bring an offering in a clean vessel into the house of the LORD.

21 And I will also take of them for priests and for Levites, saith the LORD (i.e., the priesthood will be restored to men in the final scenes).

22 For as the new heavens and the new earth (can refer to millennial earth, D&C 101:25, and celestial earth, D&C 130:9; 88:18, 19, 25, 26), which I will make, shall remain (will be eternal) before me, saith the LORD, so shall your seed (families) and your name (symbolic of celestial glory, D&C 130:11) remain (i.e., you and your families can be with me forever).

23 And it shall come to pass, that from one new moon (special Sabbath ritual at beginning of month, see Bible Dictionary, "New Moon", p. 738) to another, and from one Saybbath to another, shall all flesh come to worship before me, saith the LORD (i.e., the righteous are those who will be completely consistent and faithful during the Millennium and beyond).

24 And they (the righteous) shall go forth, and look upon the carcases of the men that have transgressed against me (they will be aware that the judgements of God did finally come upon the wicked): for their worm (a scarlet dye was made from the dried body of a certain type of female worm [coccus ilicis]. Scarlet was considered a "color-fast" dye, i.e., permanent, lasting. Hence, "their worm shall not die" implies that, even though their dead bodies can be seen, the "permanent" part of them [spirit up until the resurrection of the wicked, then their resurrected bodies] will live forever and they will thus face the consequences of their wicked choices forever.) shall not die, neither shall their fire be quenched; and they shall be an abhorring unto all flesh (a final warning from Isaiah that wickedness does not pay at all!)

Isaiah
in the
Book of Mormon
Made Easier

Compiled by

David J. Ridges

1 NEPHI 20

Note: Every verse in this chapter reads differently than in Isaiah 48 in the Bible. Nephi lived just 100 years after Isaiah which puts him much closer to the original records containing Isaiah's writings, including the brass plates. Also note that Nephi's main reason for teaching his people from Isaiah is to give them hope, not to condemn them. See 1 Nephi 19:23-24. We would do well to keep this major message of Isaiah in mind also, rather than seeing him only as a dismal prophet of doom as so many people do.

1 Hearken and hear this, O house of Jacob (the 12 Tribes of Israel), who are called by the name of Israel (Jacob), and are come forth out of the waters of Judah, or out of the waters of baptism, who swear (make covenants) by the name of the Lord (Just as we, today, make covenants in the name of Jesus Christ), and make mention of (pray to and talk about) the God of Israel, yet they swear not in truth nor in righteousness (i.e., the problem is that they claim to be the Lord's people but break covenants, don't live the gospel).

2 Nevertheless, they call themselves of the holy city (claim to be the Lord's people), but they do not stay themselves (rely) upon the God of Israel, who is the Lord of Hosts; yea, the Lord of Hosts is his name.

3 (In the next several verses, Isaiah reminds Israel that there is no lack of obvious evidence that the true God exists.) Behold, I (the Lord) have declared the former things (prophecies) from the beginning (so you would have plenty of evidence that I exist); and they (prophecies) went forth out of my mouth, and I showed them. I did show them suddenly (so you can know I really am your God, and your idols are false; see Isaiah 42:9).

4 And I (the Lord) did it because I knew that thou art obstinate, and thy neck is an iron sinew (you are not humble, won't bend your neck in humility), and thy brow brass (thick-headed, i.e., it is hard to get anything through your thick skulls);

5 And I have even from the beginning declared to thee (prophesied things); before it (the prophesied events) came to pass I showed them thee; and I showed them for fear lest thou shouldst say__mine idol hath done them, and my graven image, and my molten image hath commanded them (I have shown you my power via prophecies so you couldn't claim your idols have power).

6 Thou hast seen and heard all this (all this obvious evidence that I exist); and will ye not declare (acknowledge) them? And that I have showed thee new things (things you couldn't possibly have known in advance) from this time, even hidden things, and thou didst not know them (didn't pay attention).

7 They are created now (the prophesied events are happening now), and not from the beginning (you couldn't have guessed they were going to happen back then when the prophecies were given), even before the day when thou heardest them not (back then when there was no clue that the prophesied events would take place) they were declared unto thee (I told you in advance), lest thou shouldst say__Behold I knew them.

8 Yea, and thou heardest not (you ignored the prophecies); yea, thou knewest not; yea, from that time thine ear was not opened (you refused to listen); for I knew that thou wouldst deal very treacherously, and wast called a transgressor from the womb (I've had trouble with you Israelites right from the start!).

9 Nevertheless, for my name's sake (i.e., I, the Lord, have a reputation to uphold, of being merciful) will I defer mine anger, and for my praise (German: glory, honor; reputation) will I refrain from thee, that I cut thee not off (I'll not destroy you completely).

10 For, behold, I (the Lord) have refined thee (Israel), I have chosen thee (German: I will make you) in the furnace of affliction (i.e., I will purify you in the refiner's fire).

11 For mine own sake (because I love you. See verse 14), yea, for mine own sake will I do this (refine and purify you in the furnace of affliction), for I will not suffer my name to be polluted (German: lest my name be

slandered for not keeping my promise), and I will not give my glory unto another (I will remain true to you. See Jeremiah 3:14; good advice for marriage partners).

12 Hearken unto me, O Jacob, and Israel my called (i.e., you have a calling; see Abr. 2:9-11. The theme of verses 12-17 is that Israel is called to serve), for I am he (Christ); I am the first, and I am also the last (i.e., I am your Savior; Jesus was there at the creation and will be there at final judgement).

13 Mine hand hath also laid the foundation of the earth (i.e., I am the creator), and my right hand (covenant hand; hand of power) hath spanned the heavens (spread out, i.e., created, the skies). I call unto them (Israel in verses 12 and 14) and they stand up together (i.e., let them, Israel, all stand up and listen; this goes with the first part of verse 14).

14 All ye, assemble yourselves, and hear; who among them (perhaps referring to Israel's idols; see verse 5.) hath declared these things (prophecies; see verses 3, 6 etc.) unto them (Israel)? The Lord hath loved him (Israel); yea, and he (the Lord) will fulfill his word which he hath declared by them (the prophets); and he will do his pleasure on Babylon, and his arm shall come upon the Chaldeans (Southern Babylon; i.e., Babylon will eventually be destroyed, just as prophesied).

15 Also, saith the Lord; I the Lord, yea, I have spoken; yea, I have called him (Israel) to declare (Israel has a

job to do), I have brought him, and he shall make his way prosperous (God will help; could also mean that Heavenly Father called Christ to prophesy; also that Christ called Isaiah to prophesy).

16 Come ye (Israel) near unto me; I have not spoken in secret (I have been very open about the gospel etc.); from the beginning, from the time that it was declared have I spoken; and the Lord God, and his Spirit, hath sent me (the Father sent Christ; or perhaps this means that Christ sent Isaiah).

17 And thus saith the Lord, thy Redeemer (Christ), the Holy One of Israel; I have sent him (Israel; see verses 12 and 19; or, dualistically, this could refer to Isaiah), the Lord thy God who teacheth thee to profit (German: for your profit, benefit), who leadeth thee by the way thou shouldst go, hath done it.

18 O that thou hadst hearkened to my commandments (applies directly to Laman and Lemuel)__ then had thy peace been as a river (you could have had peace flowing constantly into your lives), and thy righteousness as the waves of the sea (steady, constant).

19 Thy seed also had been (would have been) as the sand; the offspring of thy bowels (your descendants) like the gravel (grains of sand) thereof; his (Israel's) name should not have been cut off nor destroyed from before me (i.e., Israel could have had it very good, and avoided such great destruction).

20 Go ye forth of Babylon (stop being wicked), flee ye from the Chaldeans (wickedness; Chaldeans were residents of southern Babylon), with a voice of singing (be happy about being righteous) declare ye, tell this, utter to the end of the earth; say ye: The Lord hath redeemed his servant Jacob (Israel can be saved, including Laman and Lemuel, if they will repent).

21 And they thirsted not; he led them through the deserts; he caused the waters to flow out of the rock for them; he clave the rock also and the waters gushed out (i.e., just look what the Lord can do for those who trust in him!).

22 And notwithstanding (even though) he hath done all this, and greater also, there is no peace, saith the Lord, unto the wicked (a major message for Laman and Lemuel and all of us).

1 NEPHI 21

1 And again: Hearken, O ye house of Israel, all ye that are broken off and are driven out (i.e., scattered; Isaiah is speaking prophetically to scattered Israel) because of the wickedness of the pastors (leaders and teachers) of my people; yea, all ye that are broken off, that are scattered abroad, who are of my people, O house of Israel. Listen, O isles (far away nations and lands, including those across the sea), unto me (Israel; see verse 3), and hearken ye people from far; the Lord

hath called me (Israel) from the womb (foreordination); from the bowels of my mother hath he (the Lord) made mention of my name (Israel has had a job to do since the beginning).

2 And he hath made my mouth like a sharp sword (Israel is to spread the gospel, which is hard on the wicked, but enables the righteous to cut through falsehood); in the shadow (shade; protection) of his hand hath he hid me, and made me a polished shaft (i.e., an effective servant, such as Joseph Smith, Isaiah or any faithful Israelites); in his quiver hath he hid me;

3 And said unto me (Israel): Thou art my servant, O Israel, in whom I will be glorified (Israel will yet fulfill its stewardship).

4 (In verses 4-12, Isaiah represents the loneliness of Israel waiting for the restoration) Then I said, I have labored in vain (i.e., I haven't been a very good servant), I have spent my strength for naught and in vain (in false religions and riotous living); surely my judgment is with the Lord, and my work with my God.

5 And now, saith the Lord__that formed me from the womb that I (especially Ephraim) should be his servant, to bring Jacob again to him__though Israel be not gathered, yet shall I be glorious in the eyes of the Lord (i.e., if I do my best, I'll be OK, even if people reject my message), and my God shall be my strength.

6 And he (the Lord) said: It is a light

thing (German: not enough) that thou (Israel) shouldst be my servant to raise up the tribes of Jacob, and to restore the preserved (remnant) of Israel (the job of the Church today). I will also give thee (another assignment) for a light to the Gentiles (quite a prophecy in Isaiah's day when almost any nation that wanted to could walk all over Israel), that thou mayest be my salvation unto the ends of the earth (to everyone).

7 Thus saith the Lord, the Redeemer of Israel, his (Israel's) Holy One, to him (Israel) whom man despiseth, to him whom the nation abhorreth (German: to the nation abhorred by others), to servant of rulers (for much of past history, Israel has been servants and slaves to many nations): Kings shall see and arise (out of respect for Israel), princes (leaders of nations) also shall worship, because of the Lord that is faithful.

8 Thus saith the Lord: In an acceptable time (beginning with the restoration and Joseph Smith) have I heard thee, O isles of the sea (far continents beyond Asia such as America, Africa etc), and in a day of salvation have I helped thee; and I will preserve thee, and give thee my servant (prophets, including Joseph Smith) for a covenant of the people, to establish the earth, to cause to inherit the desolate heritages (i.e., the gathering will take place; see verse 19);

9 That thou mayest say to the prisoners (the living and the dead in spiritual darkness): Go forth; to them

132

that sit in darkness: Show yourselves. They shall feed in the ways, and their pastures shall be in all high places (they will partake of the gospel).

10 They shall not hunger nor thirst, neither shall the heat nor the sun smite them; for he that hath mercy on them shall lead them, even by the springs of water shall he guide them (benefits of accepting and living the gospel).

11 And I will make all my mountains a way, and my highways shall be exalted.

12 And then (in the days of gathering), O house of Israel, behold, these (Israel) shall come from far; and lo, these from the north and from the west; and these from the land of Sinim (Strong's Exhaustive Bible Concordance says this might refer to inhabitants of southern China).

13 Sing, O heavens; and be joyful, O earth; for the feet of those who are in the east shall be established; and break forth into singing, O mountains; for they shall be smitten no more; for the Lord hath comforted his people, and will have mercy upon his afflicted (the Lord will eventually redeem Israel).

14 But, behold, Zion (Israel) hath said: The Lord hath forsaken me, and my Lord hath forgotten me (wicked Israel's complaint)__but he will show that he hath not.

15 For can a woman forget her sucking child, that she should not have compassion on the son of her womb? Yea, they may forget, yet will I not forget thee, O house of Israel (a promise!).

16 Behold, I have graven thee upon the palms of my hands (I will be crucified for you; just as a workman's hands bear witness of his work, so shall nail prints in my hands bear witness of my work for you); thy walls are continually before me (I'll not forget you).

17 Thy children shall make haste against thy destroyers (your descendants will finally gain the upper hand against your enemies); and they that made thee waste shall go forth of thee (will flee from you, i.e., the tables will be turned in the last days).

18 Lift up thine eyes (i.e., let me show you—complaining Israel in verse 14—the future) round about and behold; all these gather themselves together (You thought you were going to be wiped out completely, but look at all your descendants in the future!), and they shall come to thee. And as I live, saith the Lord, thou shalt surely clothe thee with them all, as with an ornament, and bind them on even as a bride (a bride puts on her finest clothing for the occasion, i.e., Israel will have her finest descendants in the last days).

19 For thy waste and thy desolate places, and the land of thy destruction (you've been trodden down for centuries), shall even now be too narrow by reason of the inhabitants (you will have so many people you'll seem to be running out of room; latter-day gathering of Israel); and they (your former enemies) that swal-

lowed thee up shall be far away.

20 The children (converts to the true gospel) whom thou shalt have, after thou hast lost the first (via apostasy, war etc.), shall again in thine ears say: The place is too strait for me (there's not enough room for us all); give place to me that I may dwell.

21 Then shalt thou (Israel) say in thine heart: Who hath begotten me these (where in the world did all these Israelites come from!), seeing I have lost my children, and am desolate, a captive, and removing to and fro (scattered)? And who hath brought up these? Behold, I was left alone (I thought I was finished off, done for); these, where have they been?

22 (The Lord now answers the question, "Where did all these come from?") Thus saith the Lord God: Behold, I will lift up mine hand to the Gentiles, and set up my standard (the Church, true gospel of Christ) to the people; and they (the gentiles) shall bring thy sons in their arms, and thy daughters shall be carried upon their shoulders (i.e., gentile nations will help gather Israel).

23 And kings shall be thy nursing fathers, and their queens thy nursing mothers (example: Great Britain sponsored the return of the Jews to Palestine in 1948); they (the leaders of nations) shall bow down to thee with their face towards the earth, and lick up the dust of thy feet (the tables will be turned in the last days); and thou shalt know that I am the Lord; for they shall not be ashamed that

wait for (trust in) me.

24 For shall the prey (Israel) be taken from the mighty (enemies), or the lawful captives (the Lord's covenant people) delivered (set free, i.e., Israel asks how they can be freed from such powerful enemies)?

25 But thus saith the Lord, even the captives (Israel) of the mighty (powerful enemies) shall be taken away, and the prey (victims) of the terrible (tyrants) shall be delivered (set free); for I (the Lord) will contend with him that contendeth with thee (Israel), and I will save thy children (i.e., the answer to Israel's question in verse 24 is that the Lord will save them).

26 And I will feed them (Israel's enemies) that oppress thee with their own flesh; they shall be drunken (out of control) with their own blood as with sweet wine (your enemies will turn against each other and destroy themselves); and all flesh shall know that I, the Lord, am thy Savior and thy Redeemer, the Mighty One of Jacob.

2 NEPHI 7

Note: This chapter speaks of the future as if it had already happened.

1 (The Lord asks the question, "Did I divorce you or did you divorce me?" i.e., "Did I leave you or did you leave me?") Yea, for thus saith the Lord: Have I put thee away (divorced you), or have I cast thee off forever? For thus saith the Lord: Where is the bill

of your mother's divorcement? To whom have I put thee away, or to which of my creditors have I sold you (i.e., Was it I who sold you)? Yea, to whom have I sold you? Behold, for your iniquities have ye sold yourselves (i.e., you brought it upon yourselves!), and for your transgressions is your mother (your apostate nation; Hosea 2:2) put away.

2 Wherefore (this is why), when I (Jesus) came, there was no man (who received me as the Messiah); when I called, yea, there was none to answer (nobody responded). O house of Israel, is my hand shortened at all that it cannot redeem, or have I no power to deliver (have I lost my power)? Behold, at my rebuke (command) I dry up the sea, I make their rivers a wilderness and their fish to stink because the waters are dried up, and they die because of thirst (I haven't lost my power).

3 I clothe the heavens with blackness, and I make sackcloth their covering (I can cause the sky to be dark during the day as if it were mourning the dead. In fact it will at Jesus' crucifixion; see Matt 27:45).

4 The Lord God (the Father) hath given me (Jesus; see verse 6) the tongue of the learned (i.e., Father taught me well), that I should know how to speak a word (a strengthening and comforting word) in season unto thee, O house of Israel. When ye are weary he waketh morning by morning. He waketh mine ear to hear as the learned (German: He, the

Father, is constantly communicating with me and I hear as his disciple).

5 The Lord God (the Father) hath opened mine ear, and I was not rebellious (hint, hint, Israel), neither turned away back (I accomplished my calling, the atonement; you should do yours as given in 1 Nephi 21:6).

6 (Isaiah now prophecies some details surrounding Christ's crucifixion.) I gave my back to the smiter (scourging; see Matt. 27:26), and my cheeks to them that plucked off the hair (pulled out whiskers of my beard). I hid not my face from shame and spitting (as my time for crucifixion came).

7 For the Lord God (Father) will help me, therefore shall I not be confounded (I'll not be stopped). Therefore have I set my face like a flint (I have braced myself for the ordeal), and I know that I shall not be ashamed (will not fail).

8 And the Lord (the Father; see verse 9; could refer to Isaiah too) is near, and he justifieth me (i.e., approves of everything I do). Who will contend with me (i.e., who is willing to go against such odds)? Let us stand together (go to court as in a court of law). Who is mine adversary? Let him come near me (face me), and I will smite him with the strength of my mouth.

9 For the Lord God (the Father) will help me. And all they who shall condemn me, behold, all they shall wax old as a garment, and the moth shall eat them up (the wicked will

have their day, then reap the punishment).

10 Who is among you that feareth (respects) the Lord, that obeyeth the voice of his servant (prophets), that walketh in darkness and hath no light? (Answer. No one because the Lord blesses his followers with light.)

11 Behold all ye (the wicked) that kindle fire, that compass (surround) yourselves about with sparks, walk in the light of your fire and in the sparks which ye have kindled (trying to live without God, according to your own philosophies). This shall ye have of mine hand__ye shall lie down in sorrow (i.e., misery awaits those who try to live without God).

2 NEPHI 8

1 Hearken unto me, ye that follow after righteousness (i.e., the Lord is now speaking to the righteous). Look unto the rock (i.e., the good, solid rock—Abraham and Sarah) from whence ye are hewn, and to the hole of the pit (the rock quarry) from whence ye are digged (consider your origins; i.e., you are really somebody!).

2 Look unto Abraham, your father, and unto Sarah, she that bare you (side by side with Abraham in importance); for I called him alone (when he was childless), and blessed him (see Abraham 2:9-11).

3 For the Lord shall comfort Zion, he will comfort all her waste places; and he will make her wilderness like Eden, and her desert like the garden of the Lord (the Garden of Eden). Joy and gladness shall be found therein, thanksgiving and the voice of melody (wonderful reward for the righteous).

4 Hearken unto me (Christ), my people; and give ear unto me, O my nation; for a law shall proceed from me (teachings, doctrines; see Isaiah 51:4, footnote a), and I will make my judgment to rest for a light for the people (i.e., my laws will bring light to the nations).

5 My righteousness (my ability to save you; triumph) is near; my salvation is gone forth, and mine arm shall judge the people. The isles (nations of the world) shall wait (trust, rely) upon me, and on mine arm (my power) shall they trust.

6 Lift up your eyes to the heavens, and look upon the earth beneath; for the heavens shall vanish away like smoke (D&C 29:23-24), and the earth shall wax old like a garment; and they that dwell therein shall die in like manner. But my salvation (the salvation I bring) shall be forever, and my righteousness (triumph, victory) shall not be abolished (glad message of hope; compare with D&C 1:38).

7 Hearken unto me, ye that know righteousness (i.e., you who are righteous), the people in whose heart I have written my law (you who have taken my gospel to heart), fear ye not the reproach (insults) of men, neither be ye afraid of their revilings (stinging criticisms).

8 For the moth shall eat them (the

wicked who revile against the righteous) up like a garment (they will vanish like moth-eaten clothing), and the worm shall eat them like wool. But my righteousness (salvation and deliverance) shall be (last) forever, and my salvation from generation to generation (i.e., throughout eternity).

9 (Righteous Israel now replies, invites the Lord to exercise his power in their behalf like he did in ancient times.) Awake, awake! Put on strength, O arm (symbolic of power) of the Lord; awake as in the ancient days (help us like you did in days gone by). Art thou not he that hath cut Rahab (i.e., trimmed Egypt down to size. Rahab is a mythical sea monster and symbolically represents Satan and nations who serve him), and wounded the dragon (Satan; see Rev. 12:7-9)?

10 Art thou not he who hath dried the sea (Red Sea), the waters of the great deep; that hath made the depths of the sea a way (pathway) for the ransomed (redeemed, i.e., you redeemed the Children of Israel from Egypt; symbolic of the Atonement's redeeming us from our sins) to pass over (parting of the Red Sea)?

11 Therefore (i.e., because of your power), the redeemed of the Lord shall return (the gathering), and come with singing unto Zion; and everlasting joy and holiness shall be upon their heads; and they shall obtain gladness and joy; sorrow and mourning shall flee away (ultimate results of righteousness).

12 (The Lord now replies to right-eous Israel's request in verse 9). I am he; yea, I am he that comforteth you. Behold, who art thou, that thou shouldst be afraid of man (mortal man), who shall die (i.e., trust in God, not man), and of the son of man (mortal men), who shall be made like unto grass (short-lived glory)?

13 And forgettest the Lord thy maker, that hath stretched forth the heavens, and laid the foundations of the earth (i.e., how could you forget me, your Creator, after all I've done for you?), and hast feared continually every day, because of the fury of the oppressor (Israel's captors who have oppressed them; see 2 Nephi 8, footnote 13c), as if he were ready to destroy (German: whose intent is to destroy, i.e., why should you live in fear of mortal men)? And where is the fury of the oppressor? (If you live righteously, the day will come when enemies won't be able to hurt you anymore.)

14 The captive exile hasteneth, that he may be loosed (i.e., the day will come when Israel will be set free; see Isaiah 52:1-2), and that he should not die in the pit (i.e., not die in captivity), nor that his bread should fail (i.e., run out; famine etc.)

15 But I am the Lord thy God, whose waves roared (as they drowned Pharaoh's armies in the Red Sea; see 1 Nephi 4:2); the Lord of Hosts is my name.

16 And I have put my words in thy mouth (i.e., have given you my gospel), and have covered (protected)

thee in the shadow of mine hand, that I may plant the heavens and lay the foundations of the earth (I created the heavens and the earth), and say unto Zion: Behold, thou art my people (I haven't deserted you).

17 Awake, awake, stand up, O Jerusalem, which hast drunk at the hand of the Lord the cup of his fury__thou hast drunken the dregs (bitter residue at the bottom) of the cup of trembling wrung out (you have paid a terrible price for your wickedness)__

18 And none to guide her (Israel) among all the sons she hath brought forth (i.e., you have spent many years without prophets); neither that taketh her by the hand, of all the sons she hath brought up (You have spent many years without prophets).

19 These two sons (two prophets in the last days who will help keep enemies of the Jews from totally destroying them; see Rev. 11) are come unto thee, who shall be sorry for thee (who will care about you)__thy desolation and destruction, and the famine and the sword__and by whom shall I comfort thee?

20 Thy sons (your people) have fainted (German: are on their last leg), save these two (the two prophets in Rev. 11); they (your people) lie at the head of all the streets (German: are being destroyed right and left); as a wild bull in a net (implies that they are trapped in a net woven by their own wickedness), they are full of the fury of the Lord (i.e., they are catching the

full fury of the Lord), the rebuke of thy God (the punishments of God).

21 Therefore hear now this, thou (Israel) afflicted, and drunken (out of control), and not with wine (rather, with wickedness):

22 Thus saith thy Lord, the Lord and thy God pleadeth the cause of his people (I have not deserted you); behold, I have taken out of thine hand the cup of trembling, the dregs of the cup of my fury; thou shalt no more drink it again (Christ will save the Jews in the last days; see 2 Nephi 9:1-2).

23 But I will put it (the cup in verse 22) into the hand of them that afflict thee (your enemies will get what they gave you); who have said to thy soul: Bow down, that we may go over (i.e., lie down while we walk all over you!)__and thou hast laid thy body as the ground and as the street to them that went over (i.e., you have been walked on by your enemies).

24 Awake, awake, put on thy strength, O Zion (return to the proper use of the priesthood; see D&C 113:7,8); put on thy beautiful garments (i.e., dress in your finest and prepare to be with the Savior; see Rev. 21:2-3), O Jerusalem, the holy city; for henceforth there shall no more come into thee the uncircumcised and the unclean (i.e., the wicked).

25 Shake thyself from the dust (from being walked on, verse 23; see also 2 Nephi 13:26); arise (from being walked on, verse 23), sit down (in dignity, redeemed at last), O

Jerusalem; loose thyself (free your-self) from the bands of thy neck (from captivity, bondage, wickedness), O captive daughter of Zion.

2 NEPHI 12

Note: Chapters 12, 13 and 14 go together. Also note that of the 433 verses of Isaiah quoted in the Book of Mormon, over half of them are given differently than in the King James Bible, while about 200 of them are the same; see 2 Nephi 12, footnote 2a. Thus, the Book of Mormon is a major source of clarification and help for understanding Isaiah.

1 The word that Isaiah, the son of Amoz, saw concerning Judah and Jerusalem:

2 And it shall come to pass in the last days, when the mountain ("high place", i.e., temples will be estab-lished) of the Lord's house shall be established in the top of the moun-tains, and shall be exalted above the hills (you can get "higher", i.e., closer to God in the temples through covenant-making than on the highest mountains), and all nations (the gath-ering involves people from every nation) shall flow unto it.

3 And many people shall go and say, Come ye, and let us go up to the mountain (temple) of the Lord, to the house (temples) of the God of Jacob (Israel); and he will teach us of his ways, and we will walk in his paths (we will be obedient); for out of Zion

shall go forth the law, and the word of the Lord from Jerusalem ("law" and "word" are synonyms).

4 And he shall judge among the nations, and shall rebuke many people: and they shall beat their swords into plow-shares (i.e., then the Millennium will come), and their spears into pruning-hooks (there will be peace)__nation shall not lift up sword against nation, neither shall they learn war any more (Millennium).

5 (Isaiah now switches from the future back to his own time and people.) O house of Jacob (Israel), come ye and let us walk in the light of the Lord; yea, come, for ye have all gone astray, every one to his wicked ways.

6 Therefore (this is the reason why), O Lord, thou hast forsaken thy people, the house of Jacob (the Israelites), because they be replen-ished from the east (are adopting false eastern religions), and hearken unto soothsayers like the Philistines (are into witchcraft, sorcery etc.; see 3 Nephi 21:16), and they please them-selves in the children of strangers (are mixing and marrying with foreigners, people not of covenant Israel).

7 Their land also is full of silver and gold, neither is there any end of their treasures (have become materialistic); their land is also full of horses, neither is there any end of their chariots (horses and chariots represent military equipment and preparations for war).

8 Their land is also full of idols;

they worship the work of their own hands, that which their own fingers have made (an absurd thing to do; emphasizing that wickedness does not promote rational thought, a theme Isaiah pursues throughout his writings).

9 And the mean (poor, low in social status) man boweth not down, and the great (wealthy, powerful, high in social status) man humbleth himself not, therefore, forgive him not (nobody is humble, therefore, no forgiveness!).

10 O ye wicked ones, enter into the rock (caves; see verse 19), and hide thee in the dust, for the fear of the Lord and the glory of his majesty shall smite thee (you will not be able to stand the brightness of his glory at the Second Coming and will thus be consumed; see D&C 5:19).

11 And it shall come to pass that the lofty looks (pride) of man shall be humbled, and the haughtiness of men shall be bowed down, and the Lord alone shall be exalted in that day (i.e., will demonstrate power over all things at the Second Coming).

12 For the day of the Lord of Hosts (2nd Coming) soon cometh upon (Hebrew: "against") all nations, yea, upon every one (who is wicked); yea, upon the proud and lofty, and upon every one who is lifted up, and he shall be brought low.

13 Yea, and the day of the Lord shall come upon all the cedars (high and mighty people) of Lebanon, for they are high and lifted up (pride); and

upon all the oaks (people) of Bashan;

14 And upon all the high mountains, and upon all the hills, and upon all the nations which are lifted up (in pride etc.), and upon every people;

15 And upon every high tower, and upon every fenced wall (man-made defenses);

16 And upon all the ships of the sea, and upon all the ships of Tarshish (noted for ability to travel long distances, carry large cargos and strength as warships), and upon all pleasant pictures (pleasure ships upon which the wealthy traveled).

17 And the loftiness (pride) of man shall be bowed down, and the haughtiness of men shall be made low; and the Lord alone shall be exalted in that day.

18 And the idols he shall utterly abolish.

19 And they (the wicked) shall go into the holes of the rocks (caves), and into the caves of the earth, for the fear of the Lord shall come upon them and the glory of his majesty shall smite them (D&C 5:19), when he ariseth to shake terribly the earth.

20 In that day (2nd Coming) a man shall cast his idols of silver, and his idols of gold, which he hath made for himself to worship (an absurd thing to do), to the moles and to the bats (creatures who live in darkness; symbolical of wicked people who live in spiritual darkness);

21 To go into the clefts of the rocks, and into the tops of the ragged rocks, for the fear of the Lord shall come

upon them and the majesty of his glory shall smite them (D&C 5:19), when he ariseth to shake terribly the earth.

22 Cease ye from man, whose breath is in his nostrils; for wherein is he to be accounted of (why trust in man, i.e., why trust in the arm of flesh when God is truly powerful and can save you)?

2 NEPHI 13

Note: In this chapter as well as others, Isaiah uses a literary technique known as "chiasmus", a writing form in which the author says certain things, then repeats them in reverse order for emphasis.

1 For behold, the Lord, the Lord of Hosts, doth take away from Jerusalem (chiasmus A), and from Judah, the stay (supply) and the staff (support), the whole staff of bread,(chiasmus B) and the whole stay of water (the Lord is going to pull the props out and the whole thing will collapse)__

2 The mighty man, (chiasmus C) and the man of war, the judge, and the prophet, and the prudent, and the ancient (all the stable, capable leaders will be gone);

3 The captain of fifty, and the honorable man, and the counselor (chiasmus D), and the cunning artificer (skilled craftsman), and the eloquent orator (all capable leaders will be gone).

4 And I will give children unto them

to be their princes (leaders), and babes (chiasmus E) shall rule over them (immature, irresponsible leaders will take over).

5 And the people shall be oppressed, (chiasmus F) every one by another (anarchy), and every one by his neighbor; the child shall behave himself proudly against the ancient, (chiasmus E') and the base against the honorable (no respect for authority).

6 When a man shall take hold of his brother of the house of his father, and shall say: Thou hast clothing, be thou our ruler (chiasmus D'), and let not this ruin come under thy hand (don't let this happen to us)__

7 In that day shall he swear (protest), saying: (chiasmus C')I will not be a healer (I can't defend and protect you!; for in my house there is neither bread (chiasmus B') nor clothing (I've got my own problems); make me not a ruler of the people.

8 For Jerusalem is ruined, (chiasmus A') and Judah is fallen, because their tongues and their doings have been against the Lord, to provoke the eyes of his glory (in word and actions, the people are completely against the Lord).

9 The show of their countenance doth witness against them (they even look wicked), and doth declare their sin to be even as Sodom (i.e., wicked through and through, including homosexuality; see Gen. 19, footnote 5a), and they cannot hide it (blatant sin, can't be rationalized away or hidden from God). Wo unto their souls, for

they have rewarded evil unto themselves (i.e., they are getting what they deserve)!

10 Say unto the righteous that it is well with them; for they shall eat the fruit of their doings (righteousness will pay off).

11 Wo unto the wicked, for they shall perish; for the reward of their hands shall be upon them! (As ye sow, so shall ye reap.)

12 And my people, children (immature leaders) are their oppressors, and women rule over them (breakdown of traditional family; men are weak leaders). O my people, they who lead thee cause thee to err and destroy the way of thy paths (leadership without basic gospel values causes terrible damage).

13 The Lord standeth up to plead (Hebrew: contend, i.e., you are in big trouble), and standeth to judge the people.

14 The Lord will enter into judgment with the ancients (the wicked elders) of his people and the princes (leaders) thereof; for ye have eaten up (ruined, destroyed) the vineyard and the spoil of the poor in your houses (you were supposed to protect them, but, instead, you ruin them).

15 What mean ye (what have you got to say for yourselves)? Ye beat my people to pieces, and grind the faces of the poor, saith the Lord God of Hosts.

16 (Isaiah now shows what happens when women get as wicked as men, and points out that when this happens,

society is doomed; see verses 25 and 26.) Moreover, the Lord saith: Because the daughters of Zion are haughty (full of wicked pride), and walk with stretched-forth necks and wanton (lustful) eyes, walking and mincing (short, rapid steps; see Isaiah 3, footnote 16e) as they go, and making a tinkling with their feet (German: wearing expensive shoes so people will notice them)__

17 Therefore (for these reasons) the Lord will smite with a scab the crown of the head (German: make them bald; perhaps the "scab" is a result of being shaved as slaves) of the daughters of Zion, and the Lord will discover their secret parts (expose their evil deeds).

18 In that day the Lord will take away the bravery (German: decoration, beauty) of their tinkling ornaments (German: expensive shoes), and cauls, and round tires like the moon (female ornamentations representing high status in materialistic society);

19 The chains and the bracelets, and the mufflers (veils);

20 The bonnets, and the ornaments of the legs, and the headbands, and the tablets (German: musk boxes, perfume boxes), and the ear-rings;

21 The rings, and nose jewels;

22 The changeable suits of apparel (German: party clothes), and the mantles (German: gowns, robes), and the wimples (medieval womens' head covering), and the crisping-pins (German: money purses);

23 The glasses (German: mirrors; Hebrew: see-through clothing; see Isaiah 3, footnote 23a), and the fine linen, and hoods (turbans), and the veils (Isaiah has described female high-society fashions, arrogance and materialism in terms of such things in his day).

24 And it shall come to pass, instead of sweet smell there shall be stink (from corpses of people killed by invading armies; also slavery); and instead of a girdle (German: nice waistband), a rent (torn rags); and instead of well set hair, baldness (slaves had shaved heads); and instead of a stomacher (a nice robe), a girding of sackcloth; burning (branding, a mark of slavery; see Isaiah 3, footnote 24d) instead of beauty.

25 Thy men shall fall by the sword and thy mighty in the war (wars will deplete your male population).

26 And her (Jerusalem's; see verse 8) gates shall lament and mourn; and she shall be desolate (empty, cleaned out; see Isa. 3, footnote 26d), and shall sit upon the ground (i.e., Jerusalem, symbolic of the wicked, will be brought down completely).

2 NEPHI 14

Note: The Joseph Smith Translation, the Hebrew Bible and the German Bible put this next verse at the end of Isaiah, chapter 3 (which would be 2 Nephi 13 in the Book of Mormon). Thus, 2 Nephi 14:1 fits in the context of Jerusalem's destruction and the scarcity

of men resulting from that invasion. See Isaiah 4, footnote 1a.

1 And in that day (referred to in chapter 13:25 & 26), seven women shall take hold of one man, saying: We will eat our own bread, and wear our own apparel (we will pay our own way); only let us be called by thy name to take away our reproach (the stigma of being unmarried and childless).

2 (This verse starts a new topic, namely conditions during the Millennium.) In that day shall the branch of the Lord (The "branch" can have dual meaning. In Jer. 23:5 and footnote 5b, this branch refers to Christ. In Isa. 60:21; 61:3, it refers to righteous people during the Millennium) be beautiful and glorious; the fruit of the earth excellent and comely (pleasant to look at) to them that are escaped of Israel (the righteous who have escaped the destruction of the wicked).

3 And it shall come to pass, they (the righteous remnant) that are left in Zion and remain in Jerusalem shall be called holy (i.e., will be the righteous), every one that is written among the living (those saved by approval of the Messiah) in Jerusalem__

4 When the Lord shall have washed away the filth of the daughters of Zion (when the Lord has cleansed the earth), and shall have purged the blood of Jerusalem from the midst thereof by the spirit of judgment (Hebrew: carrying out a sentence; punishment) and by the spirit of burning (the earth will be cleansed by fire).

143

5 (The Angel Moroni quoted verses 5 and 6 to Joseph Smith in reference to the last days. See Messenger and Advocate, April, 1835, p. 110.) And the Lord will create upon every dwelling-place of mount Zion, and upon her assemblies, a cloud and smoke by day (represents the presence of the Lord as in Exodus 19:16-18) and the shining of a flaming fire by night (presence of God); for upon all (everyone) the glory of Zion shall be a defence.

6 And there shall be a tabernacle (shelter; can symbolize Hebrew marriage canopy, thus representing the remarriage of Christ and his people invited in Jer. 3:1) for a shadow (protection) in the daytime from the heat, and for a place of refuge, and a covert (protection) from storm and from rain (millennial peace and protection. Verses 5 and 6 could be dual, referring to the stakes of Zion as protection, defense, refuge in the last days—see D&C 115:6—as well as millennial conditions).

2 NEPHI 15

1 And then will I sing (Isaiah composes a song or poetic parable of a vineyard, showing God's mercy and Israel's unresponsiveness) to my well-beloved a song of my beloved (Christ), touching his vineyard (Israel). My well-beloved (the Lord of Hosts; see verse 7) hath a vineyard (Israel; see verse 7) in a very fruitful hill (i.e., in Israel).

2 And he fenced it (protected it), and gathered out the stones thereof (removed stumbling blocks etc., i.e., gave it every chance to succeed), and planted it with the choicest vine (the men of Judah; see verse 7), and built a tower (put prophets) in the midst of it, and also made a wine-press therein (indicates potential for a good harvest); and he looked that it should bring forth grapes (the desired product, i.e., faithful people), and it brought forth wild grapes (apostasy, wickedness).

3 And now, O inhabitants of Jerusalem, and men of Judah, judge, I pray you, betwixt me (Christ) and my vineyard (apostate Israel; i.e., I'll give you the facts and you be the judge).

4 What could have been done more to my vineyard that I have not done in it (the main question, i.e., have I not done my job)? Wherefore (Why), when I looked (planned) that it should bring forth grapes it brought forth wild grapes (apostasy).

5 And now go to (German: All right. That's settled); I will tell you what I will do to my vineyard (Israel)__I will take away the hedge thereof (divine protection), and it (Israel) shall be eaten up (destroyed); and I will break down the wall (withdraw my protection) thereof, and it shall be trodden down;

6 And I will lay it waste; it shall not be pruned nor digged (the Spirit will withdraw; no prophets); but there shall come up briers and thorns (apostate doctrines and behaviors); I will

also command the clouds that they rain no rain upon it (drought, famine).

7 For the vineyard of the Lord of Hosts (Christ) is the house of Israel, and the men of Judah his pleasant plant; and he looked for judgment (justice, fairness, kindness etc.), and behold (instead), oppression; for righteousness, but behold, a cry (riotous living).

8 Wo unto them (the powerful, wealthy) that join house to house, till there can be no place, that they (the poor) may be placed alone in the midst of the earth (those in power cheat and push the poor farmers off their land)!

9 In mine ears (German: Isaiah's ears), said the Lord of Hosts, of a truth many houses shall be desolate, and great and fair cities without inhabitant (great troubles are coming because of your wickedness).

10 Yea, ten acres of vineyard shall yield one bath (about 8 1/4 U.S. gallons), and the seed of a homer (6 1/2 bushel of seed) shall yield an ephah (1/2 bushel of harvest; i.e., famine is coming!).

11 Wo unto them that rise up early in the morning, that they may follow strong drink, that continue until night, and wine inflame them (i.e., unrighteous, riotous lifestyle)!

12 And the harp, and the viol (Hebrew: lyre), the tabret (drums or tambourines), and pipe (Hebrew: flute; i.e., musical instruments associated with worship of the Lord), and wine are in their feasts; but they regard not the work of the Lord, neither consider the operation of his hands (their worship is empty, hypocritical; they do not actually acknowledge God).

13 Therefore (this is why), my people are gone into captivity (prophecy about Israel's future), because they have no knowledge; and their honorable men are famished, and their multitude dried up with thirst (dual: fits with Amos 8:11-12 about a famine of hearing the words of the Lord; also, literal results of famine).

14 Therefore (this is why), hell hath enlarged herself (they've had to add on to hell to make room for you!), and opened her mouth without measure; and their (the wicked) glory, and their multitude, and their pomp, and he that rejoiceth (in wicked, riotous living), shall descend into it.

15 And the mean (poor) man shall be brought down (humbled), and the mighty (wealthy, powerful) man shall be humbled, and the eyes of the lofty (proud) shall be humbled (everyone needs humbling).

16 But the Lord of Hosts shall be exalted (upheld) in judgment, and God that is holy shall be sanctified in righteousness (i.e., the Lord will triumph).

17 Then shall the lambs feed (graze where the Lord's vineyard, Israel, once stood; i.e., destruction is complete) after their manner (German: where the city once stood), and the waste places of the fat ones shall strangers (foreigners) eat.

18 Wo unto them that draw (pull) iniquity with cords of vanity, and sin as it were with a cart rope (you are tethered to your sins; they follow you like a cart follows the animal pulling it!);

19 That say: Let him (the Lord) make speed, hasten his work, that we may see it (it is up to God to prove to us that he exists); and let the counsel (plans) of the Holy One of Israel draw nigh and come, that we may know it (we are "calling his bluff"; tell him to follow through with his threats so we can know he really exists!).

20 Wo unto them that call evil good, and good evil, that put darkness for light, and light for darkness, that put bitter for sweet, and sweet for bitter!

21 Wo unto the wise in their own eyes (full of evil pride) and prudent in their own sight (i.e., the wicked, who make their own rules)!

22 Wo unto the mighty to drink wine, and men of strength to mingle strong drink (i.e., riotous living);

23 Who justify the wicked for reward (take bribes, i.e., corrupt judicial system etc.), and take away the righteousness of the righteous from him (deprive the innocent of his rights)!

24 Therefore, as the fire devoureth the stubble, and the flame consumeth the chaff, their root shall be rottenness, and their blossoms shall go up as dust (not bear fruit, no posterity in the next life and destruction of many in this life); because they have cast away the law of the Lord of Hosts, and despised the word of the Holy One of Israel.

25 Therefore (for these reasons), is the anger of the Lord kindled against his people, and he hath stretched forth his hand against them, and hath smitten them; and the hills did tremble, and their carcasses were torn in the midst of the streets (terrible destruction resulting from Israel's wickedness). For all this his anger is not turned away, but his hand is stretched out still (despite all this, you can still repent, Jacob 6:4).

26 And he will lift up an ensign (flag, rallying point; the true gospel) to the nations from far, and will hiss (whistle; a signal to gather) unto them from the end of the earth; and behold, they (the righteous) shall come with speed swiftly (because of modern transportation?); none shall be weary nor stumble among them.

27 None shall slumber nor sleep; neither shall the girdle of their loins be loosed, nor the latchet of their shoes be broken (perhaps meaning that they will travel so fast via modern transportation that they won't need to change clothes or even take their shoes off);

28 Whose arrows shall be sharp, and all their bows bent, and their horses' hoofs shall be counted like flint, and their wheels like a whirlwind, their roaring like a lion (trains, airplanes?).

29 They shall roar (airplanes etc.?) like young lions; yea, they shall roar,

and lay hold of the prey (passengers, converts), and shall carry away safe, and none shall deliver (no enemies can stop them or prevent the gathering).

30 And in that day (the last days) they shall roar against them like the roaring of the sea; and if they look unto the land, behold, darkness and sorrow, and the light is darkened in the heavens thereof (perhaps referring to conditions in the last days, war, smoke, pollutions etc.).

2 NEPHI 16

1 (This chapter deals with Isaiah's call, either his initial call or a subsequent call to a major responsibility.) In the year that king Uzziah died (about 750-740 BC), I (Isaiah) saw also the Lord (Jesus; see verse 5) sitting upon a throne, high and lifted up (exalted), and his train (skirts of his robe; Hebrew: wake, light) filled the temple.

2 Above it stood the seraphim (angelic beings); each one had six wings (symbolic of power to move, act etc. in God's work; see D&C 77:4); with twain he covered his face, and with twain he covered his feet, and with twain he did fly.

3 And one cried unto another, and said: Holy, holy, holy (repeated three times means the very best in Hebrew, i.e., superlative), is the Lord of Hosts; the whole earth is full of his glory.

4 And the posts of the door moved (shook) at the voice of him that cried, and the house was filled with smoke (symbolic of God's presence, as at Sinai, Ex. 19:18).

5 Then said I (Isaiah): Wo is unto me! for I am undone (completely overwhelmed); because I am a man of unclean lips (I am so imperfect, inadequate!); and I dwell in the midst of a people of unclean lips; for mine eyes have seen the King, the Lord of Hosts (the Savior).

6 Then flew one of the seraphim unto me, having a live coal (symbolic of the Holy Ghost's power to cleanse "by fire") in his hand, which he had taken with the tongs from off the altar (the atonement; i.e., Christ was sacrificed for us on the "altar" cross);

7 And he laid it upon my mouth (i.e., applied the Atonement to me), and said: Lo, this has touched thy lips; and thine iniquity is taken away, and thy sin purged (results of the atonement).

8 Also I heard the voice of the Lord, saying: Whom shall I send, and who will go for us (plural deity)? Then I (Isaiah) said: Here am I; send me (the cleansing power of the atonement gave Isaiah the needed confidence to accept the call).

9 And he (the Lord) said: Go and tell this people__Hear ye indeed, but they understood not; and see ye indeed, but they perceived not (Isaiah's task is not to be easy with that kind of people).

10 Make the heart (chiasmus A) of this people fat, and make their ears

(chiasmus B) heavy, and shut their eyes (chiasmus C)__lest they see with their eyes (chiasmus C'), and hear with their ears (chiasmus B'), and understand with their heart (chiasmus A'), and be converted and be healed.

11 Then said I: Lord, how long (will people be like this)? And he said: Until the cities be wasted without inhabitant, and the houses without man, and the land be utterly desolate (i.e., as long as people are around);

12 And the Lord have removed men far away, for there shall be a great forsaking (many deserted cities) in the midst of the land.

13 But yet there shall be a tenth (remnant of Israel), and they (Israel) shall return, and shall be eaten (pruned, as by animals eating the limbs, leaves and branches; i.e., the Lord "prunes" his vineyard, cuts out old apostates etc., destroys old unrighteous generations so new may have a chance), as a teil-tree (lime tree? See Bible Dictionary, p. 780), and as an oak whose substance (sap) is in them when they cast their leaves (shed the old, non-functioning leaves and look dead in winter); so the holy seed shall be the substance thereof (Israel may look dead, but there is still life in it).

2 NEPHI 17

1 And it came to pass in the days of Ahaz (a wicked, idol-worshipping king of Judah about 734 BC) the son of Jotham, the son of Uzziah, king of Judah, that Rezin, king of Syria, and Pekah the son of Remaliah, king of Israel (the 10 Tribes, i.e., Northern Israel), went up toward Jerusalem to war against it, but could not prevail against it (didn't win, but they did kill 120,000 men of Judah and take 200,000 captives in one day; see 2 Chr. 28:6-15).

2 And it was told the house of David (Jerusalem), saying: Syria is confederate (has joined) with Ephraim. And his (Ahaz's) heart was moved (shaken), and the heart of his people, as the trees of the wood are moved with the wind (i.e., the people of Judah were trembling with fear, "shaking in their boots").

3 Then said the Lord unto Isaiah: Go forth now to meet Ahaz (king of Judah living in Jerusalem), thou and Shearjashub (Hebrew: the remnant shall return) thy son, at the end of the conduit of the upper pool in the highway of the fuller's field (i.e., Ahaz is hiding where the women do their laundry, i.e., he is hiding behind the women's skirts, a coward);

4 And say unto him (King Ahaz): Take heed, and be quiet (Relax!); fear not, neither be faint-hearted for (because of) the two tails of these smoking firebrands (Syria and Israel), for the fierce anger of Rezin with Syria, and of the son of Remaliah (don't worry about continued threats from Syria and Israel; they think they are "hot stuff" but are nothing but smoldering stubs of firewood, i.e., "have beens").

5 Because Syria, Ephraim (Northern Israel), and the son of Remaliah (Northern Israel's king), have taken evil counsel (are plotting) against thee, saying:

6 Let us go up against Judah and vex it, and let us make a breach therein for us, and set a king in the midst of it (let's set up our own king in Jerusalem), yea, the son of Tabeal.

7 Thus saith the Lord God: It shall not stand, neither shall it come to pass (the plot will fail, so don't worry about it, Ahaz).

8 For the head (capital city) of Syria is Damascus, and the head (leader) of Damascus, Rezin; and within three score and five years (65 years) shall Ephraim (the Ten Tribes) be broken that it be not a people (within 65 years the Ten Tribes will be lost).

9 And the head (capital city) of Ephraim is Samaria, and the head (leader) of Samaria is Remaliah's son. If ye (Ahaz and his people, the tribe of Judah) will not believe surely ye shall not be established (not be saved by the Lord's power; see Isa. 7, footnote 9b).

10 Moreover, the Lord spake again unto Ahaz, saying:

11 Ask thee a sign (to assure you that the Lord is speaking to you) of the Lord thy God; ask it either in the depths, or in the heights above (i.e., ask anything you want).

12 But Ahaz said: I will not ask, neither will I tempt (test) the Lord (refuses to follow prophet's counsel;

is deliberately evasive because he is already secretly depending on Assyria for help).

13 And he (Isaiah) said: Hear ye now, O house of David (Ahaz and his people, Judah); is it a small thing for you to weary men, but will ye weary my God also (try the patience of God)?

14 Therefore (because of your disobedience), the Lord himself shall give you a sign_ Behold, a virgin shall conceive, and shall bear a son, and shall call his name Immanuel (the day will come when the Savior will be born).

15 Butter and honey (curd and honey, the only foods available to the poor at times; see Isa. 7, footnote 15a) shall he eat, that he may know to refuse the evil and to choose the good.

16 For before the child shall know to refuse the evil and choose the good (in as many years as it takes for the child to be old enough to know good from evil, i.e., just a few years), the land (Northern Israel) that thou (Judah) abhorrest (are afraid of) shall be forsaken of both her kings (i.e., both Syria and the Northern 10 Tribes will be taken by Assyria; see Isa. 8:4, 2 Nephi 17:17).

17 The Lord shall bring upon thee (Ahaz), and upon thy people (Judah), and upon thy father's house, days that have not come from the day that Ephraim departed (Northern 10 split) from Judah, the king of Assyria (i.e., the king of Assyria will bring troubles

like you have not seen since Israel split about 975 BC, into the Northern Kingdom under Jeroboam I, and the tribe of Judah under Rehoboam).

18 And it shall come to pass in that day that the Lord shall hiss (signal, call for) for the fly (associated with plagues, troubles, i.e., this will remind you of the plagues in Egypt) that is in the uttermost part of Egypt, and for the bee (sting) that is in the land of Assyria (i.e., the Assyrians will come like flies and bees).

19 And they shall come, and shall rest all of them in the desolate valleys, and in the holes of the rocks, and upon all thorns, and upon all bushes (your enemies will be everywhere, will over-run your land).

20 In the same day shall the Lord shave with a razor (fate of captives, slaves—for humiliation, sanitation, identification) that is hired (Assyria will be "hired" to do this to Judah), by them beyond the river, by the king of Assyria, the head, and the hair of the feet; and it shall also consume the beard (they will shave you completely, i.e., will conquer you completely).

21 And it shall come to pass in that day (after the above-mentioned devastation), a man shall nourish a young cow and two sheep;

22 And it shall come to pass, for the abundance of milk they (the few remaining domestic animals) shall give he shall eat butter; for butter and honey shall every one eat that is left in the land (not many people left, so a few animals can supply them well).

23 And it shall come to pass in that day, every place shall be, where there were (used to be) a thousand vines at a thousand silverlings (worth a thousand pieces of silver), which shall be for briers and thorns (formerly valuable, cultivated land will become overgrown with weeds; apostasy).

24 With arrows and with bows shall men come thither, because all the land shall become briers and thorns (previously cultivated land will become wild and overgrown such that hunters will hunt wild beasts there).

25 And all hills that shall be digged with the mattock (that were once cultivated with the hoe), there (you) shall not come thither (because of) the fear of briers and thorns; but it shall be for the sending forth (pasturing) of oxen, and the treading of lesser cattle (sheep or goats, i.e., your once cultivated lands will revert to wilds; apostasy).

2 NEPHI 18

1 Moreover, the word of the Lord said unto me: Take thee a great (large) roll (scroll), and write in it with a man's pen, concerning Maher-shalal-hash-baz (Hebrew: to speed to the spoil, he hasteneth the prey).

2 And I (Isaiah) took unto me faithful witnesses to record, Uriah the priest, and Zechariah the son of Jeberechiah (required witnesses and legal authorities for a proper Hebrew wedding).

3 And I went unto the prophetess (Isaiah's wife); and she conceived and bare a son. Then said the Lord to me: Call his name, Maher-shalal-hash-baz.

4 For behold, the child shall not have knowledge to cry, My father, and my mother, before the riches of Damascus (Syria) and the spoil of Samaria (Northern Israel) shall be taken away before (by) the king of Assyria (i.e., before my son is old enough to say "Daddy", "Mommy", Assyria will attack Northern Israel and Syria).

5 The Lord spake also unto me (Isaiah) again, saying:

6 Forasmuch as this people (Judah, Jerusalem) refuseth the waters of Shiloah (the gentle help of Christ, John 4:14) that go softly (mercifully), and rejoice in (pay attention to) Rezin and Remaliah's son (Syria and Northern Israel instead of the Lord);

7 Now therefore, behold, the Lord bringeth up upon them (Judah) the waters of the river (i.e., you'll be flooded with Assyrians), strong and many, even the king of Assyria and all his glory (his pomp, armies etc.); and he shall come up over all his channels, and go over all his banks (a flood of Assyrians).

8 And he (Assyria) shall pass through Judah; he shall overflow and go over, he shall reach even to the neck (you will be up to your neck in Assyrians; can also mean "will reach clear to Jerusalem, the head or capital city", which Assyria did before being stopped via death by plague of 185,000 soldiers; see 2 Kings 19:32-36); and the stretching out of his wings (Assyria) shall fill the breadth of thy land (Judah), O Immanuel (i.e., the land of the future birth of Christ).

9 Associate yourselves (if you form political alliances for protection rather than turning to God), O ye people (of Judah), and ye shall be broken in pieces; and give ear all ye of far countries (foreign nations who might rise against Judah); gird yourselves (prepare for war), and ye (foreign nations who attack Judah) shall be broken in pieces; gird yourselves, and ye shall be broken in pieces (note that "broken in pieces" is repeated three times for emphasis; 3 times in Hebrew is a form of superlative).

10 Take counsel together (go ahead, plot against Judah, you foreign nations), and it shall come to naught (won't succeed); speak the word, and it shall not stand; for God is with us (Judah won't be destroyed completely).

11 For the Lord spake thus to me (Isaiah) with a strong hand (with power), and instructed me that I should not walk in the way of this people (Judah), saying:

12 Say ye not, A confederacy, to all to whom this people shall say, A confederacy; neither fear ye their fear, nor be afraid ("Isaiah, don't endorse Judah's plan for confederacy with Assyria. Don't tell them what they want to hear.").

13 Sanctify the Lord of Hosts

himself, and let him be your fear, and let him be your dread ("Isaiah, you rely on the Lord, not public approval.").

14 And he (the Lord) shall be for a sanctuary (for you, Isaiah); but for a stone of stumbling, and for a rock of offense (a rock that makes them fall rather than the Rock of their salvation) to both the houses of (wicked) Israel, for a gin (a trap) and a snare to the inhabitants of Jerusalem.

15 And many among them shall stumble and fall, and be broken, and be snared, and be taken.

16 Bind up the testimony (record your testimony, Isaiah), seal the law among my disciples (righteous followers).

17 And I (Isaiah) will wait upon (trust) the Lord, that hideth his face from the house of Jacob (Israel), and I will look for him.

18 Behold, I and the children whom the Lord hath given me are for signs and for wonders in Israel from the Lord of Hosts, which dwelleth in Mount Zion.

19 And when they (the wicked) shall say unto you: Seek unto them (spiritualists, mediums, fortune tellers etc.) that have familiar spirits (i.e., who contact dead relatives etc.), and unto wizards that peep and mutter (into their "crystal balls" etc.)_ should not a people seek unto their God for the living to hear from the dead?

20 To the law and to the testimony (to the scriptures); and if they (the

spiritualists and their media) speak not according to this word (the scriptures), it is because there is no light in them (the fortune tellers, mediums etc).

21 And they (the wicked of Judah) shall pass through it (the land; the trouble described in verses 7 & 8 etc.) hardly bestead (severely distressed) and hungry; and it shall come to pass that when they shall be hungry, they shall fret themselves (become enraged), and curse their king and their God, and look upward (proud, defiant).

22 And they shall look unto the earth (will look around them) and behold (see only) trouble, and darkness, dimness of anguish (gloom; Hebrew: dark affliction), and shall be driven to darkness (thrust into utter despair; results of wickedness).

2 NEPHI 19

Note: King Ahaz of Judah ignored the Lord's counsel and made an alliance with Assyria.

1 (This verse is the last verse of chapter 8 in the Hebrew Bible and in the German Bible. It serves as a natural transition from chapter 18 to verse 2.) Nevertheless, the dimness (affliction referred to in 18:22) shall not be such as was in her vexation, when at first (the first Assyrian attacks in Isaiah's day) he lightly (German: strictly) afflicted the land of Zebulun (the Nazareth area, part of

Northern Israel; see maps 5 & 14 in the new LDS Bible), and the land of Naphtali (in Northern Israel), and afterwards did more grievously afflict (Hebrew: gloriously bless, German: brought honor to) by the way of the Red Sea beyond Jordan in Galilee of the nations (Jesus grew up in Galilee and righteous Israel has been gloriously blessed through him, whereas wicked Israel has been grievously afflicted as a result of rejecting him).

2 The people that walked in darkness (spiritual darkness; apostasy and captivity) have seen a great light (the Savior and his teachings); they that dwell in the land of the shadow of death, upon them hath the light shined.

3 Thou (the Savior) hast multiplied the nation, and increased the joy__they joy before thee according to the joy in harvest, and as men rejoice when they divide the spoil (Christ and his faithful followers will ultimately triumph and divide the spoils, i.e., reap the rewards).

4 (Isaiah continues prophesying about the future.) For thou (the Savior) hast broken the yoke of his burden (Israel's captivity, bondage), and the staff of his shoulder, the rod (power) of his (Israel's) oppressor.

5 For every battle of the warrior is with confused noise, and garments rolled in blood; but this shall be with burning (the burning at the 2nd Coming, according to Joseph Smith; see Isa. 9, footnote 5b) and fuel of fire.

6 For unto us a child (Christ) is born, unto us a son is given; and the government shall be upon his shoulder; and his name shall be called, Wonderful, Counselor, The Mighty God, The Everlasting Father, The Prince of Peace.

7 Of the increase of government and peace there is no end, upon the throne of David, and upon his kingdom to order it, and to establish it with judgment (fairness) and with justice from henceforth, even forever. The zeal of the Lord of Hosts will perform this.

8 (The Lord now continues his message of warning to the Northern Ten Tribes.) The Lord sent his word unto Jacob (Israel) and it hath lighted upon Israel.

9 And all the people shall know, even Ephraim (Northern Israel) and the inhabitants of Samaria (Northern Israel), that say (boast) in the pride and stoutness of heart:

10 The bricks are fallen down, but we will build with hewn stones (boastful Northern Israel claims they can't be destroyed successfully, but would simply rebuild with better materials than before); the sycamores are cut down, but we will change them into cedars.

11 Therefore (this is why, i.e., because of wicked pride) the Lord shall set up the adversaries of Rezin (Syria) against him (the Northern 10), and join his enemies together;

12 The Syrians before (on the East) and the Philistines behind (on the West); and they shall devour Israel

with open mouth. For all this his anger is not turned away, but his hand is stretched out still (the Lord will still let you repent if you will turn to him; Jacob 6:4 & 5; see also Isa. 9, footnote 12d. Laman and Lemuel need this message of mercy, as do we in our day).

13 For the (wicked) people turneth not unto him (the Lord) that smiteth (punishes) them, neither do they seek the Lord of Hosts (the people won't repent; they are going through the pain without learning the lesson).

14 Therefore (for this reason) will the Lord cut off from Israel head (leaders) and tail (false prophets), branch (Hebrew: palm branch, i.e., triumph, John 12:13) and rush (reed, i.e., people low in social status) in one day.

15 The ancient, he is the head; and the prophet that teacheth lies, he is the tail.

16 For the leaders of this people cause them to err; and they that are led of them are destroyed.

17 Therefore the Lord shall have no joy in their young men, neither shall have mercy on their fatherless and widows (all levels of society have gone bad; no one qualifies for mercy); for every one of them is a hypocrite and an evildoer, and every mouth speaketh folly. For all this his anger is not turned away, but his hand is stretched out still (please repent).

18 For wickedness burneth as the fire (wickedness destroys like wildfire); it shall devour the briers and thorns, and shall kindle in the thickets of the forests, and they shall mount up like the lifting up of smoke.

19 Through the wrath of the Lord of Hosts is the land darkened (bad conditions prevail), and the (wicked) people shall be as the fuel of the fire; no man shall spare his brother.

20 And he shall snatch on the right hand and be hungry; and he shall eat on the left hand and they shall not be satisfied; they shall eat every man the flesh of his own arm (the wicked will turn on each other)__

21 Manasseh, Ephraim; and Ephraim, Manasseh; they together shall be against Judah. For all this his anger is not turned away, but his hand is stretched out still (you can still repent; please do!).

2 NEPHI 20

1 Wo unto them that decree unrighteous decrees (unrighteous laws), and that write grievousness (oppression) which they have prescribed;

2 To turn away the needy from judgment (fair treatment), and to take away the right from the poor of my people, that widows may be their prey (victims), and that they may rob the fatherless (i.e., they are greedy)!

3 And what will ye (the wicked) do in the day of visitation (punishment), and in the desolation which shall come from far (from Assyria)? to whom will ye flee for help? and where will ye leave your glory (wealth etc)?

4 Without me (the Lord) they shall bow down under the prisoners (huddle among the prisoners), and they shall fall under the slain (be killed). For all this his anger is not turned away, but his hand is stretched out still (you can still repent).

5 O Assyrian, the rod (tool of destruction used by the Lord to punish Israel) of mine anger, and the staff in their hand is their indignation.

6 I will send him (Assyria) against a hypocritical nation (Israel), and against the people of my wrath (i.e., Israel) will I give him (Assyria) a charge (an assignment) to take the spoil, and to take the prey (Israel), and to tread them (Israel) down like the mire of the streets (see 2 Nephi 8:23).

7 Howbeit he meaneth not so, neither doth his heart think so (the king of Assyria doesn't realize he is a tool in God's hand, thinks he doing it on his own); but in his heart it is to destroy and cut off nations not a few (i.e., he is a wicked man).

8 For he (Assyrian king) saith (boasts): Are not my princes (military commanders) altogether kings (just like kings in other countries)?

9 Is not Calno as Carchemish? Is not Hamath as Arpad? Is not Samaria as Damascus (cities conquered by Assyria; see Map 10 in new LDS Bible; see also 2 Kings 19:8-13 for Sennacherib's boastful letter to Hezekiah, King of Judah)?

10 As my hand (Assyria's) hath founded (Hebrew: acquired) the kingdoms of the idols, and whose graven images did excel them of Jerusalem and of Samaria (i.e., I've taken many cities whose idols are more powerful than those of Jerusalem and Samaria);

11 Shall I not, as I have done unto Samaria and her idols, so do to Jerusalem and to her idols (Assyria's king boasts that other nations' idols, gods, did not stop him and neither will Jerusalem's)?

12 Wherefore it shall come to pass that when the Lord hath performed his whole work upon Mount Zion and upon Jerusalem (i.e., when the Lord is through using Assyria to punish Israel), I (the Lord) will punish the fruit of the stout heart of the king of Assyria, and the glory (German: pompousness) of his high looks (when I'm through using Assyria against Israel, then proud, haughty Assyria will get its deserved punishment).

13 For he (the Assyrian king) saith: By the strength of my hand and by my wisdom I have done these things; for I am prudent; and I have moved the borders of the people, and have robbed their treasures, and I have put down the inhabitants like a valiant man (bragging);

14 And my hand hath found as a nest the riches of the people; and as one gathereth eggs that are left have I gathered all the earth (i.e., I'm mighty powerful!); and there was none that moved the wing, or opened the mouth, or peeped (everybody is afraid of me!).

15 Shall the ax (King of Assyria)

boast itself against him (the Lord) that heweth (chops) therewith? Shall the saw magnify itself against (German: defy) him that shaketh it (uses it)? As if the rod (wooden club) should shake itself against them that lift it up, or as if the staff should lift up itself as if it were no wood (i.e., as if the staff were not simply a piece of wood)!

16 Therefore (i.e., because of the King of Assyria's wicked deeds and cocky attitude) shall the Lord, the Lord of Hosts, send among his fat (powerful) ones, leanness (Hebrew: disease, i.e., trouble is coming to Assyria); and under his (Assyria's) glory he shall kindle a burning like the burning of a fire (i.e., the Lord will trim Assyria down to size).

17 And the light of Israel (Christ) shall be for a fire, and his (Israel's) Holy One (Christ) for a flame, and shall burn and shall devour his (Assyria's) thorns and his briers in one day (185,000 Assyrians died of devastating sickness in one night as they prepared to attack Jerusalem; see 2 Kings 19:35-37);

18 And shall consume the glory of his forest (Assyria's armies), and of his fruitful field, both soul and body; and they shall be as when a standard-bearer fainteth (as when the last soldier falls, and the flag with him; i.e., your armies will be destroyed).

19 And the rest of the trees of his forest (i.e., the remnants of Assyria's army) shall be few, that a child may write them (so few Assyrians will remain that a small child could count

them with his limited counting ability).

20 And it shall come to pass in that day (the last days), that the remnant of Israel, and such as are escaped (survive) of the house of Jacob (Israel), shall no more again stay (be dependent) upon him (Israel's enemies) that smote them (Israel), but shall stay (depend) upon the Lord, the Holy One of Israel, in truth.

21 The remnant shall return, yea, even the remnant of Jacob, unto the mighty God (Dual: 1. A remnant remains in the land after Assyrian destruction. 2. A future righteous remnant; see 2 Nephi 21:11-12).

22 For though (although) thy people Israel be as the sand of the sea, yet a remnant of them shall return (German: only a remnant will be converted; gathering); the consumption decreed (destruction at the end of the world) shall overflow with righteousness (under God's direction; see verse 23).

23 For the Lord God of Hosts shall make a consumption, even determined (decreed; see Isa. 10, footnote 23a) in all the land.

24 Therefore, thus saith the Lord God of Hosts: O my people that dwellest in Zion, be not afraid of the Assyrian; he shall smite thee with a rod, and shall lift up his staff against thee, after the manner of Egypt (like Egypt did in earlier times).

25 For yet a very little while, and the indignation shall cease, and mine anger in their (Assyrians) destruction.

26 And the Lord of Hosts shall stir up a scourge for him (the Assyrians) according to (like) the slaughter of Midian at the rock of Oreb (Judges 7:23-25 where Gideon and his 300 miraculously defeated the Midianites); and as his rod was upon the sea so shall he lift it up after the manner of Egypt (God will stop Assyria like he did the Egyptians when they pursued the Children of Israel).

27 And it shall come to pass in that day that his (Israel's enemies', i.e., Assyria etc.) burden shall be taken away from off thy (Israel's) shoulder, and his yoke (bondage) from off thy neck, and the yoke shall be destroyed because of the anointing (because of Christ).

28 (Isaiah now tells Judah that it will look like Assyria will not be stopped; Assyrians will easily take several cities leading right up to the outskirts of Jerusalem and it will look like Jerusalem is doomed despite Isaiah's prophecies to the contrary in verse 26.) He (Assyria) is come to Aiath, he is passed to Migron; at Michmash he hath laid up his carriages (symbolic of military might).

29 They (Assyria) are gone over the passage; they have taken up their lodging at Geba; Ramath is afraid; Gibeah of Saul is fled.

30 Lift up the voice (weep!), O daughter of Gallim; cause it to be heard unto Laish, O poor Anathoth.

31 Madmenah is removed; the inhabitants of Gebim gather themselves to flee.

32 As yet shall he (Assyria) remain at Nob (just outside of Jerusalem) that day; he shall shake his hand against the mount of the daughter of Zion (Jerusalem), the hill of Jerusalem.

33 Behold, the Lord, the Lord of Hosts shall lop the bough with terror (when Assyrian armies get right to Jerusalem, the Lord will "trim them down to size", "clip their wings", stop them in their tracks); and the high ones (leaders of Assyrian armies) of stature shall be hewn down; and the haughty shall be humbled.

34 And he shall cut down the thickets of the forests (Assyria) with iron (an axe), and Lebanon shall fall by a mighty one (the Lord did stop Assyria by killing 185,000 of them in one night as they camped outside Jerusalem; see 2 Kings 19:32-35).

2 NEPHI 21

1 And there shall come forth a rod (Hebrew: "twig") out of the stem of Jesse (Christ), and a branch shall grow out of his roots.

2 (Christ-like qualities of leadership are described next) And the Spirit of the Lord shall rest upon him, the spirit of wisdom and understanding, the spirit of counsel and might, the spirit of knowledge and of the fear of the Lord;

3 And shall make him of quick understanding in the fear of the Lord; and he shall not judge after the sight

of his eyes, neither reprove after the hearing of his ears.

4 But with righteousness shall he judge the poor, and reprove with equity for the meek of the earth; and he shall smite the earth with the rod of his mouth, and with the breath of his lips shall he slay the wicked.

5 And righteousness shall be the girdle of his loins, and faithfulness the girdle of his reins (desires, thoughts).

6 The wolf also shall dwell with the lamb, and the leopard shall lie down with the kid (young goat), and the calf and the young lion and fatling together; and a little child shall lead (herd) them (Millennial conditions).

7 And the cow and the bear shall feed (graze); their young ones shall lie down together; and the lion shall eat straw like the ox.

8 And the suckling child shall play on the hole of the asp (viper), and the weaned child shall put his hand on the cockatrice's (venomous serpent) den.

9 They shall not hurt nor destroy in all my holy mountain, for the earth shall be full of the knowledge (Hebrew: devotion) of the Lord, as the waters cover the sea.

10 And in that day there shall be a root of Jesse (probably Joseph Smith, but we don't know for sure), which shall stand for an ensign of the people; to it shall the Gentiles seek; and his rest shall be glorious.

11 And it shall come to pass in that day that the Lord shall set his hand again the second time (dual: after Babylonian captivity / last days) to recover the remnant of his people which shall be left, from Assyria, and from Egypt, and from Pathros, and from Cush, and from Elam, and from Shinar, and from Hamath, and from the islands of the sea.

12 And he shall set up an ensign (the Church in the last days) for the nations, and shall assemble the outcasts of Israel, and gather together the dispersed of Judah from the four corners of the earth.

13 The envy of Ephraim also shall depart, and the adversaries of Judah shall be cut off; Ephraim shall not envy Judah, and Judah shall not vex Ephraim (the USA and others will be on good terms with the Jews).

14 But they (the Jews, with Ephriam's help) shall fly upon the shoulders of the Philistines towards the west (attack the western slopes that were once Philistine territory); they shall spoil them of the east together; they shall lay their hand upon Edom and Moab; and the children of Ammon shall obey them (the Jews will be powerful in the last days rather than easy prey for their enemies).

15 And the Lord shall utterly destroy the tongue of the Egyptian sea (productivity of Nile River ruined? See Is. 19:5-10); and with his mighty wind he shall shake his hand over the river, and shall smite it in the seven streams, and make men go over dry shod.

16 And there shall be a highway for the remnant of his people which shall

be left, from Assyria, like as it was to Israel in the day that he came up out of the land of Egypt.

2 NEPHI 22

1 (This chapter refers to the Millennium.) And in that day thou shalt say: O Lord, I will praise thee; though thou wast angry with me thine anger is turned away, and thou comfortedst me.

2 Behold, God is my salvation; I will trust, and not be afraid; for the Lord JEHOVAH (Jesus) is my strength and my song; he also has become my salvation.

3 Therefore, with joy shall ye draw water ("living water", John 7:38-39) out of the wells of salvation.

4 And in that day shall ye say: Praise the Lord, call upon his name, declare his doings among the people, make mention that his name is exalted.

5 Sing unto the Lord; for he hath done excellent things; this is known in all the earth.

6 Cry out and shout, thou inhabitant of Zion; for great is the Holy One of Israel (Christ) in the midst of thee.

2 NEPHI 23

1 The burden of (message of doom to) Babylon, which Isaiah the son of Amoz did see.

2 (The Lord will gather his righteous forces, verses 2-5.) Lift ye up a banner upon the high mountain, exalt (raise) the voice unto them (the right-

eous), shake the hand (wave the hand, signal), that they may go into the gates of the nobles (i.e., gather with the righteous).

3 I have commanded my sanctified ones, I have also called my mighty ones, for mine anger is not upon them that rejoice in my highness.

4 The noise of the multitude in the mountains like as of a great people (the gathering), a tumultuous noise of the kingdoms of nations gathered together, the Lord of Hosts mustereth the hosts of the battle.

5 They come from a far country, from the end of heaven, yea, the Lord, and the weapons of his indignation, to destroy the whole land (the wicked).

6 Howl ye (the wicked), for the day of the Lord (2nd Coming) is at hand; it shall come as a destruction from the Almighty.

7 Therefore shall all hands be faint (hang limp), every man's (wicked men) heart (courage) shall melt;

8 And they shall be afraid; pangs and sorrows shall take hold of them; they shall be amazed (will look in fear) one at another; their faces shall be as flames (burn with shame).

9 Behold, the day of the Lord (2nd Coming) cometh, cruel both with wrath and fierce anger, to lay the land desolate; and he shall destroy the sinners thereof out of it (a purpose of the 2nd Coming).

10 For the stars of heaven and the constellations thereof shall not give their light; the sun shall be darkened in his going forth, and the moon shall

not cause her light to shine (signs of the times).

11 And I will punish the world for evil, and the wicked for their iniquity; I will cause the arrogancy of the proud to cease, and will lay down the haughtiness of the terrible (tyrants; typical Isaiah repetition to drive home a point).

12 I will make a man more precious (scarce) than fine gold; even a man than the golden wedge of Ophir (a land rich in gold, possibly in southern Arabia; i.e., there will be relatively few survivors of the 2nd Coming).

13 Therefore, I will shake the heavens, and the earth shall remove out of her place, in the wrath of the Lord of Hosts, and in the day of his fierce anger.

14 And it (dual: Babylon; also the wicked in general) shall be as the chased roe (hunted deer), and as a sheep that no man taketh up (no shepherd, no defense); and they shall every man turn to his own people, and flee every one into his own land (foreigners who have had safety in Babylon, because of Babylon's great power, will return back to homelands because Babylon is no longer powerful and safe).

15 Every one that is proud shall be thrust through (stabbed); yea, and every one that is joined to the wicked shall fall by the sword.

16 Their children, also shall be dashed to pieces before their eyes; their houses shall be spoiled and their wives ravished (fate of Babylon; the wicked).

17 Behold, I will stir up the Medes against them (a very specific prophecy; Medes, from Persia, conquered Babylon easily in 538 BC), which shall not regard silver and gold, nor shall they delight in it (you Babylonians will not be able to bribe the Medes not to destroy you).

18 Their bows shall also dash the young men to pieces, and they shall have no pity on the fruit of the womb (babies); their eyes shall not spare children.

19 And Babylon, the glory of kingdoms, the beauty of the Chaldees' excellency, shall be as when God overthrew Sodom and Gomorrah (Babylon will be completely destroyed and never inhabited again).

20 It shall never be inhabited, neither shall it be dwelt in from generation to generation: neither shall the Arabian pitch tent there; neither shall the shepherds make their fold there.

21 But wild beasts of the desert shall lie there; and their houses (the ruins) shall be full of doleful creatures (such as owls); and owls shall dwell there, and satyrs (male goats) shall dance there.

22 And the wild beasts of the islands shall cry in their desolate houses, and dragons (hyenas, wild dogs, jackals) in their pleasant palaces; and her time is near to come, and her day shall not be prolonged (Babylon's time is up, her days are almost over). For I will

destroy her speedily; yea, for I will be merciful unto my people (the righteous), but the wicked shall perish.

2 NEPHI 24

Note: Isaiah uses very colorful style and imagery as he now prophesies concerning the future downfall of the King of Babylon and, symbolically, the downfall of Satan's kingdom.

1 For the Lord will have mercy on Jacob (Israel), and will yet choose Israel, and set them in their own land (One historical fulfillment of this was when Cyrus the Great of Persia allowed Jewish captives in Babylon to return, 538 BC; another group returned in 520 BC. This is also being fulfilled in our day.); and the strangers shall be joined with them (foreigners will live with them), and they shall cleave to the house of Jacob.

2 And the people (many nations who will help Israel return) shall take them (Israel) and bring them to their place; yea, from far unto the ends of the earth; and they (Israel) shall return to their lands of promise. And the house of Israel shall possess them and the land of the Lord shall be for servants and handmaids; and they (Israel) shall take them (nations who used to dominate Israel) captives unto whom they (Israel) were captives; and they (Israel) shall rule over their oppressors (i.e., the tables will be turned in the last days).

3 And it shall come to pass in that day (millennium) that the Lord shall give thee rest, from thy sorrow, and from thy fear, and from the hard bondage wherein thou wast made to serve (Israel will finally be free from subjection by foreigners).

4 And it shall come to pass in that day, that thou shalt take up this proverb (taunting saying) against the king of Babylon (dual: literally King of Babylon. Refers also to Satan plus any wicked leader), and say: How hath the oppressor ceased (what happened to you!), the golden city ceased (your unconquerable city, kingdom, is gone)!

5 The Lord hath broken the staff of the wicked, the scepters (power) of the (wicked) rulers.

6 He (dual: Babylon; Satan) who smote the people in wrath with a continual stroke (never ceasing), he that ruled the nations in anger, is persecuted (is now being punished), and none hindereth (nobody can stop it).

7 The whole earth is at rest, and is quiet (Millennium); they break forth into singing (during the Millennium).

8 Yea, the fir-trees (people) rejoice at thee (i.e., at what has happened to Satan), and also the cedars (people) of Lebanon, saying: Since thou art laid down (since you got chopped down) no feller (tree cutter, lumberjack) is come up against us.

9 Hell (spirit prison) from beneath is moved for thee (is getting ready to

receive you) to meet thee at thy coming; it stirreth up the dead for thee, even all the chief ones (dead wicked leaders) of the earth; it hath raised up from their thrones all the (wicked) kings of the nations.

10 All they shall speak and say unto thee (dual: Satan; King of Babylon): Art thou also become weak as we (what happened to your power)? Art thou become like unto us (did you get your wings clipped too, like us)?

11 Thy pomp is brought down to the grave (was destroyed with you); the noise of thy viols (royal harp music) is not heard; the worm is spread under thee, and the worms cover thee (Maggots are destroying your dead body just like they destroyed ours. You're no better off here in hell than we are, so hah, hah, hah! Refers to the King of Babylon since Satan has no mortal body.).

12 How art thou fallen from heaven (What happened to you?), O Lucifer, son of the morning! Art thou cut down to the ground, which did weaken the nations (you used to destroy nations; now your power is destroyed)!

13 For thou hast said in thy heart (these were your motives): I will ascend into heaven, I will exalt my throne above the stars of God (I will be the highest); I will sit also upon the mount of the congregation, in the sides of the north (mythical mountain in the north where gods assemble);

14 I will ascend above the heights of the clouds; I will be like the Most High (Moses 4:1 indicates he wanted

to be the Most High!).

15 Yet thou (Lucifer) shalt be brought down to hell, to the sides of the pit (to the lowest part of the world of the dead, i.e., outer darkness).

16 They (the residents of hell) that see thee (Lucifer; King of Babylon) shall narrowly look upon thee (scorn you, mock you), and shall consider (look at) thee, and shall say: Is this the man that made the earth to tremble, that did shake kingdoms?

17 And made the world as a wilderness, and destroyed the cities thereof, and opened not the house of his prisoners (refused to free his prisoners)?

18 All the kings of the nations, yea, all of them, lie in glory, every one of them in his own house (all other kings have magnificent tombs etc.).

19 But thou (dual: King of Babylon literally; Satan figuratively because he doesn't even have a physical body) art cast out of thy grave like an abominable branch (pruned off and thus worthless), and the remnant of those that are slain (you are just like any other dead wicked person) , thrust through with a sword, that go down to the stones of the pit (to the very bottom); as a carcass trodden under feet.

20 Thou (King of Babylon; Satan) shalt not be joined with them in burial, because thou hast destroyed thy land and slain thy people; the seed of evil-doers shall never be renowned (none of your evil family will survive, King of Babylon).

21 Prepare slaughter for his (King

of Babylon) children for the iniquities of their fathers, that they do not rise, nor possess the land, nor fill the face of the world with cities (none of your children will rule the earth like you have).

22 For I will rise up against them (the Lord will stop Lucifer; King of Babylon), saith the Lord of Hosts, and cut off from Babylon the name, and remnant, and son, and nephew (I will destroy Babylon completely), saith the Lord.

23 I will also make it (Babylon) a possession for the bittern (owls), and pools of water; and I will sweep it with the besom (broom) of destruction (i.e., a "clean sweep"), saith the Lord of Hosts.

24 (Isaiah starts a new topic now, the fate of Assyria) The Lord of Hosts hath sworn (covenanted), saying: Surely as I have thought (planned), so shall it come to pass (here is something else I will do); and as I have purposed (planned), so shall it stand (it will happen)__

25 That I will bring the Assyrian in my land (Judah), and upon my mountains (the mountains of Judah) tread him (Assyria) under foot; then shall his yoke (Assyrian bondage) depart from off them (my people), and his burden depart from off their shoulders (dual: the Assyrian downfall in Judah, 701 BC; also, the forces of the wicked will be destroyed at the second coming and again at the end of the earth).

26 This is the purpose (the plan) that is purposed upon the whole earth; and this is the hand (the power of the Lord) that is stretched out upon all nations (the eventual fate of all wicked).

27 For the Lord of Hosts hath purposed (planned), and who shall disannul (prevent it)? And his (the Lord's) hand is stretched out, and who shall turn it back (i.e., who can stop the Lord)?

28 (The topic now switches to the Philistines.) In the year that king Ahaz died (about 720 BC) was this burden (message of doom to the Philistines).

29 Rejoice not (don't get all happy and start celebrating) thou, whole Palestina (Philistia), because the rod (power) of him (Shalmaneser, King of Assyria from 727-722 BC) that smote thee is broken; for out of the serpent's root ("snakes lay eggs", i.e., from the same source, Assyria) shall come forth a cockatrice (one "snake" is dead [Shalmaneser] and a worse one will yet come [Sennacherib, King of Assyria, 705-687 BC]. The Philistines rejoiced when Sargon, King of Assyria from 722-705 BC took over at Shalmaneser's death. Sargon was not as hard on them as his predecessor was.), and his fruit (his son, Senacherib) shall be a fiery flying serpent.

30 And the first-born of the poor shall feed, and the needy shall lie down in safety (if you Philistines will join with the Lord, repent etc., you too can enjoy peace and safety, otherwise...); and I will kill thy

(Philistines) root with famine, and he shall slay thy remnant (you will be utterly destroyed).

31 Howl, O gate; cry, O city; thou, whole Palestina (Philistia), art dissolved (reduced to nothing); for there shall come from the north a smoke (cloud of dust made by enemy army), and none shall be alone in his appointed times (the enemy army will have no cowards in it).

32 What shall then answer the messengers of the nations (i.e., what will one say when people ask "What happened to the Phillistines?")? (Answer:) That the Lord hath founded Zion, and the poor of his people shall trust in it (i.e., that the Lord is the one who caused the destruction of the wicked and established Zion).

2 NEPHI 27

1 But, behold, in the last days, or in the days of the Gentiles (i.e., when the times of the gentiles are being fulfilled; see Luke 21:24)—yea, behold all the nations of the Gentiles and also the Jews, both those who shall come upon this land (the land of the Book of Mormon) and those who shall be upon other lands, yea, even upon all the lands of the earth, behold, they will be drunken (out of control) with iniquity and all manner of abominations—(i.e., they will be hooked on wickedness)

2 And when that day shall come they shall be visited of the Lord of Hosts, with thunder and with earthquake, and with a great noise, and with storm, and with tempest, and with the flame of devouring fire (burning at the Second Coming).

3 And all the nations that fight against Zion (the Lord's work and his people), and that distress her, shall be as a dream of a night vision (i.e., will be gone suddenly); yea, it shall be unto them (wicked nations), even as unto a hungry man which dreameth, and behold he eateth (in his dream) but he awaketh and his soul is empty (he is still hungry); or like unto a thirsty man which dreameth, and behold he drinketh but he awaketh and behold he is faint, and his soul hath appetite; yea, even so shall the multitude of all the nations be that fight against Mount Zion (the Lord's work; i.e., they, the wicked, will ultimately come up empty. Persecutors of the saints never feel satisfied, can't seem to leave them alone).

4 For behold, all ye that doeth iniquity, stay yourselves and wonder (i.e., stop and think), for ye shall cry out, and cry; yea, ye shall be drunken (out of control) but not with wine, ye shall stagger but not with strong drink (i.e., you will stagger about in wickedness because you reject the prophets; see verse 5).

5 For behold, the Lord hath poured out upon you the spirit of deep sleep (spiritual darkness; compare with Alma 12:11). For behold, ye have closed your eyes, and ye have rejected the prophets; and your rulers (righteous leaders), and the seers (prophets)

hath he (the Lord) covered (i.e., taken away) because of your iniquity.

6 And it shall come to pass (in the last days, verse 1) that the Lord God shall bring forth unto you the words of a book (the Book of Mormon), and they shall be the words of them which have slumbered (people who have already passed away such as Nephi, Mormon, Moroni etc.).

7 And behold the book shall be sealed (referring to the sealed portion of the plates; see verses 10, 21; also Ether 5:1); and in the book shall be a revelation from God, from the beginning of the world to the ending thereof.

8 Wherefore, because of the things which are sealed up, the things which are sealed (the sealed portion of the plates) shall not be delivered (translated etc.) in the day of the wickedness and abominations of the people. Wherefore, the book (sealed portion) shall be kept from them.

9 But the book (the gold plates) shall be delivered unto a man (Joseph Smith), and he shall deliver (translate etc.) the words of the book, which are the words of those who have slumbered in the dust, and he (Joseph Smith) shall deliver these words unto another (refers prophetically to the incident in which Martin Harris gave a copy of characters taken from the plates to Prof. Charles Anthon; see JS-H 1:63-65);

10 But the words which are sealed (sealed portion of the plates) he shall not deliver (translate etc.), neither shall he deliver the book. For the book shall be sealed by the power of God, and the revelation which was sealed (sealed portion) shall be kept in the book (kept with the plates) until the own due time of the Lord (verse 22), that they (contents of the sealed portion) may come forth; for behold, they reveal all things from the foundation of the world unto the end thereof.

11 And the day cometh that the words of the book which were sealed (sealed portion, see verses 8 and 10) shall be read upon the house tops; and they shall be read by the power of Christ; and all things (compare with D&C 101:32-34) shall be revealed unto the children of men which ever have been among the children of men, and which ever will be even unto the end of the earth.

12 Wherefore, at that day when the book (gold plates) shall be delivered unto the man (Joseph Smith) of whom I have spoken, the book shall be hid from the eyes of the world, that the eyes of none shall behold it save it be that three witnesses (Oliver Cowdery, David Whitmer and Martin Harris; see D&C 17, heading and verse 1) shall behold it, by the power of God, besides him to whom the book shall be delivered; and they shall testify to the truth of the book and the things therein.

13 And there is none other which shall view it, save it be a few (the Eight Witnesses) according to the will of God, to bear testimony of his word

unto the children of men; for the Lord God hath said that the words of the faithful should speak as if it were from the dead.

14 Wherefore, the Lord God will proceed to bring forth the words of the book; and in the mouth of as many witnesses (missionaries etc.) as seemeth him good will he establish his word; and wo be unto him that rejecteth the word of God!

15 But behold, it shall come to pass that the Lord God shall say unto him (Joseph Smith) to whom he shall deliver the book: Take these words which are not sealed and deliver them to another (Martin Harris), that he may show them unto the learned (Professor Charles Anthon and Dr. Mitchell; see JS-History 1:64-65), saying: Read this, I pray thee. And the learned (Charles Anthon) shall say: Bring hither the book, and I will read them.

16 And now, because of the glory of the world and to get gain will they (Anthon and Mitchell) say this, and not for the glory of God.

17 And the man (Martin Harris) shall say: I cannot bring the book, for it is sealed.

18 Then shall the learned say: I cannot read it.

19 Wherefore it shall come to pass, that the Lord God will deliver again the book and the words thereof to him (Joseph Smith) that is not learned; and the man that is not learned shall say: I am not learned.

20 Then shall the Lord God say unto him (Joseph Smith): The learned shall not read them, for they have rejected them, and I am able to do mine own work; wherefore thou shalt read the words which I shall give unto thee (with the help of the Urim and Thummim etc.).

21 Touch not the things which are sealed (i.e., don't even peek at the sealed portion), for I will bring them forth in mine own due time; for I will show unto the children of men that I am able to do mine own work.

22 Wherefore, when thou (Joseph Smith) hast read the words which I have commanded thee, (i.e., finished the translation of the Book of Mormon plates), and obtained the witnesses which I have promised unto thee, then shalt thou seal up the book again, and hide it up unto me, that I may preserve the words which thou hast not read (the sealed portion), until I shall see fit in mine own wisdom to reveal all things unto the children of men.

23 For behold, I am God; and I am a God of miracles; and I will show unto the world that I am the same yesterday, today, and forever (i.e., I use the same gospel to save people; I am totally reliable, dependable); and I work not among the children of men save it be according to their faith.

24 And again it shall come to pass that the Lord shall say unto him (Joseph Smith; see JS-H. 1:19) that shall read (translate) the words that shall be delivered him:

25 Forasmuch as this people draw

near unto me with their mouth, and with their lips do honor me, but have removed their hearts far from me, and their fear towards me (i.e., their concept of God) is taught by the precepts of men—

26 Therefore, I will proceed to do a marvelous (Hebrew: "astonishing") work among this people, yea, a marvelous work and a wonder (the Restoration), for the wisdom of their wise and learned shall perish, and the understanding of their prudent shall be hid (i.e., pushed aside by revealed truth).

27 And wo unto them (the wicked) that seek deep to hide their counsel (evil plots) from the Lord! And their works are in the dark; and they say: Who seeth us, and who knoweth us? And they also say: Surely, your turning of things upside down (i.e., perversion of truth) shall be esteemed as the potter's clay (i.e., claiming they can get along without God, like the situation described in Isa. 45:9). But behold, I will show unto them (the wicked), saith the Lord of Hosts, that I know all their works. For shall the work (the pot) say of him (the potter) that made it, he made me not? Or shall the thing framed say of him that framed it (the carpenter, craftsman), he had no understanding (he doesn't know me, i.e., "God doesn't know us. We can be wicked and successfully hide from God." or, "You wicked are just as foolish as potters clay that claims it made itself into a pot and has no accountability to its maker.")?

28 But behold, saith the Lord of Hosts: I will show unto the children of men that it is yet a very little while (after the Book of Mormon comes forth) and Lebanon (the Holy Land) shall be turned into a fruitful field; and the fruitful field shall be esteemed as a forest (i.e., Israel will blossom with literal forests and with truth, spiritual growth etc. after the Restoration.).

29 And in that day shall the deaf hear the words of the book, and the eyes of the blind shall see out of obscurity and out of darkness (spiritually deaf and blind will be healed as a result of the Restoration, Book of Mormon etc.).

30 And the meek also shall increase, and their joy shall be in the Lord, and the poor among men shall rejoice in the Holy One of Israel (i.e., the righteous will know the Savior again).

31 For assuredly as the Lord liveth they shall see that the terrible one (tyrant) is brought to naught, and the scorner (scoffer) is consumed, and all that watch for iniquity (in Church leaders and members; see D&C 45:50) are cut off;

32 And they that make a man an offender for a word (via corrupt lawyers and corrupt judicial system), and lay a snare for him that reproveth in the gate (i.e., try to destroy the honest person who attempts to straighten out corrupt governments etc. The "gate" was an alcove in Jerusalem's wall where officials and citizens met to discuss matters.), and

turn aside the just for a thing of naught (i.e., destroy good people for unimportant matters).

33 Therefore, thus saith the Lord, who redeemed Abraham, concerning the house of Jacob (Israel): Jacob shall not now be ashamed, neither shall his face now wax pale (i.e., Father Jacob will no longer have to be embarrased about the behavior of his posterity).

34 But when he seeth his children (his posterity), the work of my hands (i.e., now righteous), in the midst of him, they (righteous Israel) shall sanctify my name, and sanctify the Holy One of Jacob, and shall fear (respect) the God of Israel (Christ).

35 They also that erred in spirit shall come to understanding, and they that murmured shall learn doctrine (via truths of the Restoration).

MOSIAH 14

1 Yea, even doth not Isaiah say: Who hath believed our report ("Who listens to us prophets, anyway?"), and to whom is the arm of the Lord revealed ("Who sees God's hand in things")?

2 For he (Jesus) shall grow up before him (the Father) as a tender plant (a new plant, a restoration of truth), and as a root out of dry ground (apostate Judaism); he hath no form nor comeliness (German: He has no special appearance or beauty); and when we shall see him there is no beauty that we should desire him

(normal people couldn't tell he was the Son of God just by looking at him).

3 He is despised and rejected of men; a man of sorrows (sensitive to peoples' troubles), and acquainted with grief; and we hid as it were our faces from him (wouldn't even look at him); he was despised, and we (people in Judea) esteemed him not (even his own siblings rejected him at first; John 7, heading and verse 5).

4 Surely he has borne our griefs, and carried our sorrows; yet we did esteem him stricken, smitten of God, and afflicted (we didn't recognize him as the Great Atoner, rather thought he was being appropriately punished by God).

5 But he was wounded for our transgressions, he was bruised for our iniquities; the chastisement of our peace was upon him (he was punished so that we could have peace); and with his stripes (punishments) we are healed (the Atonement and its effects).

6 All we, like sheep, have gone astray; we have turned every one to his own way (every one of us has sinned; we all need the Atonement); and the Lord hath laid on him the iniquities of us all (He took our sins upon himself).

7 He was oppressed, and he was afflicted, yet he opened not his mouth; he is brought as a lamb to the slaughter, and as a sheep before her shearers is dumb (can't speak) so he opened not his mouth.

8 He was taken from prison and from judgment (fair treatment); and who shall declare his generation? For he was cut off (killed) out of the land of the living; for the transgressions of my people was he stricken.

9 And he made his grave with the wicked (died with convicted criminals), and with the rich in his death (a rich man donated his tomb, John 19:38-42); because he had done no evil, neither was any deceit in his mouth (i.e., Christ was perfect).

10 Yet it pleased the Lord (it was the Father's will) to bruise him (to allow the Atonement); he hath put him to grief; when thou shalt make his soul an offering for sin he shall see his seed (his loyal followers, i.e., success; Mosiah 15:10-12), he shall prolong his days, and the pleasure of the Lord shall prosper in his hand.

11 He shall see the travail (labor to bring forth the Atonement) of his soul, and shall be satisfied (i.e., He will look upon the Atonement with satisfaction); by his knowledge shall my righteous servant justify (save) many; for he shall bear their iniquities.

12 Therefore will I divide him a portion with the great, and he shall divide the spoil (Jesus will receive his reward) with the strong (the righteous); because he hath poured out his soul unto death (because He gave His life); and he was numbered with the transgressors; and he bore the sins of many, and made intercession for the transgressors.

3 NEPHI 22

1 And then (in the last days) shall that which is written (i.e., the prophecies) come to pass: Sing, O barren (one who has not produced), thou that didst not bear (righteous children); break forth into singing (rejoice), and cry aloud, thou that didst not travail (go into labor) with child (in former days, you did not succeed in bringing forth that which you were supposed to, namely righteous people loyal to Christ); for more are the children of the desolate (converts from scattered Israel) than the children of the married wife (perhaps meaning converts from Israelites who remained in the Holy Land), saith the Lord (now, in the last days, you've got more righteous Israelites than you ever thought possible).

2 Enlarge the place of thy tent (make more room!), and let them stretch forth the curtains of thy habitations; spare not, lengthen thy cords and strengthen thy stakes (i.e., the Church will greatly expand in the last days as righteous Israel is gathered);

3 For thou shalt break forth on the right hand and on the left (righteous Israel will be popping up everywhere!), and thy seed shall inherit the Gentiles and make the desolate cities (cities without the gospel) to be inhabited.

4 Fear not, for thou shalt not be ashamed (you won't fail); neither be thou confounded, for thou shalt not be put to shame; for thou shalt forget the

shame of thy youth, and shalt not remember the reproach of thy youth, and shalt not remember the reproach of thy widowhood any more (you can forget the failures of the past when Israel was apostate; the once "barren" Church is going to bear much fruit in the last days).

5 For thy maker, thy husband, the Lord of Hosts is his name (i.e., you will return to your Creator in the last days); and thy Redeemer, the Holy One of Israel__ the God of the whole earth shall he be called (Millennium).

6 For the Lord hath called thee as a woman forsaken and grieved in spirit (Israel has been through some very rough times), and a wife of youth, when thou wast refused (you didn't bear righteous children), saith thy God.

7 For a small moment have I forsaken thee (because you apostatized), but with great mercies will I gather thee.

8 In a little wrath I hid my face from thee for a moment (when you rejected me), but with everlasting kindness will I have mercy on thee, saith the Lord thy Redeemer.

9 For this, the waters of Noah unto me (your situation is similar to the days of Noah and the Flood), for as I have sworn that the waters of Noah should no more go over the earth, so have I sworn that I would not be wroth with thee (i.e., just as I promised not to flood the earth again, so have I promised to accept you back as you return to me in the last days).

10 For the mountains shall depart and the hills be removed, but my kindness shall not depart from thee, neither shall the covenant of my peace be removed, saith the Lord that hath mercy on thee. (God keeps promises; Isaiah is reminding us of the true nature of God, a very kind and merciful God indeed!)

11 O thou (Israel) afflicted, tossed with tempest, and not comforted (a rough past)! Behold, I will lay thy stones with fair colors, and lay thy foundations with sapphires (I will make your eternal homes with me in heaven very beautiful, Rev. 21).

12 And I will make thy windows of agates, and thy gates of carbuncles (a bright red precious stone in Isaiah's day), and all thy borders of pleasant stones (the righteous will have it very good; see Rev. 21).

13 And all thy children shall be taught of the Lord; and great shall be the peace of thy children (likely referring to Millennium).

14 In righteousness shalt thou be established; thou shalt be far from oppression for thou shalt not fear, and from terror for it shall not come near thee (Millennial conditions).

15 Behold, they (enemies of righteousness) shall surely gather together against thee, not by me; whosoever shall gather together against thee shall fall for thy sake (I will protect you; you will finally have peace).

16 Behold, I have created the smith (the blacksmith) that bloweth the coals in the fire, and that bringeth

forth an instrument (German: weapon) for his work; and I have created the waster (German: the Destroyer) to destroy (i.e., I created and can control all things. You will be safe with me).

17 No weapon that is formed against thee shall prosper; and every tongue that shall revile against thee in judgment thou shalt condemn. This is the heritage of the servants of the Lord, and their righteousness is of me, saith the Lord (i.e, there is safety for the righteous with me).

About the Author

David J. Ridges

David J. Ridges has been teaching for the Church Educational System for 35 years and has taught for several years at BYU Campus Education Week and Know Your Religion programs. He has also served as a curriculum writer for Sunday School, Seminary, and Institute of Religion manuals.

He has served in many positions in the Church, including gospel doctrine teacher, bishop, stake president and patriarch.

Brother Ridges and his wife, Janette, are the parents of six children and make their home in Springville, Utah.

0   26575 76151   1